THE FACE OF
DISCRIMINATION

D1372585

THE FACE OF DISCRIMINATION

How Race and Gender Impact Work and Home Lives

Vincent J. Roscigno

ROWMAN & LITTLEFIELD PUBLISHERS, INC.
Lanham • Boulder • New York • Toronto • Plymouth, UK

ROWMAN & LITTLEFIELD PUBLISHERS, INC.

Published in the United States of America
by Rowman & Littlefield Publishers, Inc.
A wholly owned subsidiary of The Rowman & Littlefield Publishing Group, Inc.
4501 Forbes Boulevard, Suite 200, Lanham, Maryland 20706
www.rowmanlittlefield.com

Estover Road
Plymouth PL6 7PY
United Kingdom

Copyright © 2007 by Rowman & Littlefield Publishers, Inc.

All rights reserved. No part of this publication may be reproduced, stored in a
retrieval system, or transmitted in any form or by any means, electronic, mechanical,
photocopying, recording, or otherwise, without the prior permission of the publisher.

British Library Cataloguing in Publication Information Available

Library of Congress Cataloging-in-Publication Data

Roscigno, Vincent J.
 The face of discrimination : how race and gender impact work and home lives / Vincent
J. Roscigno.
   p. cm.
 ISBN-13: 978-0-7425-4808-4 (pbk. : alk. paper)
 ISBN-10: 0-7425-4808-2 (pbk. : alk. paper)
 ISBN-13: 978-0-7425-4807-7 (cloth : alk. paper)
 ISBN-10: 0-7425-4807-4 (cloth : alk. paper)
 1. Discrimination in employment—United States. 2. Discrimination in housing—United
States. 3. Race discrimination—United States. 4. Sex discrimination—United States.
I. Title.
 HD4903.5.U58R67 2007
 331.13'30973—dc22   2006038022

Printed in the United States of America

♾™ The paper used in this publication meets the minimum requirements of American
National Standard for Information Sciences—Permanence of Paper for Printed Library
Materials, ANSI/NISO Z39.48-1992.

This book is dedicated to those represented in the pages that follow, who stood up and challenged unfair treatment, regardless of consequence; to business owners, managers, realtors, and landlords who are not represented in this book, given their fair and just treatment of all individuals and groups; and to civil rights workers and academic researchers for setting the agenda and inspiring us to engage in what is intellectually and socially important.

Contents

Preface

*T*HE *FACE OF DISCRIMINATION* grapples with a fundamental social and socio-logical question—how and why significant inequalities by race and gen-der exist despite over forty years of intact civil rights legislation, and even in the face of declines in education, income, and skill gaps between groups. The question itself is hardly a novel one for sociologists. Scholars have been deal-ing seriously with ascription and its rigid character for quite some time, in-cluding within the seminal writings of individuals like DuBois, Weber, Mar-tineau, Marx, and Addams.

Since the 1950s, researchers have modeled race and gender inequalities, often using quantitative data and state of the art statistical methods. Such ef-forts have been quite useful, revealing broad patterns and trends in race and gender inequality, how educational and skill differences contribute to ongoing disparities, and the many consequences—material, social-psychological, health-related, and so on—of the inequalities that individuals and groups face. A particularly frustrating aspect to the research literature and our con-sumption of it, however, has been a general detachment from real people, in real workplaces, and in real residential settings. How are broader trends, pat-terns, and disparities captured in the aforementioned analyses enacted in everyday settings and lives? Does discrimination really still occur in work-places and neighborhoods and, if so, how? What happens to the victims, how do discriminatory actors justify their behaviors, and are certain populations especially vulnerable and, if so, why? These were the most intriguing questions we pondered. But, how might they be addressed?

Turning to existing literature, we found significant materials pertaining to inequality, of course, and to some degree its structural and individual foundations. The statistical residuals found in sophisticated quantitative modeling were and continue to be interpreted as capturing unmeasured discrimination, at least by sociologists. Attitudinal research, based on surveys or in-depth interviews, has lent plausibility to inferences of discrimination by revealing biases among employers, proclivities in terms of housing preferences, and a host of (often retrospective) subjective experiences pertaining to discrimination. Coupled with recent audit tests in employment and housing, these various literatures and research traditions helped hone us in on the broadest issue of interest, namely *processes of inequality*. To really study such processes would require an essentially grounded view of discrimination in actual workplaces and residential contexts. In fact, what it really would require, we thought at first, would be an ethnographic study of discrimination. Such a study would not be feasible, however, given the likely covert nature of most discriminatory actions. Moreover, even if a scholar could accomplish an ethnography of discrimination within a given workplace or neighborhood, it would be significantly constrained in terms of generalizability to a host of workplaces or residential contexts.

The effort to address discriminatory processes necessitates both grounded accounts but also significant heterogeneity across populations, workplaces, and residential areas. Here, and unlike the preponderance of inequality research, the aim is not to analyze levels of inequality but rather social closure processes wherein that inequality is produced in the everyday lives of adults on an ongoing basis. We turned to the Ohio Civil Rights Commission (OCRC), and its executive director, G. Michael Payton, and its director of operations and regional counsel, Keith McNeil. Michael and Keith, beyond helping garner access to the approximately sixty-five thousand cases of race and sex discrimination processed by the OCRC over the last fifteen years, became enthusiastic supporters of what we were attempting to do. They also provided significant insight throughout the research process on issues pertaining to case processing, evidentiary criteria, and case determination procedures. Along with investigators throughout the commission, Michael and Keith deserve great thanks not to mention applause for the work they are engaged in. Indeed, they are engaged with the incredibly important task of investigating and confronting injustice. They do so passionately, despite limited staffing and resources.

The result of gaining access to case files was ideal for the project aims: significant qualitative and quantitative materials and, indeed, grounded accounts of what unfolded from victims' points of view, from witnesses' testimony, and from the businesses' and landlords' viewpoints. Moreover, case materials also often included deposition statements from the attorney general's office and information pertaining to the job or residential context itself. Herein lied considerable variation in terms of work and residential context. Case determinations allowed for selectivity on our part. By examining primarily "serious" cases where a probable cause determination was reached—a determination based on the preponderance of evidence following both state and national civil rights guidelines—we are able to speak confidently about the process of discrimination and circumvent critique and the pitfalls of relying solely on subjective or retrospective accounts.

Most important, however, were the qualitative materials—materials that offer a grounded view of "inequality in action." Indeed, this study reflects perhaps the closest possibility of systematic, ethnographic observation of discrimination and its role in the process of stratification that one could envision. As the chapters reveal, there are important variations depending on workplace and residential contexts. And, as the qualitative portions of this book demonstrate, the production of inequality through discrimination is very real, often complex, and quite significant within individuals' work and residential lives.

Tapping into rare and valuable data is one thing. Creating a worthwhile research agenda surrounding that data and then analyzing it systematically is another. In this regard, we drew heavily from classic and contemporary scholarship on the topic, much of which seems to share our frustrations of not being able to tap into the very processes that we, as stratification scholars, are most interested in. Take, for instance, recent conclusions by important inequality scholars.

> Do employers engage in reasonable evaluation practices that accurately distinguish productive from less productive workers, or do they make such distinctions on the basis of informal criteria, which allow more leeway for the influence of stereotypes based on race and class background? . . . The large residual raises the possibility that unmeasured discrimination accounts for differential rates of employment exit and, again, intra-firm processes would shed light on the issue. (Reid and Padavic 2005)

> Data should be collected in specific organizations, where the potential exists to observe first-hand the extent to which the practices of employers structure layoffs . . . our understanding of the dynamics will be vastly improved. (Wilson and McBrier 2005)

The questions we raise, however, are not simply tied to finding the right data or employing the appropriate methodologies. Far from it. Rather, as suggested in the introduction to this book, theoretical orientations—orientations that guide prevailing research traditions and data collection—should be re-visited as well. This point was made in straightforward fashion recently by Tomaskovic-Devey, Thomas, and Johnson (2005).

> Within a status-attainment or human capital framework, we cannot observe discrimination. These are essentially theoretical models that assume a more or less meritocratic labor market allocation process. They have encouraged social scientists to collect data on individuals' characteristics and labor market attainment. Thus, discrimination is not observed, but must be inferred as a residual significant effect, once presumably meritocratic factors have been statistically accounted for. It seems unlikely that we will ever advance knowledge of discrimination mechanisms with data collected in a human capital or status-attainment framework.

Correspondingly, the introduction to this book outlines our theoretical aims pertaining to explicating processes of social closure specifically, and especially the micropolitical processes that contemporary research has tended to overlook analytically. The subsequent chapters follow through on this by examining these very processes in detail, relying on immersion into a large body of case files, content coding, and descriptive analyses. We make no apologies for not undertaking sophisticated statistical modeling in this book, for prediction is not the principal goal. Rather, what *The Face of Discrimination* offers is immersion into the world of discrimination, and an explication of process.

Such goals and the approach employed throughout are by no means competing with more macro-orientations, nor are they at odds with what quantitative modeling can tell us. Rather, we see them as quite complimentary in so much as analyses of discriminatory processes—the major focus of the chapters ahead—provide valuable lessons on what macro-orientations and quantitative analyses have speculated about for some time and, in many cases, have inferred. In this vein, we follow the lead of recent exemplary qualitative and multi-method research in the area of social stratification, not the least of which are Feagin and McKinney's *The Many Costs of Racism* (2003), Deirdre Royster's *Race and the Invisible Hand* (2003), Moss and Tilly's *Stories Employers Tell* (2001), and Devah Pager's (2003) recent audit analyses of hiring discrimination.

Many scholars and friends, all grappling with important dimensions of inequality in their own work, have been pivotal for this project and its aims from conception, to data gathering, to analyses. In particular, we owe a great deal of thanks to Donald Tomaskovic-Devey, George Wilson, Irene Padavic, Paula England, Robert Kaufman, Deirdre Royster, Verta Taylor, Martha Crowley, Liana Sayer, Korie Edwards, Steven Lopez, Randy Hodson, William Form, Rachel Dwyer, William Danaher, and Zhenchao Qian. Throughout the course of this project, these individuals took time out of their own busy schedules to provide feedback, not to mention significant encouragement that we were, and are, on to something important. We are also thankful to our friends, families, and partners for their patience throughout, and for their ongoing encouragement as we proceed on our intellectual journeys.

Finally, we are grateful to the Department of Sociology at the Ohio State University for partially funding this project through its Sociology Graduate Research Practicum. The practicum, which came to be known as the *Ohio Discrimination Project*, offered the necessary space and resources to undertake the daunting but exciting task of milling through files, content coding, scanning, reading, and analyzing the vast body of discrimination cases. Perhaps more important, it became an arena of truly exciting intellectual exchange and one wherein teaching pedagogy and research training intersected, and in a manner that greatly benefited all involved. The result was an enthusiastic, collective, team effort—an effort reflected in the pages that follow.

Introduction

Now there was nothing I could pinpoint, and say that he is actually doing it . . . because he stayed within the scope of what a supervisor might do. But since he had never done it before I felt that way, and I felt that he was probably trying to get me to be subordinate to him and . . . but I wasn't going to fall into that trap. . . . He stayed within a supervisor position. I mean, it wasn't . . . it wasn't nothing overbearing that you could put your finger on and that you could, that you could say, hey this man did this. It . . . it was very subtle.

—African American male, computer technician

DISCRIMINATION IS OFTEN a subtle phenomenon, as noted in the introductory quote—a phenomenon that may be difficult to detect, and that may even be unconscious on the part of the perpetrator. It is nevertheless influential and harmful for its victims, undermining their status in a given institutional arena and their well-being psychologically, materially, and within society at large. At other moments, discrimination is quite obvious and explicit. Take the case of a thirty-six-year-old African American man, working as an account manager, who is repeatedly taunted by coworkers with racist cartoons and jokes for a period of nearly six months; or, a twenty-four-year-old white female who, in the process of applying for a job advertised in the local paper, is told by the owner that it really does not really matter whether she fills out a job application because he simply does not hire women; or a white mother and her biracial child who are victimized by threats and racial slurs used by their apartment complex neighbors.

Such examples, be they subtle or explicit, are not merely historical, nor are they remnants and residues of history. Rather, their manifestation and prevalence are contemporary. Indeed, tens of thousands of people experienced such moments within the arenas of work and housing in the state of Ohio over the last decade. Such treatment continues to occur, perhaps even commonly, across the United States. It is thus notable that public attention has remained relatively oblivious to discrimination's extent, seriousness, and consequences. Much of this can be attributed to the fact that discrimination seldom gets reported. Victims are often unaware that it occurred, they may fear retaliation if they do report it, or they simply do not have the monetary resources, time, or emotional strength to pursue publicly visible and/or legal action.

Perhaps more paramount to the lack of public awareness and attention to discrimination is the fact that much of U.S. society believes that we have simply moved beyond the era of differential treatment toward minorities and women. Correspondingly, where claims of discrimination do garner attention, they tend to be dismissed as but a manifestation of overly sensitive minority groups. To the extent that truly discriminatory action is confirmed, it is more often than not seen as a function of the few remaining "bad seeds" in the white and male populations—bad seeds who continue to engage in exclusionary practices in what is viewed by the majority as an increasingly color and gender blind society. The reality of thousands of established incidents of discrimination every year in but one relatively representative state along with recent, high visibility, and national gender- and race-based class action suits against large restaurant and retail chains, however, straightforwardly challenge such simplistic claims and cultural blind spots.

Work and housing represent two often interconnected spheres of social life within which inequalities and discrimination by race and sex are arguably most clearly evident, even forty years after the Civil Rights Act and the Fair Housing Act—a fact reinforced by substantial social science research on these arenas of social life. Research, for instance, has denoted the role of human capital differences (Tam 1997), labor market variations in opportunity (Cohen 1998; Huffman 2004), spatial and historical patterns of residential segregation (Farley and Frey 1994; Massey and Denton 1993), and the various consequences of workplace and housing segregation (England et al. 1994; Tomaskovic-Devey 1993a; Yinger 1995). Discrimination, often inferred as a contributing mechanism, however, has received considerably less attention (for some exceptions, see Feagin 1991, Gotham 2002a, 2002b, Pager 2003, Pager and Quillian 2005, and Yinger 1995).

Limited empirical attention to discriminatory processes, while largely driven by data limitations, is also likely a consequence of theoretical conceptions of stratification and how it manifests. Indeed, while analyses of organizational or geographic variations in levels of inequality provide understanding of macrolevel sociological outcomes and relations with, for instance, racial competition across neighborhoods or gender segregation at work, they tend to offer less insight into the microinteractional processes that are most assuredly playing a role (Feagin and Eckberg 1980). This book, in an effort to address this gap, offers explicit conceptualization of inequality as a dynamic, interactive process occurring within real workplaces and residential contexts.

Background: Stratification in Work and Housing

Although certainly unique to some degree as areas of analytic foci, employment and housing represent two important and often intertwined arenas of social life. Employment status and the income derived from it shapes residential options. Housing options, in turn, can restrict opportunities for employment (Jencks and Mayer 1990; Kain 1992). Significant race and gender inequalities exist in each, and evidence suggests quite clearly that discriminatory decision making processes, among other things, are likely playing a role (Cohn 2000). Auditing studies in both literatures, for instance, which rely on quasi-experimental methods of investigation, suggest that arbitrary criteria are often utilized by gatekeeping actors when making determinations to hire for employment or rent property (Pager 2003; Yinger 1995). Moreover, as noted by Kirschenman and Neckerman (1991) and more recently Moss and Tilly (2001), key actors such as managers and landlords often begin the process of evaluation with biased perceptions of women and minorities in the first place. Such overlaps within the spheres of work and housing underlie the need for broad conceptualization of discrimination and its role in inequality—conceptualization that is certainly grounded in area specific literatures, but whose lessons crosscut those very literatures.

Stratification and Work

Much attention within the workplace stratification literature specifically has focused on race and gender wage disparities as well as variations in mobility. Although most concede that minority human capital deficits account for some outcome differences, studies have consistently found that income and wage deficits (e.g., Cotter, Hermsen, and Vanneman 1999; Marini and Fan 1997; Tomaskovic-Devey 1993b; Tomaskovic-Devey and Skaggs 2002) employment disparities (Cohn and Fossett 1995; Wilson, Tienda, and Wu 1995), and inequalities in promotion and authority (McBrier and Wilson 2004; Smith 2002; Wilson 1997; Wilson, Sakura-Lemessy and West 1999) remain even in face of human capital controls (e.g., education, training, job experience). But why?

Some attribute persistent employment inequalities to labor market sectoral differences. Cohen (1998), for instance, in his multilevel analyses of race and gender inequalities across labor markets of the United States, finds that income disparities vary rather systematically as a function of local economic conditions. A similar point has been made by Wilson (1978) in his historical overview of African American secondary sector employment in large, inner city areas of the United States. Even more recently, Huffman (2004) finds sectoral variations in employment for men and women, and empirically denotes the consequences for wage inequalities holding constant potentially influential individual background attributes.

More proximate and perhaps more meaningful may be the firms in which minorities and women work and the extent to which they are segregated. Men earn more than women even when they are in the same general occupation (U.S. Census Bureau 2003), yet occupational sex segregation remains a significant source of wage disparities (England 1992; Padavic and Reskin 2002). Kaufman (1986, 2002) recently found similar segregation of African Americans into lower skilled, race-typed jobs involving menial tasks and poor working conditions. Tomaskovic-Devey (1993a), who examines levels of both race and gender segregation for a sample of firms in North Carolina concurs, while also noting that some of the inequality he finds is likely due to *social closure*, wherein women and minorities are sorted into jobs that require fewer educational credentials and that offer less job training. Such analyses have proven incredibly useful in terms of specifying the prevalence and consequences of segregation for race and gender groups, the general devaluation of female and minority work, and corresponding wage and mobility inequalities. Less systematic attention, however, has been devoted to explicating the discriminatory processes contributing to the very segregation that has received so much attention.

Recent work has suggested that sorting mechanisms, including discretionary decision making and discrimination by employers and coworkers may be partially responsible and, thus, warrant further scholarly attention. And, there is good reason to suspect that such foci will contribute to our understanding of employment inequality. Research pertaining to downward race and gender mobility by McBrier and Wilson (2004) and employment exits by Reid and Padavic (2005) suggest that arbitrary and subjective decision making within firms may be key. Huffman and Cohen's (2004) and Petersen and Saporta's (2004) recent analyses of race and gender wage disparities, respectively, although not measuring or analyzing discrimination directly, come to the conclusion that discrimination in worker allocation and exclusion are playing a part in persistent disparities that they find.

The possibility of discrimination as an important, although seldom directly studied, mechanism is bolstered further by recent analyses of employer attitudes by Moss and Tilly (2001). These researchers demonstrate that, like subjective biases and stereotypes that pervade the more general population, employers too may hold biased views and, consequently, make skewed hiring, promotion, and firing decisions (see also Kirschenman and Neckerman 1991). Experimental and audit designs, not the least of which is Pager's (2003) recent analysis of hiring decisions, highlight more directly the centrality of employer preconceptions and especially the ways in which subjective biases translate into discriminatory behaviors (see also Laband and Lentz 1998 and Neumark, Bank, and Van Nort 1996).

For African Americans, detrimental employer biases might include, for instance, the view that they are more inclined toward criminality or less dependable employees, each of which may influence hiring and promotion decisions (Moss and Tilly 2001; Pager 2003). For women, employer biases may include the match between a prospective or current employee and gender-typed work, or an expectation that a prospective or existing employee may become pregnant or be less committed to their job due to motherhood. This may lead to exclusion, stagnation in mobility, or sexual harassment—particularly when gender expectations are violated and males attempt to reify gender hierarchies (e.g., Gruber 1998; Gutek and Cohen 1987; Padavic and Orcutt 1997). In-depth analyses of such interactions at work, the contexts within which they occur, and processes of discrimination provides much needed leverage on the issue of workplace relations and the social processes implicated in the reproduction of race and gender boundaries and inequalities (Vallas 2003).

Stratification in Housing

Housing research reveals racial residential segregation to be a persistent social problem in the United States. According to Charles's (2003) analysis of the fifty largest metropolitan areas in the United States, black–white segregation is extreme in twenty-nine of these areas while there has been little to no change in the remainder over the last two decades. This spatial isolation and its consequences for the concentration of disadvantage only exacerbate a variety of other social problems, including high rates of out-of-wedlock births, crime rates, and unemployment (e.g., Massey and Denton 1993; Krivo and Peterson 2000; Wilson 1978, 1990). Charles (2003; 198) concludes, "as a consequence of residential segregation, the vast majority of blacks experience residential circumstances that are—to a greater or lesser degree—detrimental to their future social mobility."

How does one make sense of high and persistent segregation levels, even forty years after passage of the Fair Housing Act? The most obvious possibility revolves around economic differentials. Yet, to date, scholars have only found mixed support for the role of economic differences in the perpetuation of segregation patterns. While there is evidence to suggest that achieving racial economic parity would have a significant impact on residential choices for African Americans, some conclude that racial differences in the ability to afford housing and in tastes for housing services only explain a small proportion of residential segregation. Indeed, even wealthy blacks and wealthy whites and poor blacks and poor whites remain segregated from one another (Charles 2003; Denton and Massey 1988; Farley 1977; Taeuber 1965).

Residential preferences offer an alternative possibility. We know from survey analyses that a majority of whites feel uncomfortable when more than 20 percent of their neighborhood becomes black, and that negative stereotypes, fear of crime, and decreasing property values may be playing a role (Farley et. al. 1994; Krysan 2002). Blacks, for their part, similarly may prefer to live in neighborhoods that are predominantly black, yet this appears to be driven by fear of intimidation, violence, or hostility by potential white neighbors (Krysan and Farley 2002). While certainly useful for addressing our understanding of social psychological processes that may be driving individual residential choices, the focus on preferences ultimately leaves unexplored concrete behaviors and the ways in which residential preferences may, in fact, be constrained by institutional gatekeeping processes as well as more informal interactional processes of inequality and social closure. Massey and Denton (1993), credited with bringing racial residential segregation to the forefront of scholarly debates surrounding the plight of the black urban underclass with their publication *American Apartheid*, certainly concur that discriminatory action is to blame.

A few studies, often relying on case analytic methods, nevertheless have begun to emerge that take as the principal focus discriminatory treatment by more powerful institutional actors. Especially notable in this regard are studies such as Gotham's (2002a, 2002b) analysis of 1970s neighborhood racial transition and the role of realtor blockbusting in Kansas City. Drawing from insights pertaining to vested interests in political economic development (Gottdiener and Feagin 1988) and the role of stratification struggles and status distinctions in defining and reifying spatial boundaries (Feagin and Parker 1990), Gotham shows how key actors (school officials, real estate firms) undertook behaviors that effectively led to racial turnover. While racial composition, segregation, and change are a portion of the focus (as it is in much of the segregation literature), the real analytic concern lies in the processes involved and the behaviors of actors. Correspondingly, such work represents an important development in research on contemporary housing stratification—a development that incorporates agency into theoretical conceptions of inequality creation and reproduction. And, like more specific housing audits conducted over the last two decades, such grounded analyses also denote the dynamic and interactional nature of housing inequality.

Housing audit (or racial testing) studies, in contrast to more aggregate, quantitative work and case-specific sociological investigations, have been used by fair housing groups as a systematic means of uncovering actual discrimination. Two, racially distinct, though similarly situated, individuals or "testers" (one minority and one white) are sent into similar circumstances in the housing market. With efforts to control for social and human capital characteristics, such tests have served as an effective way to uncover discrimination and, thus, violations of the law. Beginning in 1977, HUD launched the Housing Market Practices Survey (HMPS), which conducted 3,264 tests in 40 metropolitan areas. The study provided evidence of significant discrimination against blacks in sales and rental markets and played a role in the passage of the 1988 amendment to the Fair Housing Act. A second national study in 1989 (The Housing Discrimination Study) covered 25 metropolitan areas and revealed that discrimination had not decreased (Yinger 1995). Initial analyses from the most recent nation-wide HUD audit indicate that African Americans and Hispanics continue to face significant discriminatory barriers when searching for a home to rent or buy (Ross and Turner 2005).

Numerous other housing market audit studies, conducted in individual cities, have reached similar conclusions. Generally, discrimination may be more intense in integrated neighborhoods than segregated neighborhoods and "steering"—a realtor suggesting more or less desirable alternatives based on the race of the client—is a common mechanism (Turner, Struyk, and Yinger 1991; Yinger 1986, 1995). Black and Hispanic home buyers can expect to encounter approximately one act of discrimination every time they interact with a real estate broker (Yinger 1991). Moreover, there appears to be widespread discrimination by landlords, including fewer offers of rental assistance and showing fewer units to minorities (Ondrich, Stricker, and Yinger 1999). Similar evidence is reported from analyses of rental inquiries by phone (Massey and Lundy 2001) and interactions with mortgage lenders and homeowner's insurance agents (Smith and Cloud 1996; Squires and Velez 1988).

Clearly, the audit methodology is a useful method for assessing levels of discrimination faced by potential residents. There are, however, obvious disadvantages. Some, such as Fix and Struyk (1993), have argued that testers (i.e., individuals conducting the audit) may be predisposed to find discrimination.

Audit studies are also constrained by the sampling frame of the study (i.e. units advertised in major metropolitan newspapers), and may not be as useful for studying complex transactions, such as lending processes (Fix and Struyk 1993; Yinger 1998). Even more noteworthy, auditing studies have seldom been extended to issues of gender discrimination in housing and, specifically, federal protections based on family status (e.g., a single mother with children)—issues that, given complexities of family poverty, single parenthood, and preexistent racial stereotypes, may be especially pronounced for African American women. And, finally, audit studies can only reveal exclusionary discrimination. That is, by design, such research overlooks day-to-day processes of antagonism, harassment, intimidation, and differential treatment once actually housed; all illegal forms of discrimination, as defined by the Fair Housing Act, may be equally or even more psychologically devastating for minorities and women.

Stratification, Closure, and Processes of Discrimination

A sound understanding of stratification brings together awareness of structure and action and their potentially reinforcing and/or conditional nature (Giddens 1984; Lawler, Ridgeway, and Markovsky 1993). For the purposes of this book and the goals underlying it, this entails not only consideration of prior research on race and gender disparities in employment and housing, but also serious consideration and theoretical development pertaining to the very social processes that create and reinforce those disparities. Without doing so, conceptions of inequality remain overly structural, with little room for, or acknowledgment of, agency on the part of gatekeeping actors within institutional and organizational contexts, as well as that often exercised by those victimized by inequality. Acknowledgement of agency within structural/organizational bounds is consistent with theorizing on social justice, inequality, and reproduction, such as that by Blau (1967), Foucault (1980), and Young (1990). At its theoretical core is the premise that social closure, the exercise of power, and inequality are fundamentally relational and interactional.

We draw from perspectives pertaining to social closure given their emphases on how inequality is created and maintained rather than merely its extent. Social closure often occurs through institutional exclusion and dominant group positioning. It also comes about, consciously and unconsciously, within the context of everyday interaction—interaction that, through language, symbolic acts, and/or physical control or force, has as its aim status–hierarchy preservation and the various advantages/disadvantages it affords (Weber

1978; Blau 1977; Young 1980). Indeed, for Weber (1978), social closure reflects the process by which collectivities seek to maximize advantage by restricting access and privileges to others. Parkin (1979) elaborates further by stressing the two-pronged, dynamic nature of stratification, wherein dominant group members undertake actions (closure) to preserve privilege while subordinate groups hold some capacity to resist and change prevailing stratification arrangements (usurpation) (see also Murphy 1988). Reskin (2003) has reinvigorated such themes more recently by pushing stratification scholars to not only delineate the extent or forms of inequality, but perhaps more important, pertinent processes and mechanisms (see also Charles 2003; Feagin and Eckberg 1980; Tomaskovic-Devey 1993a). Rather than merely delineating the extent of inequality, then, social closure as a sociological construct directs us toward an in-depth understanding of the processes through which stratification hierarchies are both defined and maintained.

Figure I.1 provides a general conceptual model of social closure and its dimensions relative to group inequality as applied to any given institutional

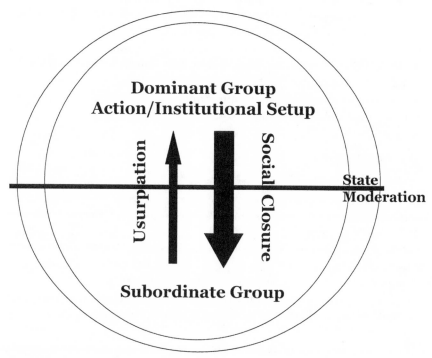

FIGURE I.1
Structural and Interactional Dimensions of Social Closure

realm. The inner circle reflects organizational structure, including mandated procedures and practices. The outer circle represents, generally, extraorganizational and institutional structures (e.g., labor markets, spatial demographics, and competition patterns) that may influence the more proximate patterning of organizational and institutional practices and the inequality that they may produce. Of course, the state (federal or local, captured by the horizontal line) may intrude, and certainly has historically, in a manner that shapes organizational and extraorganizational dynamics pertaining to group access and treatment.

The preponderance of current and previous research pertaining to race and gender inequality in housing and work has focused on relations between the two rings and group well being. This includes research pertaining to workplace race/gender composition, labor market processes, organizational practices (i.e., in realty and lending and in human resource departments), and racially competitive processes across geographic space. While useful in documenting aggregate relations between structure and group outcomes, such empirical literature has remained significantly underdeveloped on the question of social relations and interactions, captured by the inner arrows of the diagram. How do superordinate and subordinate actors, knowingly or not, play a role within this process and engage in inequality production, reduction, and/or maintenance within the constraints of preexistent workplace and housing structures? To achieve this objective, the various chapters examine the multidimensional nature of discriminatory forms themselves, reflect on the embeddedness of discrimination within context, and pay significant attention to consequences and how victims respond.

Discriminatory Forms

Whether undertaken by sociologists or by fair hiring and housing advocacy groups, much of the research on work and housing tends to highlight exclusionary elements of discrimination. Discrimination, both sociologically and legally, however, involves much more than exclusion. It also entails differential treatment once employed or once housed, where the outcome is status hierarchy maintenance. It is on this point that research has been largely limited to but a small handful of experiential and retrospective analyses.

Feagin (1991), for instance, provides insight into the day-to-day and often informal aspects of discrimination in his analyses of experiences reported by thirty-seven African Americans across several U.S. cities. In particular, he notes various forms of discriminatory treatment in public spaces. Consistent with the theoretical goals in the pages that follow, he delineates "sites" or contexts of discrimination, the interactive and process-oriented nature of discriminatory acts, as well as African Americans' varying responses to such behavior.

More recently, Feagin and McKinney (2003) elaborate on the significant physical, psychological, familial, and community costs of discrimination, including discrimination encountered in workplaces, drawing from detailed interviews. What is notable in their account is that respondents often reflect back negatively on supervisor and coworker behavior that is mundane and very much day-to-day in character, yet race-specific in its targeting, rather than on issues of wages or promotion. Thus, there is a disjuncture, to some extent, between the types of discrimination highlighted or inferred in quantitative analyses, which tend to focus on objective workplace rewards, and that which is more effectively captured using case or in-depth, interviewing techniques. Retrospective and experiential accounts of sexual harassment at work (e.g., DeCoster, Estes, and Mueller 1999; Rogers and Henson 1997; Rospenda, Richman, and Nawyn 1998) and more general differential treatment of women within particular occupations and workplace contexts (e.g., Rosenberg, Perlstadt, and Phillips 1993) similarly seem to suggest that, alongside possible efforts to exclude women from certain forms of employment or from promotion ladders, discriminatory actions are often aimed towards reifying gender hierarchies among those already employed.

Although such studies can be critiqued for relying on perceptions of discrimination and small samples, not to mention retrospective biases, they nevertheless add a much needed social and interactional dimension to our understanding of inequality (in this regard, see also West and Zimmerman 1987). Moreover, they direct attention toward discrimination beyond its purely exclusionary form. Rather than relying simply on perceptions, the data described shortly focus on thousands of concrete incidences (i.e., cases) of discrimination wherein the complaint received investigative validation by a neutral, third-party, governmental agency. Importantly, and relative to the discussion above, the data allow for analyses of (1) exclusionary forms of workplace and housing discrimination, (2) forms that impact mobility and expulsion from the workplace, and (3) more informal manifestations in housing and work that appear to have as their goal hierarchy maintenance.

These distinctions are important. Indeed, particular discriminatory forms shape the target's objective housing or employment status and often require complicit behavior or neglect on the part of more powerful institutional actors. More informal manifestations (e.g., harassment, intimidation, sexual harassment), in contrast, may be carried out by actors with or without (i.e., neighbors, coworkers) institutional authority. Although one's objective status in housing or employment may not be impacted, such discrimination is nevertheless quite consequential for victims, and often occurs in an ongoing manner. Simply, the ability to distinguish between types of discrimination and address its multiple consequences is essential.

The Contexts and Complexities of Discrimination

Despite some level of agency by those engaging in discriminatory behavior and those responding to it, expressions of agency and processes of discrimination are fundamentally bounded and conditioned by the organizational and local environments within which they occur (Feagin and Eckberg 1980). That is, actors in the stratification process, and certainly those in housing and employment contexts, are typically constrained or enabled to a greater or lesser degree by broader societal processes as well as organizational procedures, attributes, and directives. It is for this reason that many of the chapters that follow highlight the contexts within which discrimination unfolds.

Particular economic sectors, such as the core or manufacturing specifically, have historically witnessed significant antagonism directed toward previously excluded minorities and women. Conversely, the public sector has been friendlier to minorities and women, and has also been historically active in initiating nondiscrimination policies and procedures (see Wilson and McBrier 2005). Variations in discrimination across sectors, to the extent they exist, may also reveal more than historical precedent. Indeed, research pertaining to the labor process, especially that dealing with managerial discretion, workplace bullying, and shop-floor social relations, suggest quite clearly that particular sectors are characterized by poor organization and limited bureaucracy—a reality that often lends itself to significant managerial discretion and abusive treatment of employees (or prospective employees) (Hodson 2001; Roscigno and Hodson 2004).[1] Such bullying and abuse may take the form of targeted discrimination against racial/ethnic minorities and women.

Minority and female composition at the organizational level (in the case of workplace discrimination) or neighborhood level (in the case of housing discrimination) may be consequential as well for the prevalence and forms of discrimination one might find—something we deal with explicitly in chapters 6 and 10. Sociologists have long speculated about gender composition and its effects on tokenism (Kanter 1993), queuing (Reskin and Roos 1990), resistance by men (Reskin 1988), and mobility and wage inequalities (e.g., England 1982). Similar arguments, grounded in Blalock's (1967) conception of race concentration and competitive threat, have provided empirical leverage in understanding racial disparities in employment entry, mobility, inequality, and poverty (Cohen 1998; Tomaskovic-Devey 1993b; Tomaskovic-Devey and Roscigno 1996). These bodies of literature often infer discrimination as a mechanism. Although few if any studies to date have been able to investigate directly the linkages between race/gender composition and the degree and forms of discrimination, predictions center upon isolated and integrated settings.

The sociological understanding of housing discrimination, its occurrence, and its persistence can likewise be bolstered by recognition of local conditions and the ways in which they are systematically linked to discriminatory behaviors. According to racial competition theorizing, the compositional attributes of neighborhoods and the extent to which a competition threshold is reached will be key. Historical accounts certainly suggest that discrimination by landlords, realtors, and even neighbors is most likely to manifest in areas that are either homogenous (i.e., the protection of white space) or on the threshold of racial turnover (i.e., competitive threat) (Charles 2003; Massey and Denton 1993; Farley and Frey 1994). While these accounts provide insight, particularly on the issue of discriminatory exclusion, analyses of other forms and the processes of housing discrimination as they unfold in varying neighborhood contexts are lacking. Moreover, little if any literature deals directly with the issue of gender discrimination in housing, which is illegal and by no means a rare occurrence. We know, at the very least, that women face multiple compounding burdens and vulnerabilities pertaining to race, class, and maternal status (e.g., Collins 1990; Harris 1993). These vulnerabilities play a part in access and treatment within a variety of institutional realms, and housing is no exception.

Discrimination's Consequences

By devoting limited empirical attention to *processes* of social closure, workplace and housing stratification research has generally neglected several consequences of discrimination that are quite important to those experiencing it. Indeed, while outcomes that are objectively measurable, such as segregation levels, wage and promotion disparities, and levels of hiring or firing, have received some attention either directly or by inference, the sociopsychological impact and the capacity of individuals to respond to discrimination have received much less treatment. This is unfortunate. Discrimination is quite consequential to overall well-being of minorities and women—minorities and women who often adopt strategies to cope with, avoid, and resist discriminatory actors and interactions.

Analyses of minority mental health have been relatively clear on the role that perceived discrimination plays in creating psychological distress and in shaping physical and mental health across a wide variety of outcomes (Krieger et al. 1993; Williams 1995; Williams and Collins 1995). The causal effect itself may be relatively direct, through actual face-to-face discriminatory experiences, or indirect through discrimination's influence on socioeconomic well-being. Although less often focused upon, one might expect a similar pattern to hold for women given objective and subjective differences in workplace experiences and rewards (Ross and Mirowsky 1996) and direct forms of discrimination that women may face within employment and residential contexts.

Analyses of discriminatory processes, especially when coupled with first-party interpretations of what occurred and its consequences—all foci of the chapters that follow—provide significant empirical insight on discrimination's multiple costs. Such analyses also provide a more grounded view of responses to discrimination. Indeed, as Feagin's (1991) analysis of minority discriminatory experiences and Rogers and Henson's (1997) research on women and workplace sexual harassment reveal, women and racial ethnic minorities on the receiving end of discriminatory actions, despite suffering negative outcomes, are more than passive recipients. Rather, they are active agents often engaged in complex strategies of coping, avoiding, and confronting the discrimination they face. The qualitative data reported in the following pages speaks quite clearly to the implications of discrimination for its victims as well as the ways that victims react and try to deal with what they are facing.

Data

The data used in the following chapters were collected through an agreement with the Ohio Civil Rights Commission (OCRC). It includes as the main sampling frame all employment and housing discrimination suits filed in the state of Ohio from 1988 through 2003. The base quantitative data include a case ID number; the charging party's race and sex; the respondent (e.g., employer, manager, coworker, landlord, mortgage company, etc.) and their location; the basis of the charge (e.g., race, gender, religion, etc.); the harm or injury that occurred (e.g., exclusion, promotion, firing, sexual harassment, etc. for employment cases; exclusion, harassment, differential treatment, sexual harassment, etc. for housing cases); industry SIC codes (for employment cases), the outcome of the investigation; and a host of geographic identifiers (zip codes, MSA codes, and county FIPS codes).

Ohio's laws prohibiting discrimination (OCRC 4112) have remained relatively constant during the fifteen year period of the case data, and are "substantially equivalent" to federal laws. As such, cases filed with the OCRC are usually also filed with the Equal Opportunity Employment Commission (EEOC) (employment cases) and the U.S. Department of Housing and Urban Development (HUD) (housing cases). In fact, the EEOC actually relies on

OCRC findings unless the case falls into an already existent EEOC investigation, litigation, or national initiative. HUD, which has a small staff and only two offices in Ohio (relative to OCRC's five offices), similarly relegates most Ohio cases to the OCRC for investigation. Thus, the data reported throughout reflect discrimination in a state that, given heterogeneity in its industrial structure, significant minority composition in quite large urban areas (i.e., Cincinnati, Akron, Cleveland, Toledo, Dayton, Columbus), and laws that mirror federal protections, is a reasonably generalizable case in point.

Since our aim is to contribute to stratification literature in general, but specifically that pertaining to race and gender, analyses are limited to cases in which the self-reported basis of the charge is race/ethnicity and/or sex. Charging parties can list up to two bases of their suit, and there is a relatively small subsample of cases where both race and sex discrimination are alleged. Although other forms of discrimination (i.e., religion, disability, and age) are interesting and perhaps an avenue for future investigation, they are simply beyond the scope of this project.

The resulting data equates to approximately 60,743 cases of sex and/or race discrimination in employment, and 3,941 housing cases in which either race/ethnicity and/or sex was the basis of charge. This large data set holds significant potential for analyses of spatial and institutional patterns of discrimination and the types of harm experienced within varying workplace and residential contexts. Having detailed information on the issue/injury also allows for explicit analyses of exclusion versus other forms of discrimination.

It would, of course, be erroneous to assume that a discrimination *claim* necessarily implies that discrimination occurred. The OCRC's case determination (and a probable cause finding in particular) helps distinguish cases with little supporting evidence from those with significant and supporting evidence in favor of the charging party's claim. Along with probable cause findings, settlement of a case in the charging party's favor (prior to litigation) is often deemed as supporting evidence from the point of view of legal scholars who both study and testify in discrimination suits. For this reason, both qualitative and quantitative analyses presented in the following pages focus on cases where probable cause determinations were reached or favorable settlements for the charging party were brokered by a neutral third party (OCRC or district attorney's office)—a neutral third party whose job it is to collect evidence, eyewitness accounts, and case histories, and to weigh the preponderance of all evidence following HUD and EEOC guidelines.

Selecting "serious" cases has, no doubt, the effect of underestimating discrimination by excluding cases where there simply was not enough evidence. Yet, it simultaneously bolsters confidence in the ability to conclude that the processes uncovered pertain directly to serious cases of discrimination (rather

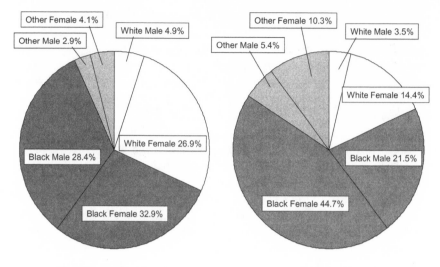

Serious Employment Cases (N = 14,091)   Serious Housing Cases (N = 757)

FIGURE I.2
Distribution of Serious Race and Sex Discrimination Cases by Race and Sex, for both Employment and Housing

than alleged or perceived discrimination). Figure I.2 offers a visual representation of these more serious employment (n = 14,091) and housing (n = 757) cases, broken down by the race and gender attributes of the charging party (note: "other" represents combined categories of Asian, Hispanic, and other race/ethnic minorities.) Given limited representation of "other" racial/ethnic minorities, our analyses focus largely on African Americans.

Discrimination in housing and work will also be underestimated by virtue of the fact that a case must be reported. Specifically, someone discriminated against must (1) understand their rights under the law, (2) interpret their treatment as discrimination, (3) actively seek out a civil rights commission office, and (4) enter the office and go through an entire investigative process. There is undoubtedly a subjective element to the process, and to the "serious" cases analyzed—one wherein a charging party's subjective interpretation of the discrimination experience and their corresponding filing of a charge aligns with the law and meets investigative criteria. Although certain populations may be more or less likely to experience discrimination, interpret it, and/or file a charge, it remains unclear as to where such bias may lie. Are more educated individuals likely to file and have their grievances confirmed by investigation? Or are lower status individuals more likely to file given that they live and work within contexts wherein discrimination is either more prevalent or where others around them (and like them) can share grievances and information pertaining to civil rights?

Literature has been somewhat unclear in the aforementioned regards, although there is piecemeal evidence that women and younger individuals may be least likely to either interpret or lodge complaints (e.g., Uggen and Blackstone 2004). Such bias (to the extent it exists) should not be problematic for the analytic aims of the following chapters. Indeed, *the intent is not to predict overall levels of discrimination.* Rather, although some of the analyses that follow compare and analyze rates across labor market sectors, by race/gender composition of workplaces, and across neighborhoods, the principal aim remains to clarify how discrimination plays out in work and residential contexts, who it effects, and the various consequences. Relative to prior work on discrimination, which has tended to focus on a particular group, singular industries, or large urban contexts, this data provides significant variation in who is filing.

Quantitative Overview

For employment, racial discrimination is the primary basis of charge for approximately 55 percent of cases, while sex discrimination is the primary basis for the remaining 45 percent. For housing cases, approximately 60 percent of cases have as their primary basis of charge racial discrimination, while the remaining 40 percent denote gender and familial status discrimination as the primary claim.

The data include approximately twenty-five categories of issue/injury for both workplace and housing, ranging from outright exclusion, to demotion/promotion, to wages, to advertising of jobs and housing, to intimidation, harassment, and sexual harassment. In the chapters that follow, we collapse these into theoretically and substantively meaningful categories of harm. Notably, a large portion of cases deal with harassment and other forms of discriminatory treatment once employed or housed, above and beyond exclusion. There is also a quite high level of expulsion, or firings and layoffs, for employment—a pattern consistent with recent analyses of employment exits and race and gender inequalities (e.g., Reid and Padavic 2005; see also Wilson and McBrier 2005).

There is also quite significant spatial (for housing) and industrial variation (for employment) within this sample of serious cases—a fact that speaks to issues of sample representation and potential generalizability. The entire pool of housing cases are distributed across more than one hundred towns and cities, as are the more serious ones. There are similarly significant variations

in employment cases across major industrial sectors, as reported in the following chapters.

Such quantitative data holds considerable promise for developing our understanding of the types of discrimination women and minorities may disproportionately face, as well as the ways in which the likelihood of discrimination may vary by spatial, labor market, and/or industrial context. In and of
themselves, however, such analyses cannot reveal the social-interactional dimensions of discrimination, the ways in which discrimination might occur,
and the role of gatekeepers. To capture these dimensions of the stratification
and closure process, we turn to content coding and qualitative material from
a random subsample of (serious) case files themselves.

Case Material and Qualitative Data

The chapters that follow make significant use of case materials. In legal
terms, once a case is filed with the OCRC and a final case determination is
reached, the case file and the information contained within it become public
information, available to any citizen or agency—a point that both charging
parties and respondents are made aware of. These files, ranging from 20 to 120
pages, include the following:

Detailed, first hand accounts of what occurred from the charging party's
  viewpoint, often in their own words.
A response and/or explanation from the respondent as to what happened.
Witness statements as to what occurred.
Whether the charging party or respondent are represented legally or by an
  advocacy group.
Who carried out the discrimination (i.e., supervisor, owner, coworkers,
  landlord, bank, etc.).
A deposition of testimony, taken by the attorney general's office, if the case
  reached that point.
The occupation of the charging party, or occupation in question, for em-
  ployment cases.
The equivalent of EEOC race and gender composition data for the work-
  place.

Qualitative materials were gathered from these files and a content coding
device was used to systematically gather further material (e.g., perpetrator status, race/gender composition, occupational title) from approximately 850
randomly selected cases. This randomly selected subsample, which mirrors
the larger sample in terms of race/gender breakdown and the distribution of

injuries reported, allows for: (1) analyses of occupational differences in the degree and types of discrimination, (2) insight into who precisely the actors are in discriminatory processes, and (3) examination of compositional contexts. On this last point, recent work has suggested that firm-level compositional data, such as that provided on EEOC forms, is much more reliable and useful for studying segregation and its impact (Robinson et al. 2005). Correspondingly, this will be the first study of its kind linking firm-level race and gender compositional data to data and qualitative material detailing the specific discrimination occurrence and what it entailed precisely. All individual and business names have been changed in the qualitative reporting of what occurred in the pages that follow.

Within the content-coded subsample, there is considerable variation in race and gender workplace composition (ranging from 1 to 87, and 1 to 90 percent, respectively) and organization size (from 3 to 1,743 employees); a multitude of discriminatory actors (neighbors, landlords, banks, coworkers, supervisors, etc.); and significant heterogeneity in charging party occupational status and prestige.

Analyzing Discrimination, and the Chapters Ahead

Studying discrimination and its relation to inequality is a daunting task owing to the difficulties in finding and using relevant data and the complexities of the phenomenon itself. This book does so, nevertheless, with relatively rare data—data that speaks to many of the complexities of stratification outlined previously and that provides a grounded view of how discrimination impacts people in their everyday work and residential lives.

Chapters 1 through 4 focus straightforwardly on fundamental issues pertaining to race and gender discrimination in employment. Most notable, particularly in chapter 1 (race) and chapter 3 (sex), is attention to the prevalence of certain discriminatory forms and their manifestations within particular sectors of the economy. Chapters 2 and 4 highlight, and in significant detail, fundamental issues in both race and sex discrimination, including the disjuncture between racial discriminatory treatment and employer justifications (chapter 2), and sexual harassment at work (chapter 4), respectively—two major threads of theoretical speculation in the race and gender literatures that have received limited empirical attention.

Chapters 5 through 8 focus on and capture what are arguably contextual and intersectional complexities pertaining to workplace inequality and discrimination. Chapters 5 and 6 analyze variations in the discriminatory experience across public and private sector workers, and then in workplaces of varying gender and racial compositions. These discussions and analyses are quite important given expectations in the workplace stratification literature that, owing to lack of adequate data at sectoral, organizational, and interactional levels, have been seldom examined empirically. Chapters 7 and 8 address the possibility of intersectionalities and, more concretely, whether gender, race, and social class intersect in ways that make experiences and processes of discrimination unique. Chapter 7 focuses specifically on black and white women of varying social class positions, while chapter 8 assesses the African American male experience of discrimination and the ways it may differ depending on occupational status.

Just as social closure and discrimination in employment is activated in various ways, and conditioned to some degree by context, so is that pertaining to housing. The remaining chapters address how. Chapter 9 assesses forms of housing discrimination, their prevalence, and how racial/ethnic minorities are impacted, while chapter 10 details how these relations vary by the context of residential settings. These discussions are important, extending how one should think about racial residential discrimination, its complexities, and its manifestation in minority's everyday residential lives. Chapter 11 takes the question a step further by examining how discrimination in housing is often rooted in sex and familial status—a fact rarely addressed in the research literature or in public and media discussions of housing inequality.

The very interactional complexities and contextual variations highlighted throughout this book speak to the difficulties in addressing discrimination and inequality from a policy standpoint, yet the analyses offered, including the "grounded" nature of the everyday interactions reported, do provide both insight and leverage. The conclusion revisits emerging patterns and themes, discusses them relative to prior research and theorizing on workplace and housing stratification, and provides what we believe to be a digestible synthesis of lessons—lessons that are intellectual in nature but also concrete and useful for efforts geared toward creating fair and just workplaces and living arrangements.

Note

1. See especially McCall (2001) on variations across labor market sectors and geographic areas.

1

Race Discrimination in Employment

with Lisette Garcia

As I have stated before, I don't want to ever have anyone suffer the way I
have with this company. And I want the company to know that it is subject to the rules of the U.S. Constitution, just as every citizen and organization is.

—African American male, police officer

IN RECENT YEARS, a significant body of employment and inequality research
has highlighted the impact of labor market dynamics on persistent inequalities, including those pertaining to race (Beggs 1995; Semyonov, Raijman, and
Yom-Tov 2002). Specifically, scholars have denoted quite nicely the effects of
economic structure on the racial wage gap (Huffman and Cohen 2004; McCall
2001), racial competition in labor markets and the consequence for group
economic well-being (Semoyonov, Raijman, and Yom-Tov 2002), and how
business concentration in particular sectors has shaped or, in some cases, undermined black employment (McCall 2001).

Traditionally, labor market analyses divided the economy into two primary
sectors, the core and the periphery (Bibb and Form 1977). The core sector is
characterized by high productivity and profits, high levels of capital, and large
firms, while the periphery is marked by low productivity and profits, smaller
firms, and a high level of competition. These differences and where particular
groups are concentrated, it has been shown, influence overall levels of economic well-being (see, for instance, Wilson 1978 and McCall 2001).

The organization of work itself also varies across these sectors, with implications for worker experiences and well-being. Some economic sectors, for

instance, are more bureaucratic; in others, firm size, monopolization, and large-scale productivity dictate organization; some, owing to specialization, professionalism, and training, are organized with certain protections; and finally, certain sectors are disorganized, with less formalized structure and process and, correspondingly, more chaos (Hodson 2001; Roscigno and Hodson 2004). Such attributes and their variations lead to differences in workplace rewards and experiences, including but not limited to levels and forms of racial inequality and discrimination (Wilson 1978).

It is important to consider industrial sector because it patterns the employment experience, and especially the extent to which actors are enabled or constrained from acting in discretionary and, indeed, discriminatory ways. More formalized economic sectors (e.g., state sector, high-wage sector, core sector, etc.) with formal and bureaucratized procedures, for instance, may provide procedural constraints to arbitrary and ascriptively oriented managerial and coworker conduct. The low-wage service sector, in contrast, is often poorly organized with significant managerial flexibility in terms of hiring, firing, and promotion. This lends itself to potential abuses of that flexibility (Roscigno and Hodson 2004). Indeed, we suspect that supervisory discretion in particular and its variations by sector may be a crucial avenue through which discrimination by race is played out in contemporary workplaces.

Racial Discrimination as a Possibility

A comprehensive understanding of racial inequality in employment necessitates exploration of the day-to-day processes and actors implicated in reinforcing the inequality that has been so well documented (Vallas 2003). In this regard, numerous studies attest to the likely persistence of racial discrimination in everyday encounters (Feagin 1991; Feagin and Vera 1995; Forman, Williams, and Jackson 1997; Hughes and Thomas 1998; Kessler, Mickelson, and Williams 1999). Workplace stratification research is no exception, particularly in its emphasis on employer attitudes garnered through interviews.

Employer interviews are one method of assessing why blacks and whites may experience differential treatment and outcomes in the workplace. Indeed, the use of aggregate data can typically only tap into and allow for analyses of "hard skills," measured by human capital, skill, and experience. Since employer discretion and screening methods often rely on justifications surrounding "soft skills," employer surveys remain an effective analytic method. Especially notable here is that employers consistently rate blacks lower in soft skills such as interactional ability and motivation (Kirschenman, Moss, and Tilly 1995; Kirschenman and Neckerman 1991; Moss and Tilly 1995).

Moss and Tilly (2001) show that differential assessment of soft skills can be problematic and lead employers to claim that "blacks don't know how to get a job," or are lazy, unmotivated, undependable, and "just don't care." They argue that these assessments, however, are subjective and rooted in stereotypes. Correspondingly, employers also contend that blacks are defensive and combative in their interactions, and that their speech patterns and language usage make them less desirable employees. Further, notions of fear and intimidation stemming from media images of black men also seem to result in employers' unwillingness to hire black employees. And finally, as noted by Moss and Tilly, employers hesitate to hire African Americans given perceptions that, as a group, black employees are too sensitive to discrimination.

There remains significant slippage, however, between what employers say versus what they may actually do in the course of workplace decision making. In fact, behavior can be influenced by such things as social desirability, interactions with individuals, and situational factors—all of which do not always directly follow from attitudes (Pager and Quillian 2005). Correspondingly, audit methodologies may be more effective at gauging discriminatory processes and behaviors themselves.

Audit studies, as noted in the introduction, attempt to place qualified minorities and white actors into economic and social settings to measure how each group will fare (Bertrand and Mullainathan 2004). These studies have been instrumental in informing us on topics surrounding discrimination. For instance, in 2004, Bertrand and Mullainathan, sent resumes to employers in several metropolitan areas that were identical in all respects except they simulated the race of the concocted job candidates by choosing names that sounded black or white. The authors found that a candidate with a "white" sounding name (e.g., Emily Walsh) was more likely to receive a call back for an interview compared to a candidate with a "black" sounding name (e.g., Jamal Jones). These researchers tested for several other causes, including resume quality,[1] a possible proxy for human capital, and found that enhanced resume quality does not operate as a benefit for blacks in the same way that it does for whites.[2]

A more recent audit study by Pager and Quillian (2005) explored the relationship between employer attitudes about hiring ex-offenders by race, and then employers' actual behavior. They first sent "testers" with similar qualifications and appearance into the same work environment, only varying race and ex-offender status. Findings indicated large and significant effects of both race and ex-offender status. African Americans and ex-offenders were less likely to be invited back for second interviews with black offenders experiencing the greatest disadvantages. This audit study was then followed by a telephone survey which allowed employers to express their hiring preferences.

Employers reported a far greater willingness to hire ex-offenders than the audit study illustrated. Their results suggest that what employers say does not necessarily match what they actually do in practice.

Despite the obvious benefits of the audit design, it can only shed light on one form of discrimination, exclusion in hiring. Audit analyses also provide limited understanding of the interactional nature of inequality or even differential mobility within the workplace. Audit designs nevertheless move us in a needed direction by bringing human actors back into the equation and by asking how, precisely, the inequalities so effectively highlighted in more aggregate, quantitative racial stratification research are being created.

Analyzing Workplace Racial Discrimination

The stratification and work literatures provide solid starting points. Background attributes are important and must be acknowledged, yet these differences in human capital are hardly the sole mechanism underlying contemporary inequalities. Varying structures of local opportunity and levels of labor market organization matter in important ways. The industrial sector and the organization of work are mechanisms which pattern work experiences and stratification. Sectors that allow for more managerial flexibility in terms of hiring, firing, and promotion are arguably more likely to witness discretionary and, thus, discriminatory behavior. But, what is discriminatory behavior?

As noted at the outset, we conceive of discriminatory acts as multidimensional: (1) shaping institutional access, (2) influencing mobility differentially, and (3) reifying a racial hierarchy through interaction and harassment in general. One of the more important of these, at least historically, has been the *limiting of institutional access* either through exclusion (not hiring) or purging through expulsion (firing). Recent audit analyses reveal the contemporary importance of hiring discrimination. Less overall attention has been given to expulsion, although it may be just as important. With regard to *mobility*, much recent work has suggested that discrimination via managerial discretion is likely occurring, yet few if any have been able to systematically detail and examine such behavior.

No work of which we are aware, aside from Feagin and McKinney (2003), grapples seriously with the issue of *general harassment* and racial hierarchy maintenance in the arena of work. This is quite unfortunate. Although the consequences of general harassment may not affect a victim in terms of shaping their objective work status (e.g., getting the job, promotion, or salary increase), there is good reason to suspect that such discrimination holds quite significant sociopsychological consequences for its victims.

As already noted, we limit our analyses to those where a determination of probable cause was made or the case was settled in the charging party's favor (prior to litigation). For race discrimination, this equates to 7,710 cases. Figure 1.1 reports basic descriptives pertaining to these cases across economic sectors for the fifteen year time period being considered. As the reader will note, the majority of serious cases are in the low-wage service sector (38.2 percent) compared to core industries (29.7 percent), high-wage service jobs (19.2 percent), and the public sector (12.9 percent).

Although the patterns above make intuitive sense, given poorer overall organization, less formalized procedure, and a correspondingly lower level of managerial constraint in the low-wage service sector, the variation reported may very well be a consequence of black over-representation in lower status service sector work to begin with. To address this possibility, we control for black sectoral population size, drawn from the Integrated Public Use Microdata Series (IPUMS) 5 percent sample for 2000 (see figure 1.2).[3] The interpretation is relatively straightforward. Where the discrimination bar is larger in magnitude than black population concentration in a particular sector (i.e., IPUMS bar), it suggests that discrimination charges are disproportionately more likely. Conversely, where the discrimination bar is smaller, discrimination is arguably less prevalent.

In figure 1.2 we see that the percentage of claims filed in the high-wage service sector and in the public sector are actually higher than the IPUMS estimate of statewide sectoral concentration of African Americans. This indicates a disproportionate representation of discrimination cases. Although the numerical majority of cases are occurring in the core and low-wage service sectors, this seems to be largely driven by higher overall levels of minority

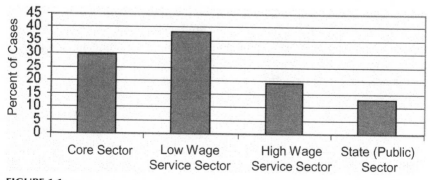

FIGURE 1.1
Distribution of Serious Race-Employment Discrimination Cases, by Industrial Sector

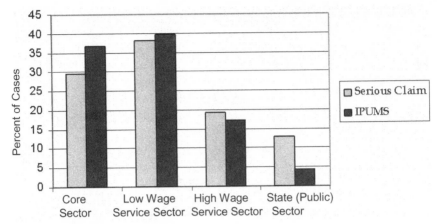

FIGURE 1.2
Distribution of Serious Race-Employment Discrimination Cases and Overall Sectoral Representation of African Americans

representation in these sectors where the opportunity to discriminate, based on pure numbers, is much higher. But what forms does discrimination take within and across sectors? To answer this, we turn toward finer breakdowns in figure 1.3.

Each cluster in figure 1.3 represents proportional breakdown within sector, while the dark bar presented on the far right of each cluster, labeled IPUMS, reflects how the African American population as a whole is distributed across sectors within the state. Although the representation of discriminatory forms differs significantly by industrial sector, no one sector stands out as being much worse than the others. There are, nevertheless, some noteworthy patterns.

Expulsion in the form of discriminatory firing is the most common discriminatory form across most sectors, and disparately so relative to population concentrations. Indeed, firing accounts for 63.6 percent of serious discrimination cases in the core sector, 68.4 percent in the low-wage service sector, and 65.8 percent in the high-wage service sector (65.8%).[4] The exception to this general pattern appears in the state (or public) sector. Although firing remains high, it is overshadowed by general racial harassment while on the job. Perhaps the state sector provides some bureaucratic protections against arbitrary firing, but less shielding from harassment while on the job. Possible variation between the public and private sectors is an issue we revisit in detail in chapter 5. The high rates of discriminatory firing and harassment, taken together, are particularly interesting in light of the fact that prior re-

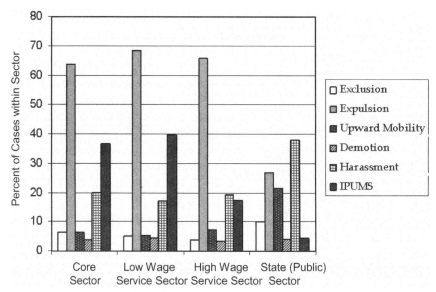

FIGURE 1.3
Distribution of Discriminatory Forms by Industrial Sector, Relative to Overall Minority Representation (IPUMS)

search takes as its principal analytic foci not these forms of discrimination and inequality, but rather hiring and mobility.

Comparison with IPUMS estimates provides some insight into whether these patterns are a function of population size in a given industrial sector. Recall that if the estimated count from the IPUMS is less than the observed percentage of claims filed, then discrimination is higher than expected given African American population size. To illustrate, consider expulsion in the core industries, the low-wage service sector, and the high-wage service sector. The percentage of claims filed is greater than the estimated black representation for those sectors, suggesting that there is disparate representation of firing within them. Also interesting to note is that the percentage of claims filed in the high-wage service sector alleging harassment is greater than the estimated population representation. This may very well reflect managerial or coworker resistance aimed at upwardly mobile African Americans.

Public-sector patterns—something we revisit in detail in chapter 5—are worthy of attention and we briefly make note of them here. Interestingly, in a sector where one would arguably find the greatest protections against discrimination, we find disparate representation of almost all forms of discrimination compared to the estimated population size (except exclusion and demotion).[5] While this is likely a function of a low estimate of African American representation in the state sector, according to the IPUMS, it may also reflect a generally more educated African American population aware of its political rights and avenues of redress.

The Process of Discriminatory Hiring and Firing

Exclusion through hiring is the fourth most common (6 percent) discriminatory form, while discrimination pertaining to expulsion or firing is the most pronounced (60 percent of cases). Although hiring discrimination is less obvious in these data, it is likely the case that individuals experiencing exclusion never find out who obtained the job and, thus, seldom recognize that they have been discriminated against. Under certain circumstances, particularly when extra information is accorded to the victim, the discrimination does become more obvious. Take, for instance, William Hawkins, a young black man seeking employment with a landscaping company, Green Grass, Inc. He submitted an application for employment and over the course of nearly a year was continually told there were no openings. William, however, had a friend employed at the same company who kept informing him of openings.

> Every time I went down and said, "Bob, man, I'm ready—I need to get in here." Bob would always somehow tell me that this person either out-qualified me in one way or the other. But my friend Mike Foote was assuring me all along that he had to train these people, that these people had no more qualifications than I did, and on a couple of occasions they didn't even have the qualifications that I had. Bob was hiring people as I was looking for a job, while he was telling me that he was doing no hiring, he was continuously hiring people and putting them into work and not letting me know that he was doing this.

Not only was William told that there were no openings, but he encountered other obstacles as well. During the course of the year in which he sought employment with this company, his application was lost and he was asked to complete a second application; he was asked to provide his driver's license so that a background check and check of his driving record could be made; and, he was asked to submit a urinalysis which was also lost resulting in him having to take a second test.

That extra information helps prompt challenge is evident in many of the cases, including that of Otis Phillips. Phillips was a security guard seeking employment as a police officer. He completed the necessary paperwork and was awaiting the results of his background investigation (common practice for civil servants) when he was told that his name had been removed from the police recruit eligibility list due to a poor credit history. Mr. Phillips alleged that he was "aware of a younger white applicant, Chris Cornwell, who also has a poor credit history and he has not been removed from the Police Recruit Eligibility list." In fact, the officer conducting the background check on the white applicant, Chris Cornwell, had this to say:

> After completing this applicant's background investigation there are several areas of concern:
>
> 1. This applicant has a very poor credit rating, he has 9 accounts up for collection. He has many civil judgments rendered against him. He attempted to file bankruptcy. It appears that he will not pay his bills at all.
> 2. This applicant has worked 13 different jobs. He doesn't seem to last too long at any job.
> 3. The oral board should take a very close look at this applicant to determine if he should be accepted for the position of police recruit.

In contrast, the officer who conducted Mr. Phillip's background check made these comments.

> The only negative thing found is the fact that the applicant is currently under a Chapter 13 judgment as a result of two divorces. He is currently meeting his financial obligations which should be completed in 2½ years. Despite his advanced age for an applicant, he appears to possess the necessary physical and mental skills for the position.

Notable in the face of the distinct recommendations above is that Phillips was removed from the list while the white applicant remained in contention for a job. Obviously, differential standards were being employed. And, although not explicitly racial in intent, the effect was nevertheless the exclusion of an African American male from the police force.

Expulsion, or firing, is the most common form of discrimination according to our data. One might assume that expulsion is so highly represented because the individual simply feels harmed and humiliated as a consequence of being let go. We remind the reader, however, that these are cases where investigators reached a probable cause determination, based on statements, evidence, and eyewitness accounts. Correspondingly, these cases do not simply represent ones in which a fired individual was simply seeking retaliation against an employer. Rather the bulk of evidence suggests that racial discrimination played a role in the firing.

Shirley Milhouse was an administrative assistant at River City Cultural Center in the early 1990s. During this time, her employer experienced a budget shortfall and some staff, including Shirley, had to be let go. Prior to her termination, however, she noticed something going on in the office around her, prompting her to write a letter to her director nearly a year before her termination. Milhouse noticed specifically that "every attempt is being made to replace and demote me on both a professional and personal basis." Several of her job responsibilities were delegated to her coworkers. As her concerns intensified, Milhouse discussed her uneasiness with her director and requested a transfer, to no avail. Several months later she was terminated. In her charge affidavit, Milhouse notes that her employer:

> knew as early as January 1992 about the pending budget cuts and probable layoffs. In June 1992 Richard Steele [supervisor] had Nancy Davis's [co-worker], white, job reclassified from Administrative Assistant to Curator effective April 1992. I had held the position of Administrative Assistant longer than Davis but, due to her job reclassification, I was no longer eligible to bump her when the layoffs occurred. I was the only Black employee in administration and my duties were divided among the white employees who were retained.

Apparently, Ms. Milhouse's supervisor had reassigned her job duties and even reclassified one of the positions in order to facilitate her termination. The act of reassigning her duties and reclassifying the other position together illustrate the lengths that he would go to in order to ensure that the sole black employee was the only one let go.

Another way in which discriminatory firing is often masked, as noted both below and in the chapters to come, is through allegations of poor performance. Chase Sanbourne, for instance, was an assistant manager of a local electronics store at the Vista Mall. He was terminated from his position at Video Warehouse for unsatisfactory sales performance. A careful review of his employment record and that of the other manager, Jason Witte, reveals Sanbourne's *superior* sales performance. Yet, he was the one fired. As he notes:

> Jason Witte, Caucasian Manager, has had consistently lower sales performance, both reported and actual, than I. My sales have even, at times exceeded those of Caucasian sales persons who did not have the managerial responsibilities that I have. I believe I was terminated from my position as assistant manager of Video Warehouse, because I am black. I was the only black person in my store.

Differential criteria and sanctions for supposedly poor performance are rampant throughout the body of case materials. In the case above, the charging party was accused of not doing his job well enough. In other cases, such as that of Elaine Pines, discussed next, the victim of discrimination is accused of either doing their job poorly or violating company policy. While certainly grounds for termination in and of itself, such termination is problematic and discriminatory when the rationale and justifications are differentially applied.

Elaine Pines, an African American woman and telephone operator at Earthly Communications, was discharged for excessive absenteeism. During the investigation, attendance records of all employees were examined and it was discovered that a white male was afforded a temporary suspension (for the same infraction), whereas Ms. Pines was not. Evidence also substantiates that the employer in this case requested that a union steward be present during the discharge of a white male who was later returned to work via settlement with the union. Ms. Pines, however, was not similarly afforded the presence of a union steward during her discharge. Finally, a white female group leader agreed to remove a white male's final written warning if he were to work six months with no absences. Ms. Pines, in contrast, was never given this opportunity.

In most cases of discriminatory expulsion, the discriminatory action itself tends to be largely covert in nature. It often entails the differential application of workplace policies in a manner that undercuts minority relative to white employees. Thus, despite what often appears to be neutral, bureaucratic procedure and policy—something we elaborate on in chapter 2—powerful actors in workplace organizations typically have flexibility and agency in whether, how, and to whom such policies will be applied. Such discretion appears to be activated across all sectors, although is arguably constrained to some extent in public relative to private sector jobs.

Upward and Downward Mobility

Discrimination is multidimensional, limiting not only institutional access through exclusion and expulsion but also mobility. Approximately 12 percent of the cases report racial discrimination in mobility as the primary injury. Discrimination in mobility can include denials for promotion as well as demotions. A more complete breakdown indicates that 8 percent of all race and employment discrimination cases entail blocked upward mobility (i.e., promotion), whereas 4 percent reported discriminatory downward mobility (i.e., demotion).

Upward mobility is key to institutional power and access. Yet, we continue to find such mobility being denied to individuals based on their race. The rationale for such denials often revolves around employer discretionary judgment pertaining to soft skills. Quinn Fine, for instance, worked for a national auto repair shop for nearly ten years—six of which as an assistant manager. He consistently expressed interest in serving as manager, yet was consistently passed over for promotion while less-qualified white individuals were promoted. Civil rights investigators note that all of those who had been promoted during Mr. Fine's tenure were Caucasian, and were promoted to management positions within a relatively short period of time after being hired. Witness testimony substantiates that the area manager, Al Bright, hand picked who he wanted to be manager. The company itself had no formal procedure for promoting individuals. Consequently, the application process was by word of mouth and promotion was merely based on managerial preference.

Rory Jones, a park ranger, had a somewhat different experience. As a sergeant, he sought promotion to ranger lieutenant. Two such positions were available, and he was eventually passed up for both. According to Jones himself,

> Respondent's reason for not promoting me to lieutenant is a pretext. Respondent never told me that I lacked the ability to make decisions or that my writing needed improvement. My performance evaluations will definitely show that I have performed all of my duties in an outstanding manner.

In this first statement, Jones addresses his employer's main rationale for denying his promotion, that Mr. Jones was simply not qualified. Yet, a review of his file and yearly assessments suggest that he was indeed qualified. Jones goes on to state:

> the respondent assigned me the working title of sergeant with no increase in pay for the position. Respondent let it be known to me that any other promotions to lieutenant would have to come from the sergeant's position.

If Mr. Jones's performance was indeed substandard and not up to the same level of his peers, why then was he assigned to the sergeant's position—the prerequisite for becoming the ranger lieutenant? For Jones, it became clear that criteria and policies were being differentially applied:

> Ronald Sullinger and Terence Foster were not required to work as a sergeant without the pay in order to be promoted to lieutenant. Heretofore, respondent [had] promoted the most senior person. When I became the senior person, the practice stopped (Terence Foster was promoted even though he is less senior).

Often employers use "soft skills," such as reliability, as the justification for denying mobility to African Americans. Consider, for instance, the case of Melody Barnes. Mrs. Barnes was employed at a large medical facility where she sought promotion to the supervisory nurses position. In a letter to her employer Mrs. Barnes writes:

> It is now obvious that there was no intent to seriously consider me for this position. I am aware that the decision to hire the other applicant was made prior to my second interview and the interview only served as a formality to appease me. Lisa Davenport was given the position despite the fact that she was trained by me

and that she has only been employed with you for 15 months; I for seven years. In the seven years I have been employed, I have trained 15 assistants and have taken on many managerial duties. [You have] no legitimate reason to deny me this promotion.

Barnes claims that more attention was given to her personal life, rather than whether or not she was qualified for the position. Several times her reliability was questioned as was her "past record." Discussion of prior absences, in fact, dominated the interview discussion, despite the fact that these absences that were clearly documented as excused in her employment file. She goes on to add that the problem in her workplace is indeed more pervasive and is not limited to failure to promote.

> Several times I have been insulted. Once a doctor turned off the lights and said all he could see was my teeth. . . . [T]here is definitely a problem here. . . . I have just recently been subjected to jokes demonstrating racial insensitivities. Being compassionate to other people's feelings should be a criteria [for medical professionals] . . . so it still leaves me, as well as other minorities, in a climate that is blatantly unfair.

The use of soft skills criteria are evident in a plethora of these cases, including that of Delia Jordan. Ms. Jordan worked for an insurance company and found herself in a situation very similar to that of Mrs. Barnes. She was the person primarily responsible for training new hires—new hires eventually promoted over her. Notably, Ms. Jordan had received many awards and commendations for her work. Investigative materials pertaining to the case suggest that management felt she did not "present herself" as well as the other candidates. In particular, management asserts that she was too "negative," did not focus enough on the positive aspects of her work history, and did not make enough eye contact with the interviewer. In contrast, white candidates presented themselves "clearly," "positively," and "concisely."

Though cases alleging demotion are less prevalent in number, they are still significant. Whereas promotion can open up further opportunities, resources, and power, demotion all but precludes such access. Notable is the similarity with promotion cases and especially the often veiled means by which such discrimination is accomplished. Consider, as a case in point James Lewis, who was employed first as the store manager (and later as sales manager) at a fairly large retail store.

> I was running the number one store in the region . . . however, Brad Smith [white, regional manager], fired me from my store manager position. Smith later called and told me to forget the firing and re-hired me for a Sales Manager position, which was a demotion. . . . I had always received favorable performance

reviews. Smith did not discipline me or notify me of any position performance problems prior to my demotion or discharge. Respondent demoted Logan Moss, white, from Store Manager to Sales Manager, but did not reduce his pay, as they reduced mine. . . . I was the only black Store Manager and Sales Manager employed by Respondent. Respondent immediately replaced me with George Carter, white, who had much lower performance reviews than I.

During their investigation, investigators uncovered that Smith had repeatedly told one of the other store managers that there was something about Lewis that he did not like and often referred to black males as "niggers." Although these comments are not direct evidence of discriminatory treatment, they do support the possibility that there were discriminatory motives on the part of the regional manager.

In another case, Andre Marshall, a manufacturing superintendent at a large electrical manufacturing plant, was demoted to production scheduler, with a corresponding reduction in salary for allegedly violating the company car policy. In his charge Mr. Marshall states:

I know that I did not violate the company car policy procedure as used at Washington Electric and I am aware of numerous other management personnel at the higher echelon than myself who have either done what I did, or much worse and have never been disciplined or reprised by demotion, loss of wages, or anything else. In my twenty years with the Respondent, with the exception of myself, I know of no one else to be demoted for a disciplinary infraction.

During the course of the investigation it became clear that the current vice president of the company did not want Mr. Marshall to continue in his employ and was willing to go to whatever lengths necessary to force him out. Mr. Marshall goes on to state:

The committee gave me the option of quitting with a mutually satisfactory release or being demoted. I refused to quit and the HRM committee decided on my new job placement which, for the first time in my life, was not a supervisory position and required me to report to the same manager who brought the charges against me. I am in an intolerable situation.

As is the case in many of these examples as well as those reported earlier pertaining to firing, we see managerial discretion in the application of company rules and procedures. Alleged violations of policy, when differentially enforced, can lead to discriminatory firings and demotions. Discretionary judgment, particularly with regard to soft skills, and when accompanied by vague promotion policies, can have differential and discriminatory effects for African American employees vying for promotion.

Racial Antagonism and Harassment on the Shop Floor

Interactional processes are important to consider in studies of stratification at work. And, the inequality that may result from workplace interactions is not, strictly speaking, only tied to objective workplace outcomes such as hiring, firing, mobility, promotion, or pay. This is quite evident in our data, which includes a significant number of cases (21 percent) pertaining to racial harassment and differential treatment on the job. Such cases, as the earlier figures revealed, seem to occur disparately in public-sector work. As a case in point, consider the experiences of Buddy Johnson, a policeman in a large metropolitan area. He had been reassigned to various shifts within his department before winding up as the patrolman assigned to the local hospital. He was rather shocked at what unfolded next.

> On June 26th, 1987, I had been reassigned from general duty to "intake officer" . . . One Friday afternoon, Lt. Dooley came into the E/R lobby, where I was sitting, walked over to me, bent over to my ear, and in a very low voice stated to me, "You know Buddy, you're a very lucky nigger."

Johnson had talked about this instance, and several others that occurred, with the city administration. They provided no remedy or response, however, to the hostile environment in which he worked.

> This is a regular routine. The various city administrators promise I won't be harassed any longer, then soon after the oral promise I am subjected to every indignity imaginable. It is late in my career and I would like to be able to enjoy the remaining years.

Mr. Johnson's work environment was barely tolerable and there seemed no solution to the problem. Unfortunately, his experience is by no means rare, as noted by the example of Penny Mitchell, as well as others discussed in subsequent chapters. Penny worked as a secretary at a medical clinic, but was eventually terminated by her employer "because things were not working out" and her work was "substandard." Interestingly, she bore the brunt of racial harassment throughout the tenure of her employment. Consequently, when the clinic offered to have her reinstated after she filed a discrimination suit, she refused to go back. According to her lawyer:

> Mrs. Mitchell is no longer interested in being reinstated to her prior position with the Clinic. We believe that due to the nature and extent of her discrimination as well as the extreme humiliation which she suffered at the clinic as a result of employee actions, reinstatement is not an alternative for which we can consider. For example, a notice was posted on her office door broadcasting Mrs.

Mitchell's termination. Also, there have been instances of extreme racial discrimination such as an instance which occurred on May 8, 1989, where she was
referred to as a monkey. Under these circumstances, I would not recommend re-
instatement to my client.

Such day-to-day interactions and encounters, while perhaps not shaping
one's objective status at work, hold several consequences. For victims, such
treatment clearly leads to despair, distress, and a sense of isolation, particularly
when internal grievance channels do nothing to rectify the situation. More
broadly, and as many of the cases throughout the remainder of this book reveal, racial harassment on the job does something else—it reifies racial hierarchy, and makes race all the more salient within the context of workplaces.

Conclusion

A significant body of literature has demonstrated that racial inequality in the
American labor market shapes allocative issues, such as variations in labor
market opportunities and wage differentials. This line of research has been
beneficial in contributing to our overall knowledge and understanding of inequality. It has done less, however, to address the mechanisms through which
workplace inequality persists. Even as early as Peter Blau and Otis Duncan's
monumental work, the *American Occupational Structure*, sociologists were
suggesting that stratification is itself a social process, and one that is dynamic
in nature. Unfortunately, however, limited data availability continues to leave
us with a relatively static picture.

In this chapter, we have drawn from unique data to explore processes of discrimination quite directly. Some noteworthy findings emerged. First, workplace racial discrimination is, numerically speaking, more prevalent in the
low-wage service sector. This appears to be a function of high minority representation, although there is good reason to suspect that the organization of
low-status, low-reward workplaces may be playing a role. Lack of worker protection, limited formalization, and significant managerial discretion may be
especially key, at least as suggested by many of our examples. The public sector—an explicit focus of chapter 5—in contrast, seems plagued by greater instances of harassment. Perhaps the level of bureaucratization constrains how
discrimination plays out in formalized settings, diverting exclusionary tendencies toward day-to-day mistreatment and racial harassment on the job.

Understanding the day-to-day processes and actors implicated in discrimination is essential for a comprehensive understanding of racial inequality in
employment. Managerial discretion and justifications that make use of soft skill

criteria are often subjective and quite problematic for racial inequality and the ways it is reinforced. This is a theme that reemerges in later chapters pertaining to the unique experience of black women (chapter 7) and black men (chapter 8). Notably, it also resonates with evidence pertaining to gender discrimination (chapter 3) and exclusionary processes in housing (chapters 9 and 11).

We elaborate, in chapter 2, on interpretational issues revolving around race discrimination, most notably disjunctures between victims' accounts of what occurred and employer justifications for differential treatment. This extended focus is important, in our view, and addresses fundamental issues pertaining to racial inequality and ideology, as well as organizational culpability.

Notes

1. Higher quality resumes typically had more work experience, fewer gaps between employment, and were more likely to have some form of degree certification and foreign language skill (Bertrand and Mullainathan 2004).

2. Whites with higher quality resumes received 30 percent more call backs than whites with lower quality resumes. This effect was not as large for blacks (Bertrand and Mullainathan 2004).

3. The IPUMS offers generally reliable estimates of population size by industry across the state.

4. Within sectors bars sum to 100 percent.

5. The IPUMS 5 percent sample estimate for this sector, 4.4 percent, is actually an underestimation of the percent of the workers in the public sector that are black. It is likely that there has been some slippage in capturing a true value for this particular sector and that this figure is actually much closer to 10 percent. If that is indeed the case, then such exclusion would not meet the criteria for disparate representation.

2

Race Attitudes and the Alternative Realities of Workers and Bosses

with Ryan Light

Witness: Linda Wallace came in to see me. She was having problems mostly due to a coworker. The coworker seemed to be involved in racial discrimination. I talked to the personnel director.

Employer: In fact, Wallace had experienced considerable difficulty working with other employees within the personnel department. Her difficulties were with both coworkers and [her] immediate supervisor. . . . Wallace was a marginal employee with a long history of being difficult to work with, who was upset with her assignments . . . this was the basis for her termination.

RATHER THAN DOCUMENTING LEVELS of workplace inequality or the particular workplace contexts where such inequality plays out, attitudinal research takes as its principal analytic foci the extent to which human agents and race-based attitudes may be playing an active role. Indeed, recent work has begun to suggest that the experiences and interpretations of social actors are central.

General research on race attitudes, such as that by Schuman, Steeh, and Bobo (1985), depict shifting trends in both attitudes and the discrimination they may generate. Whites appear more likely to report increasing acceptance of diversity in their neighborhoods, workplaces, and schools, with the caveat that tolerance diminishes as minority composition magnifies across these contexts. This does not mean, however, that whites are not race conscious. Rather, whites continue to wrestle with the historical legacy of racism, have difficulty communicating about racial matters, or express outright ambivalence towards race (see Bonilla-Silva 2003).

Although some work paints an optimistic picture regarding the racial views of white America, qualitative research on black attitudes and experiences indicate that discrimination remains a persistent problem. Within employment, and as denoted in the prior chapter, a range of discriminatory experiences persists from the subtle to the more explicit (Feagin and McKinney 2003; Pierce 2003). How do we navigate the divide between the optimistic reports of general white attitudes and evidence of ongoing discrimination generally, and in the arenas of work and housing more specifically?

Recently, researchers have relied on two related analytic strategies to get at these questions. Some, such as Kirschenman and Neckerman (1991) and Moss and Tilly (2001), make use of in-depth employer interviewing and have uncovered subtle forms of racial bias and preconceptions. Specifically, they point to the subjective aspects of evaluating employees and potential hirees. Moss and Tilly (2001) locate the action of discrimination in hiring primarily within the evaluation of soft skills, such as friendliness, appearance, attitude, and commitment—a pattern related in some examples in chapter 1. Employers generally view racial differences in relation to these soft skills to the disadvantage of minorities.

Other research decodes the language used when discussing race and interaction in the workplace (Pierce 2003). Bonilla-Silva's (2003) developed treatment, which also relies on open-ended interviewing techniques and that takes as its analytic focus white attitudes and preconceptions, describes the subtle forms of discrimination underlying the way whites discuss race. Whites continue to struggle with racial identities, but this struggle appears to have taken a turn. Specifically, white Americans often express support for the meritocratic ideal regardless of a person's race—that is, they acknowledge the right of all people to the pursuit of upward mobility, or the "American Dream." They remain reticent, however, in acknowledging structural and historical impediments that continue to shape the well-being of minority groups.

The very attitudes that whites possess regarding race might complicate studies of discrimination if attitudes do not correspond to actions. Even those attitudes held in earnest may conceivably cloak, knowingly or unknowingly, discriminatory behavior. In this regard, both classic and contemporary studies (e.g., LaPiere 1934; Pager and Quillian 2005) suggest that attitudes and behaviors are often disconnected.

In general, attitudinal research adds an essential microcomponent to the general discussion of discrimination in the workplace. Yet, attitudinal research typically does not link perceptions and attitudes to actual acts of discrimination. Moreover, this research rarely, if ever, matches gatekeeper attitudes and interpretations with those of employees or potential victims. As audit studies make evident, the discrimination process is a dyadic one, between employer and employee. Little work on racial attitudes has made use of this fact, integrating what we know on racial attitudes in general and the more specific evaluative criteria, biases, and actions of employers. Such synthesis, we show below, provides important leverage for understanding how social closure occurs, how gatekeepers perpetuate it knowingly or not, and how and why discrimination persists.

Attitudes, Disjuncture, and Workplace Racial Discrimination

Simultaneous consideration of subjective experience and interpretation, on the one hand, and concrete discriminatory behavior and consequences, on the other, is essential for filling the empirical gaps pertaining to workplace racial inequality and its persistence (see also Pager and Quillian 2005). Equally important, the explicit focus on gatekeeping actors, their perceptions, and their behaviors can provide much needed theoretical elaboration on the processes and mechanisms implicated in inequality reproduction—elaboration that arguably transcends employment inequality and that has utility across a wide array of institutional arenas.

As noted in the introduction, social closure as an orienting tool invites and indeed directs us toward an in-depth understanding of the processes through which stratification hierarchies, including but not limited to the arena of work, are both defined and maintained. The benefit, beyond a more in-depth understanding of stratification in particular, also entails more explicit, rigorous theorizing. As noted by those engaged in theory construction and evaluation, effective sociological theory not only takes as its logical aim the denotation of relations (i.e., does x effect y, and in a particular manner?), but it also grapples seriously with the explication of process (i.e., how does x influence y, or what processes and mechanisms are involved in that relation?). In the first of these regards, research has been quite strong in denoting the empirical relevance of human capital attributes, segregation, and so on, concluding that discrimination is very likely occurring. In the second, however, empirical work has been much less clear. We attribute this, at least in part, to data limitations—limitations that have undoubtedly constrained which questions researchers pose in the first place, and that we attempt to rectify in our analyses. It is also likely the case that lack of theoretical development—development that explicitly delineates dimensions of social closure and discrimination, at structural and interactional levels—is partially to blame. It is for this reason that we begin below by disentangling dimensions of closure, including discrimination, through a two-by-two classification of types.[1]

Figure 2.1 provides an overview of principal mechanisms, both historical and contemporary, involved in racial inequality. The horizontal axis relates the degree of explicitness within which social closure by race occurs, while the vertical axis denotes whether the closure occurring tends to be manifested at macro- or microinteractional levels. To the extent that state-sanctioned discrimination (macroexplicit) pertains to contemporary discussions, it will tend to only be through historically driven disadvantages (macroimplicit), the persistence of explicit bigotry and action (microexplicit), or biased perceptions, standards, and rule applications (microimplicit).

Microlevel processes of social closure will certainly be conditioned by historical and macrostructural disadvantages (see arrows), but are ultimately enacted by potential gatekeeping actors whose rationales for discriminatory treatment will be either explicitly racial or implicit. Thus, although this formulation suggests unique dimensions of closure as it pertains to race, such dimensions are obviously connected both historically and contemporarily.

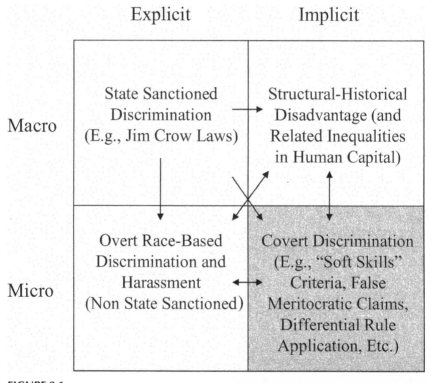

FIGURE 2.1
Typology of Social Closure, Generally, and Discriminatory Forms by Macro/Micro and Explicit/Implicit Dimensions

Prior research has established the historical legacies of formal, state-sanctioned racial exclusion and segregation. And, contemporary empirical work has denoted the ways in which macrostructural disadvantages translate into racial variations in skills, education, job experience, and thus some of the employment inequalities we continue to find. Less obvious (but see Pager 2003; Pager and Quillian 2005; Moss and Tilly 1996, 2001) have been the ways in which discriminatory treatment at the microinteractional level may be playing a role. There is, however, a broader literature on racial attitudes from which we can draw and that directs attention toward microimplicit forms of social closure that may still be occurring within the arena of work.

Grounded in liberal race theory, some researchers suggest that discrimination continues to result from pure racism (the microexplicit box) by gate-keeping actors, who have explicit aversions to hiring minority employees or to statistically discriminate given perceptions of the minority population and its attributes generally. Such perspectives dominated accounts of employment discrimination until the 1990s. Broad, observable racist behaviors, such as the use of derogatory names and the creation of a racially hostile work environment became key to discussions of the stratification process, as did racial stereotyping by employers—employers who might use race as a rough proxy for skill and human capital differences.

Although explicit racism continues to exist, as denoted by many examples used in this book, more recent trends in attitudinal data suggest that covert forms (bottom right of figure 2.1) have grown increasingly more important. Indeed, attitudinal studies suggest that explicitly racist views have been and continue to be on the decline in the United States. Notably, though, this decline does not necessarily correspond with a decline in the experience of discrimination. Rather, covert or even unconscious forms of discrimination may simply be playing a greater role in the processes of social closure.

Covert forms of discrimination, as the concept implies, are often hidden and subtle. In the workplace, contemporary discrimination is frequently shrouded in legal or meritocratic language offering a surface layer that must be dissected in order to evaluate how discrimination occurs in a given setting. Recent theorists, such as Eduardo Bonilla-Silva, Cornell West, Michael Eric Dyson, and Barbara Reskin, offer distinct approaches that move questions of discrimination beyond the predominant liberal race theories to provide insight into the evaluation of covert discrimination. A major component that weaves through each is a call to account for the microinteractional mechanisms. These mechanisms are all too obvious within narratives or stories that people tell, yet remain difficult to extrapolate in survey research. By taking accounts of discrimination from both sides' points of view seriously—something we can do with our data—we gain greater understanding of discriminatory processes and how they play out, as well as the disjunctures we find between action and interpretation.

What Employees Say and Experience

Workplaces and employers accused of discrimination are rarely willing to admit it. A few notable studies uncover patterns of discrimination within a single case, yet critics will suggest that singular cases or limited sample sizes compromise the ability to draw general conclusions. The growing body of audit studies partially addresses such criticism, yet such studies tend to be limited to but one aspect of employment, hiring. Our analyses address some of these methodological limitations by examining the interpretations of employees and employers relative to actual instances of discrimination across a wide array of workplaces.

Take, first, the case of Raymond Jackson. In 1989, the Midcity School District decided to diversify the responsibilities of its employees. Due to the summer lull in activities, a number of the district's bus drivers were asked to mow grass. Raymond, an employee of the district for over thirty years, tried his hand on the tractor. He quickly realized that he was not comfortable with his new duties. He had difficulty reaching the pedals stating that the length of his legs "makes it unsafe for me to reach the brake or clutch in an emergency." He demonstrated this hazard to several supervisors who agreed with his misgivings. However, by the end of the summer, Raymond was suspended and subsequently fired for refusing to mow grass. Another employee also demonstrated her inability to mow the grass and was allowed to continue her duties as a bus driver. Raymond felt that he was treated differently because of his race: he was black and his colleague was white. He simply wanted equal treatment in order to fulfill his duties as a bus driver.

Around the same time, in Erie Town, Jim Carson experienced an entirely different sort of impediment to his duties at an automobile parts company. Having worked for the company for sixteen years, he had recently reached a breaking point due to severe racial harassment that compelled him to go to the Ohio Civil Rights Commission (OCRC):

> For the past year a six-page letter with 114 racial jokes has been circulating throughout [the parts company]. A picture of various types of monkeys has been posted on the bulletin board, which included a picture of myself. It was posted in plain sight for all to view.

Additionally, a "nigger application for employment," a mock letter to a "jungle bunny hunter," and a cartoon of an African American woman giving birth

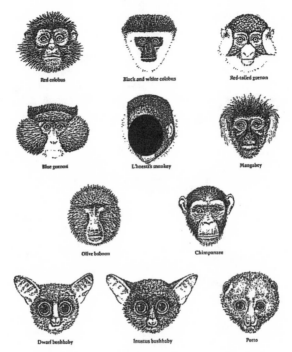

FIGURE 2.2
Racist Poster Depicting African American Male Employee (the face at the center of the poster is covered for identifiability reasons)

to a child holding a boom box were posted. This hostile climate made it difficult for Jim to perform his duties and influenced his ability to do his job.

Raymond and Jim's experiences differ in salient ways. Raymond's supervisors and colleagues did not abuse him in an overt manner. In fact, they listened to his complaints and confirmed his fears regarding the tractor. They did not use racial slurs or subject him to harassment. Raymond experienced covert discrimination. Covert discrimination occurs subtly, sometimes unknowingly, and often by gatekeepers behind closed doors. Jim, on the other hand, experienced overt racism. His colleagues indeed subjected him publicly to racial slurs and epithets.

As the prior chapter began to reveal, multiple forms of employment discrimination exist, and they range from covert to quite overt in their racial character. Figure 2.3 reports the primary charges for a subsample of serious race-related employment cases, and the grievance from the victim's point of view.

The vast majority of victims, like Raymond, experience differential treatment. Differential treatment, usually covert in nature, occurs across employment

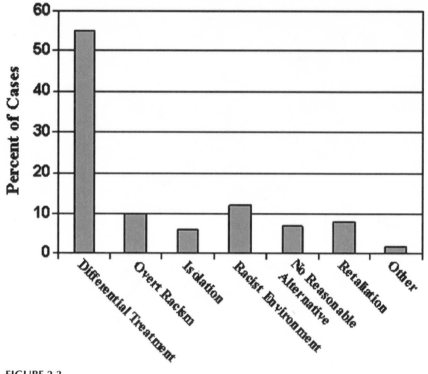

FIGURE 2.3
Principal Charge/Injury in Race-Employment Discrimination Subsample, According to the Victim

sectors and covers an array of employment outcomes. Individuals are differentially treated in hiring, firing, promotions, work assignments, and the distribution of benefits, among other occupational situations. The key theme that weaves through each employee's story of discrimination is a call for equality. People simply want to be treated fairly and like everyone else.

Consider, for instance, the case of Thomas Johnson. Thomas, a black male, worked in Northern Town. Like many workplaces in Northern Town and others across Ohio, there is strict hierarchy based on seniority within his workplace. After twenty-four years on the job, however, Thomas was informed that his position had been abolished and he was subsequently let go. Shortly thereafter, he learned that a less senior white employee, whose job was also previously terminated, had been asked back to the workplace. The employer effectively denied Thomas "the right to bump [the junior employee] out of the position." As the junior employee himself acknowledged, this right was well

established in the workplace and an unusual violation of the seniority protocol. In fact, this coworker states that the employer consistently "made decisions about [Thomas's] job duties based on their assumption that he is not as
qualified as the other Foreman" and confirms, as did the OCRC, that Thomas
possessed the appropriate qualifications for his position.

Many such cases involving differential treatment revolve around subjective
judgments of qualifications. Similar to Thomas, for instance, an African
American customer service representative was fired for failing to follow procedures, while white employees who similarly violated procedure retained
their jobs. He states that "I was denied the same privilege of continued employment." Others suffer similar fates, such as an African American mental
health professional whose contract was not renewed because, in her words,
"high profile, high priority and well-funded projects were assigned to [other
professionals], all White employees." The subjective nature of assessing
whether an employee is eligible for a promotion or whether a hiree is qualified for a position opens up the window for discrimination and the use of soft
skills by gatekeepers (see especially McBrier and Wilson 2004; Wilson 1997;
Peterson and Saporta 2004). Employers use these cues, such as clothing, demeanor, or modes of speech, to exclude otherwise capable minority candidates for promotion or hire.

Other workers experienced less prevalent, but no less egregious forms of
covert discrimination, such as isolation and no reasonable alternative for a
negative employment outcome. Isolation occurs when workplaces are overwhelmingly dominated by a single race, typically nonminority. The employees or hirees experiencing discrimination in these instances often have little
evidence of discrimination beyond numerical observations or a cursory
knowledge of the critical gatekeepers' race.

D. J. Houston, an African American machine operator in Steel County, applied for a job at a public utility company. This company had recently adopted
a formal procedure for hiring new employees. Unbeknownst to D. J., this employer required the completion of a written application form for all prospective hirees. Multiple people inside the organization refused to let D. J. know of
this change in policy despite his numerous inquiries regarding job openings at
the public utility. However, D. J. perceived that something was not right. What
he did know was that other, white applicants were being hired for the positions to which he applied:

> Since the beginning of September 1990, I and another qualified Black person
> were denied hire for the position of Assistant operator. (These positions went to
> Whites). Currently, only one out of fifty-eight individuals employed here is
> Black. Hiring and firing decisions here are made exclusively by Whites.

Similarly, an African American truck driver in Northern Town felt uncomfortable after being given "vague reasons" for his termination. Upon reflection, he came to realize that he had been consistently held to different standards compared to his white coworkers. He concludes his charge of discrimination by noting that he "was the only Black truck driver in the history of the company." In a similar case involving hiring, an African American laborer searching for employment applied for a lawn care job and was required to take a drug test. He subsequently discovered that this was not typical practice and that the company had no black employees. In these cases and others like them, a key informant, either a friend, relative, or former colleague, inside of a company shares information with the employee or hiree. This information leads the employee or hiree to conclude that their adverse employment outcome was a result of racial discrimination.

In several instances, workers somehow correctly perceive that discrimination took place without significant first-hand evidence. In such cases, workers feel that something suspicious has occurred that led to their termination or other negative consequence. The suspicion often grows over a significant period of time. Similar to the examples of isolation, these individuals perceive a pattern of discrimination; however, unlike isolation, those who see no reasonable alternative for their adverse employment outcome possess scant evidence. This lack of evidence does not mean that discrimination did not occur. Such is the case of Brenda Smith, an African American, whose job as an administrative assistant was eliminated at a historical preservation society. This society hired other minorities, but no minorities worked in her particular office. Other employees were reassigned when the society experienced financial difficulties while Brenda was let go.

Brenda is not alone in experiencing discrimination's sometimes subtle form. An African American police officer in Northern Town was "continuously denied permanent assignment" to a police cruiser for over ten years without justification beyond the fact that no one would volunteer to team with him. Such cases indicate that individual's perceptions of discrimination can be confirmed without initial evidence. Although seemingly difficult to identify, workers perceive and are greatly affected by even the most subtle forms of discrimination.

Although most employees or hirees experience covert discrimination, nearly 20 percent experience some form of overt or blatant discrimination with race at its core. Two broad categorizations capture instances of overt discrimination, namely overt racism within social interaction and a generally racist environment. The distinction between the two hinges upon the focus of the discriminatory acts.

Similar to the case of Jim Carson, mentioned previously, employees may be subject to direct racist attacks by individuals in the workplaces within the course of daily interaction. Rachel Webster, for instance, worked as a cashier at a restaurant in a hotel. The staff of the restaurant was multiracial, yet the management was exclusively white. One day, she was having difficulty understanding a new promotion for kid's meals. The white manager grew impatient with her and eventually lost his nerve exclaiming,

> What does it take to get my point across [to] you people. . . . Do I have to smack the shit out of you to get my point across?

These derogatory statements led Rachel to experience severe discomfort. In a handwritten note, she writes, "I felt that after all that happened I could not do my job to the best of my ability."

Others face similar impediments to successful job performance because of hostile treatment by bosses. In one case, a deputy clerk of courts overhears coworkers refer to her as "the nigger." In another, a custodian is continually forced to take longer routes than white employees all while he is subjected to racial slurs. Importantly, such incidents of overt racism take place across an array of job types within our data, and affect individuals regardless of gender. Although the negative employment outcomes are known—termination, decreased job performance, and so on—the broader emotional and mental impact of such experiences clearly warrants further research attention.

In contrast to either subtle discrimination based on race or overt, direct acts that occur within the context of interaction, are cases within which a racist environment permeates the workplace. Here, the discriminatory action may not be directed toward a particular individual, but rather shape day-to-day interactions and the potential well-being of any and all minorities in a given workplace. For example, a black grocery worker in Northern Town seeking a job as a supervisor states, "I believe that [Northern Town Supermarkets] discriminated against Blacks as a class by denying us promotion." An employee in a jewelry store in Steel County makes a similar claim stating that "a Caucasian manager asks Caucasians if they are interested in a position when a manager position becomes available." The manager does not provide the same courtesy to minority employees resulting in a managerial staff that is entirely white.

These general forms of discrimination as told by workers themselves depict the variety of discrimination that occurs in employment. Discrimination is multifaceted and affects a diverse array of people. Expanded analyses of discrimination must acknowledge this variety in order to capture a more complete picture of how discrimination impacts the lives of Americans. By acknowledging this diversity, particularly the important differences between covert and overt forms of discrimination, we gain a greater understanding of the mechanisms implicated in inequality.

What Employers Say

Employers are required by law to respond to discrimination charges. Like victims' perceptions, employers have a variety of reasons for the actions that led the employee to seek reprisal from the OCRC. Figure 2.4 depicts the forms of justification used by employers within our sample of cases.

It is important to recall that these are serious cases of discrimination, wherein a neutral, third-party investigation eventually found that there was probable cause that the charging party's complaint was legitimate based on the evidence, or wherein the employer eventually settled the claim to the victim's satisfaction. Conventional analyses of employers and discrimination, as the reader will recall from prior discussion, tend to rely on interview techniques to gauge employer's attitudes and capacity to discriminate. Our analyses, in comparison, evaluate official employer responses to, and justifications

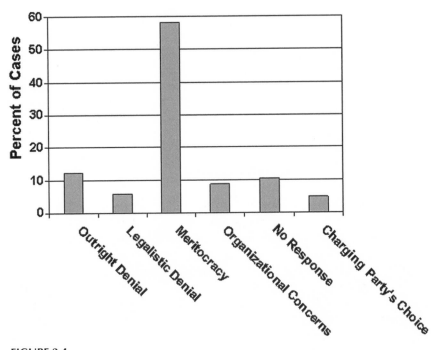

FIGURE 2.4
How Employers Respond to and Justify Discriminatory Treatment

for, actual discriminatory behaviors and treatment of employees (see Pager and Quillian 2005).

As seen in figure 2.4, the majority of employers (56.8 percent) claim that their organization is purely meritocratic in terms of employees and workplace decisions concerning employees. Their organization, as is often contended, adheres to equal opportunity employment and respects the tone of such laws. Thus, employment decisions are arguably never made on the basis of race, but rather are made through concrete and fair evaluations of worker performance. We know that this is not the case, however, based on OCRC reports, evidence, and investigative criteria. Take, for instance, the case of Raymond Jackson, the Midcity bus driver asked to operate a lawnmower, discussed earlier. A representative for Midcity School District offers this merit-based justification for Raymond's termination:

> Mr. Jackson was discharged due to the charges of Insubordination and Neglect of Duty being sustained and in consideration of his past record as it related to discipline. Specifically, Mr. Jackson refused a summer assignment mowing grass, after exhausting all other types of leave. He refused to demonstrate his claimed inability to operate the tractor/mower. He refused, on more than one occasion, to demonstrate that he could not operate the equipment by making an attempt.

As this case reveals, employers often use insubordination and neglect of duty as the meritocratic justification for negative employment outcomes. Similar to the case of Raymond Jackson, Jim Carson's employer justified his firing based upon merit and specifically "time away from work and long lunches and job performance." Yet, he was the employee mentioned previously, who suffered severe harassment in the form of racist jokes, including the poster of himself embedded among monkeys.

Evaluations based upon skill often take place in a short period of time or, as in Jim's case, without informing the employee of his/her poor performance. For example, managers made a quick decision in the case of an experienced freight operator who was fired after a week on the job:

> As Charles Howell's supervisor for the week that he was employed at our company I agreed with the decision to terminate him. I did not feel that his lift skills were at the same level as the other new hires at the same point. . . . As I do with new hires I have to rely on feedback from the people they work with to a certain degree . . . the comments about Charles was that he was still having trouble with the ties of the freight.

As these exemplify, gatekeepers often use merit to defend the decisions they make. By basing their decisions upon merit, they conform to the post–civil rights ideal of equal opportunity. The onus of these decisions, then, regardless of whether the workers have experienced covert or overt discrimination, rests on the performance of the employee and not on the climate created by, actions of, or differential treatment by the management.

Other employers deny discrimination strictly on legal grounds. In one such instance, a community-based human rights organization strongly affiliated with a local government agency addresses the charge that it discriminates against minorities. A statement from the executive committee of the organization states, "The Human Rights Organization is an independent organization with only one employee. . . . [We] understand that the Commission doesn't investigate organizations with only one employee."

In a similar vein, some employers claim that the statute of limitations has been reached or, in an extreme case, that the OCRC conspired against the employer, violating the employer's civil rights. These legalistic denials do not revert back to the performance of the employee, but challenge the legal validity of the discrimination claim. Such employers, rather than responding to the charge, simply question the jurisdiction of the OCRC. Understandably, such responses are heavily laden with legal jargon, and are often invalid in the context of cases we are examining.

Many employers perceive that their decisions, deemed discriminatory by civil rights investigators, have been made with legitimate organizational concerns in mind. For example, in the case of Brenda Smith, the administrative assistant terminated by the historical preservation society, the personnel officer for the organization cites budgetary concerns as the primary reason for her dismissal:

> Last September, due to budget cuts from the State of Ohio, we experienced a significant layoff, the result of which prompted the above charge.

Notable in her case, however, was the fact that she was laid off while all other employees (all white) were simply reassigned. Such budgetary and financial justifications are numerous throughout our data. Although business can certainly make hiring, firing, demotion, and promotion decisions with such concerns in mind, it is important that the behavior that results does not, by default or design, single out or disparately effect racial/ethnic minorities.

Many employers place the responsibility directly on the employee by stating that the adverse employment outcome, typically termination, was the employee's decision. These explanations "blame the victim" by placing the adverse employment outcome at the hands of the worker. Often the employer reacts to charges of discrimination by suggesting that the employee never sought a promotion or that the employee agreed to a transfer. In cases of firing, the employer, citing the employee's decision, makes the unusual claim that an employee "voluntarily terminated" his or herself.

The multiple and diverse justifications that employers use are evident across employment sectors and independent of the size of the workplace. Whether these justifications are honestly felt or invented to protect business interests is difficult to clarify, and are beyond the scope of any single sociological analysis. However, future analyses should continue to account for the interpretations of bosses, in addition to workers, when exploring racial discrimination at work.

Conclusions

Employees and employers have disparate perceptions regarding discriminatory acts. This chapter has highlighted the multifaceted perspectives that each of these groups hold. Indeed, analyses of justifications, especially when coupled with actual employer behaviors, reveal important clues to how inequality gets created on the ground and how it is linked to broader societal ideologies. Such ideologies may take the form of merit-based world views or views wherein simple business interests override those pertaining to fairness and equality of opportunity and treatment.

Social scientists, policy makers, and other interested parties should obviously account for both overt and covert forms of discrimination given the patterns revealed thus far. Discrimination occurs openly in hostile, racist form, but it also clearly manifests, and perhaps increasingly so, subtly and behind closed doors.

Future analysis should further account for the varied perspectives of employers. This poses particular problems for research on discrimination. When do employers tell the truth? And, when do they evade the truth in order to protect their reputation or avoid litigation? These questions and our ability to get at them provide an obstacle, to be sure, yet should not preclude serious efforts to add employers' perspectives to discussions of discrimination.

Immersion into the perspectives of employers and employees highlights the microinteractional nature of discrimination, as called for by theorists and researchers alike. Although certainly driven by structure and history, and constrained or enabled by organizational and institutional structures, inequality is fundamentally enacted or ameliorated in an ongoing manner by human beings in the course of interaction. Audit analyses, as reviewed previously, acknowledge and observe this dyadic structure. The dyad, or pairing, between the employer and employee forms the focal point.

The process of claims making in relation to actual behavior highlights the disjuncture between workers and bosses. We draw, one last time, from the case of Raymond Jackson, fired for not mowing the grass. There were obviously wildly disparate interpretations of the events that led to Raymond's termination. Raymond noted physical disability, and the fact that a white female employee who made similar claims was relegated to regular job duties. His employer, in contrast, suggested that his insubordination led to his firing. Such a gulf is not rare in our data and is reproduced time and again within the case files. Indeed, the differential treatment–meritocratic dyad, as in Raymond's case, occurs most frequently in cases of racial employment discrimination. Yet, no dyad illustrates the gulf between workers' and bosses' interpretations of discrimination as dramatically as the overt racism–meritocratic dyad. Figure 2.5 illustrates this profound disjuncture.

Here, a worker overhears his employer speak disparagingly about his performance using derogatory language. The employer responds by stating simply that the employee did not perform his duties adequately. Taken in isolation, these interpretations of the events that led to the employee's termination

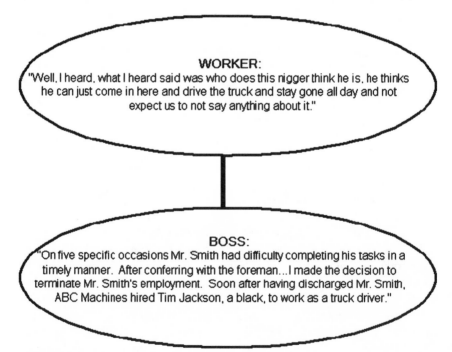

FIGURE 2.5
An Example of the Overt Racism-Meritocratic Dyad

would be incomplete. The worker's claim by itself lends credence to the persistence of overt racism, while the boss's counterclaim reaffirms the meritocratic ideal. Observed as a dyad, however, we can see the disjuncture between workers' and bosses' interpretations of discrimination and begin to dissect how this disjuncture affects worker treatment, not to mention broader public discussions of race.

Note

1. Typological classifications, such as the one we are presenting, have proven to be an invaluable theoretical tool in sociology historically, although they have been less often explicitly employed in stratification research or that pertaining to racial inequality and closure processes. Such "types" provide clarity in important dimensions, such as micro/macro, covert/overt, etc. Especially effective typologies will cover the preponderance of empirical possibilities in the real world.

3

Sex Discrimination in Employment

with Donna Bobbitt-Zeher

I feel she was discriminated against . . . no one had any problems with her except David; he didn't feel she could do the job because she was a female. David told her many times that she was doing a fine job but if there was a problem, he would put it on her. She was a scapegoat. . . . She was very capable of doing the job. She didn't deserve that treatment. They took advantage of her.

—male witness to discrimination against a female coworker

MUCH LIKE THE RACIAL INEQUALITIES discussed thus far, there remain substantial gender disparities in the arena of employment. We see this in the types of jobs men and women have, the pay they receive, and in significant differentials in where they end up on the occupational hierarchy. What accounts for these persistent gender inequalities? In this chapter, we examine existing research evidence on sex stratification in employment, much of which concludes that discrimination at institutional and interactional levels must be playing a role. Our analyses focus on the four principal discrimination issues that women face at work according to our qualitative immersion into case files. These revolve around job exclusion, expulsion, mobility, and harassment. While similar to race patterns, at least to some degree, our results and the qualitative insights in particular relate what are clearly unique barriers and discriminatory tendencies that women face on the job.

Gender Inequalities in the Labor Market

Researchers have documented persistent gender differences in both occupational position and in wages.[1] While the degree of sex segregation in occupations (a topic we deal more systematically with in chapter 6) has declined since the 1960s, men and women continue to work in different types of jobs to a considerable degree. In 2000, for instance, the top occupations for women were secretaries, school teachers, nurses, and cashiers. For men, the most popular occupations included truck drivers, retail managers, and salespersons (U.S. Census Bureau 2003). Although certain occupations have certainly integrated over time, the level of gender segregation remains large enough that more than half of women (52 percent) would have to change occupations in order to achieve sex integration of occupations (Padavic and Reskin 2002, 67).

One reason that occupational sex segregation is considered problematic is its connection to the gender wage gap. In 2003, full-time working women employed year round average 75.5 percent of what men earn (Institute for Women's Policy Research 2004). And, such gaps are found even among the youngest workers who are just beginning their careers (Marini and Fan 1997). While men earn more than women even when they are in the same general occupation, occupational sex segregation remains a significant source of these earnings disparities (England 1992; Padavic and Reskin 2002).

Why do these inequalities persist, especially in the face of women attending and completing college at equivalent or even higher rates relative to their male counterparts and contemporary ideologies that stress egalitarianism (see NCES 2005 for evidence of this trend)? As popular perceptions typically insinuate, is it simply that women and men prefer different types of work—types of work that are differentially rewarded? Do women and men have different skills, as human capital and traditional economic theories might suggest—skills that lead to distinct occupational positions and job rewards? Or are there alternative processes occurring that place women at a systematic disadvantage?

Proponents of human capital and neo-economic theorizing clearly view gender differences in occupations and wages as a consequence of gender differences in job preference, work experience, and marketable skills. Through gender socialization, the argument suggests, young men and women come to have different priorities for their careers. This shapes occupational choices, as young men seek jobs with higher earnings. Women, for their part, seek flexible positions and jobs in which they can help others (see, for instance, Daymont and Andrisani 1984). As a result of lower commitment to the labor market and greater devotion to their families, women will have less overall in the way of on-the-job skills and experience; this matters because skills and work experience affect pay (see, for instance, Budig and England 2001). In a somewhat similar vein, some have suggested that women and men have distinct, basic-skill sets, particularly when it comes to cognitive capacity. Skills associated with men tend to be utilized in jobs that are better rewarded in the labor market, and men tend to be concentrated in these jobs that require such skills (Paglin and Rufolo 1990).

While not denying the possibility that preferences, experience, and skills may be playing some role, interpretations such as those presented above downplay or neglect altogether the role that discrimination may be playing in generating unequal labor market outcomes for women and men.[2] A focus on processes of social closure, as delineated in the introduction and certainly alluded to in sociological theorizing on inequality, moves discrimination and various forms of differential treatment from the periphery to the center of analyses.

Social Closure and Sex Discrimination in Employment

Social closure, according to Tomaskovic-Devey (1993a), occurs when "a status group creates and preserves its identity and advantages by reserving certain opportunities for members of the group. Exclusionary policies ensure that the best positions and most desirable opportunities are reserved for members of more powerful status groups." As was the case in our analyses of racial inequality, attention to closure as a construct shifts analytic focus toward workplace experiences, interactions, and structures rather than the background characteristics of those on the losing end of stratification hierarchies. As Reskin (2000) notes, it also leads us to explore "discrimination in terms of the strategic, self-interested actions by members of privileged groups who intentionally exclude and exploit subordinate-group members to protect or advance their own interests." Emerging scholarly work has developed such emphases recently in highlighting how organizational policies and practices enable or constrain discrimination on the part of more powerful groups and social actors (Reskin 2000; see also Reskin and Roos 1990).

A variety of social closure processes and blocked opportunities shaping women's disadvantages in the labor market may, in fact, help maintain gender segregation and lower workplace rewards for women (Reskin 1988; Tomaskovic-Devey 1993b; Reskin and Padavic 1988; see also Reskin, McBrier, and Kmec 1999). While an extensive body of research testing neoclassical economic theory using statistical modeling generally assumes some role of discrimination in pay differentials, discrimination is most often inferred from residuals rather than empirically captured (Wood, Corcoran, and Courant 1993; see also England 1992). Case studies and interview data, however, reveal particular patterns of differential treatment that results in a host of more objectively measurable inequalities. Benokraitis and Feagin, for instance, find that gender discrimination in employment may be blatant (obvious and intentional), subtle (not as obvious and perhaps unintentional), or covert (hidden, hard to document, and intentional) and that such exclusionary practices have harmful effects on women, employing organizations, and society in general (Benokraitis and Feagin 1995).

Such discrimination is manifested in several ways. Some have found employers engaging in sex discrimination in hiring. Using an audit design, much like those already discussed pertaining to race, researchers in Philadelphia used male and female testers with comparable resumes and switched the resumes of the testers each week to prevent bias. They found that women were significantly less likely to be hired in low priced and expensive restaurants (Neumark, Bank, and Van Nort 1996). Similar evidence is culled from a study of symphony orchestras. Goldin and Rouse (2000) find that when audition procedures place potential candidates behind a screen where their sex is unknown, women are significantly more likely to be hired than when they are viewable. Here, the only change is that the auditioner's physical features are no longer known.[3]

Problems for women, however, often go further than the employment door. It appears, for instance, that employers hold women to higher standards than men when making promotion decisions (Olson and Becker 1983). Meitzen (1986) finds that sex discrimination contributes to women's higher rate of quitting jobs. He concludes that wage discrimination both exists and contributes to women's exit from their current position. Furthermore, a recent study of sexual harassment among lawyers finds that women who experience or observe such harassment have both lower job satisfaction and higher levels of intent to leave their job (Laband and Lentz 1998). This higher rate of turnover stemming from wage discrimination and harassment most likely contributes to women's lower degree of job experience.

Such patterns, resulting in female disadvantage in hiring and especially exits and mobility, would parallel to some degree our earlier and later findings pertaining to race and the role that discrimination is playing. Analyses of the processes implicated in female employment disadvantage, however, remain sparse, owing largely to data limitations. Our analyses, which follow, allow for detailed examination of workplace sex discrimination in everyday work settings, how it unfolds, its various forms, and its consequences including, but not limited to, objective indicators of job status.

Forms of Sex Discrimination in Employment

Here we consider 4,176 serious cases of sex discrimination against women. Notably, these cases are quite representative of the more general population of female workers in the state of Ohio. For example, similar to the state's population, 71 percent are white, while 14 percent are black.

Figure 3.1 reports the distribution of injury claims or, more precisely, what the discrimination entailed for these women. In almost two-thirds of cases, women experienced workplace institutional exclusion. The vast majority of these, as will be apparent to the reader, involve discriminatory firings, while another 4 percent of all cases entail women not being hired on the basis of their sex. In another 20 percent of the cases, women were harassed, either suffering general harassment (such as antagonism and intimidation) or sexual harassment. In addition, 7 percent of women experienced discrimination in mobility, with 4 percent being unfairly denied promotion and 3 percent enduring demotion on the basis of their sex. In 14 percent of the cases, women experienced some other kind of discrimination, such as unequal benefits or wages. These descriptive statistics, thus, show job exclusion and discriminatory

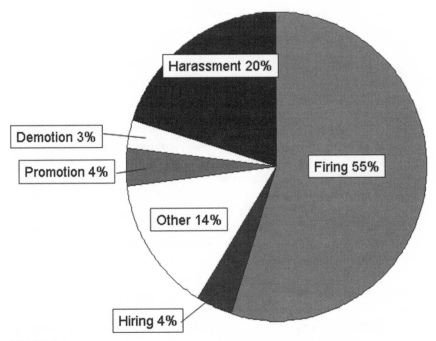

FIGURE 3.1
Distribution of Discrimination Types for Serious Cases of Sex Discrimination

firing in particular to be the principal and most pronounced form of gender discrimination, with a range of other injuries also represented in these cases.

As was the case with race, expulsion and harassment appear to be the largest discriminatory threats to women. Stratification research, in contrast to these two discrimination foci, has largely centered on issues of hiring, mobility, and wages. While certainly important foci in their own right, we suspect that methodological and analytic trends toward the use of large, quantitative data sets with easily measurable, objective indicators of job status have contributed to this. This is problematic, to be sure, to the extent that methodological leanings and general research orientations create social scientific blind spots on issues of inequality, processes of stratification, and their manifestations.

Sex Discrimination in Context

While it is important to focus on the broad, generalizable patterns of sex discrimination, it is also important to remain cognizant of distinct contexts within which women work. For example, although sex discrimination is found in all types of industries, it is more common in some industries than others. This may hold implications for discrimination and the forms that it takes. Serious claims of discrimination are found most commonly in the low-wage service (i.e., retail sales and personal services) and core (i.e., construction, manufacturing, and finance) industries. These two industries account for 70 percent of the sex discrimination claims. How sex discrimination is manifested also varies to some degree across these sectors.

Figure 3.2 suggests quite clearly that there are industrial differences in the inequalities that women are more or less likely to face. Discrimination in firing and harassment (the bulk of the cases) are most common in the low-wage service sector, while discrimination in hiring and demotion are most apparent in the core sector. Blocked upward mobility via denial of promotion appears to be most prevalent in the state sector (public administration and government). State workers also experience the second highest level of hiring discrimination. Relative to the other industries, high-wage service-sector industrial employment (i.e., information services, real estate, and professional services) does not stand out as exceptionally high on any of the measured dimensions of sex discrimination. This is most likely a function of significantly lower female representation in this economic sector.

To better understand the implications of these figures, table 3.1 compares the percentage of women workers in Ohio who are employed in each industry type to the percentage of discrimination cases in each industry. These figures show a general overrepresentation of the state and core sectors among sex discrimination cases. For example, in Ohio, 4 percent of women work in the

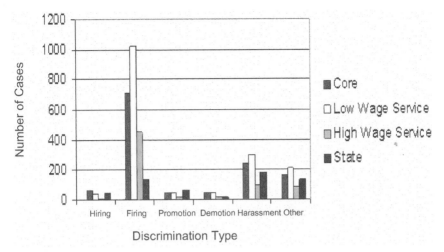

FIGURE 3.2
Serious Sex Discrimination Cases, by Form of Discrimination and Industry

state sector, yet 13 percent of sex discrimination claims are made by women working in that particular sector. Also overrepresented is the core sector. The low-wage service sector, although higher in actual number of cases, is underrepresented relative to female representation generally. The high-wage service sector has generally proportionate representation in the data. Taken as a whole, these patterns suggest that there is some variation in the types of discrimination women experience, and that this variation itself has some industrial-specific character.

TABLE 3.1
Distribution of Sex Discrimination Cases by Industry,
Relative to Women's Industrial Representation in Ohio Generally

	Core	Low Service	High Service	State	All Industries
Percentage of . . .					
Ohio Women Workers	*19%*	*59%*	*18%*	*4%*	*100%*
All Cases	30%	39%	16%	13%	100%
Hiring Cases	40%	24%	6%	30%	4%
Firing Cases	30%	44%	20%	6%	55%
Promotion Cases	27%	28%	8%	37%	4%
Demotion Cases	41%	36%	13%	10%	3%
Harassment Cases	30%	36%	11%	22%	20%
Other Cases	28%	35%	15%	22%	14%

Source: U.S. Census, 2000b.

We turn now to women's lived experiences with each of the most prevalent forms of sex discrimination. Throughout, we highlight the industrial sectoral context within which the discrimination unfolds—a strategy that lends insight into not only the variations, but also the ways in which the structure and functioning of the labor process within certain types of work may be playing a role.

Institutional Access: Sex Discrimination in Hiring and Firing

Two fundamental discrimination issues for women center around access to jobs, specifically hiring and firing. This is true across sectors, but is clearly a more pressing issue in the core industrial sector specifically.

As difficult as it is to document, with perhaps the exception of systematic audit testing, we find hiring discrimination in 4 percent of serious sex discrimination cases overall. This is quite low and undoubtedly an underestimate given that most victims of hiring discrimination are likely unaware that it actually occurred. Nevertheless, our data do hold cases, and disproportionately so in the core and state sectors. Employers in these cases—particularly employers in the core economic sector—are sometimes rather explicit about their desire to keep women out of the workplace or at least certain positions in their organization. Consider the case of Kate, a job applicant, as described by a friend who visited the business establishment with her.

> Kate asked if they had hired anyone for the job that was in the paper, the owner then replied, "No, I haven't hired anyone yet, but I don't hire women." Kate then replied that the newspaper stated that someone [was needed] . . . no experience necessary, then the owner said he didn't care what the paper said; he was the owner of the shop and he didn't hire women. Then she asked for an application for employment. He said, "No, just write your name and address down on paper," but he said it wouldn't do any good because he still wasn't going to hire any women.

Henry, the employer, is so comfortable with his right to keep women out that he states in a letter to the Ohio Civil Rights Commission (OCRC), "I feel as the owner of Leather Manufacturing Company I may choose who I want to fill the position, regardless of what color or male or female." Although he did employ women as "counter help," he blatantly refused to hire women as repair persons.

Henry's candor with the OCRC is exceptional. More often, employers justify decisions to not hire women candidates on the basis of qualifications, including the need for a man to do the job. For example, a law enforcement agency chose to hire a male candidate over a female one, citing the male's better qualifications as well as a need for a male in that position (overseeing prisoners). A review of the hiring process revealed that *by the employers' own assessment* the two candidates were virtually equally qualified, and that union procedure dictates that the more senior officer, in this case, the woman, be hired. The review also found that it was not necessary to hire a male for the position, as gender ratios could be maintained to meet standards for inmate contact. While there may be times when there are legitimate reasons to limit certain positions to members of one sex, such use of sex as a criterion for employment may very well contribute to the relatively higher numbers of substantiated discrimination claims in certain, traditionally male, state-sector jobs, most notably those pertaining to protective services.

Gaining employment is one hurdle for women. Keeping that employment is an even more prevalent problem across the cases examined. Indeed, across industries, firing is the most common type of sex discrimination, affecting more than one out of two women represented in these data. Such cases are numerically more prevalent in the low-wage service sector, where women are highly represented. In the core sector, the percentage of cases is disproportionately high relative to women's overall representation in that sector across the state.

Across sectors and types of workplaces, it is common that discriminatory firing and job termination follow from a tenure of employment during which sexist comments and general, targeted harassment takes place. Female employees at a newspaper, for instance, note that the editor frequently made derogatory comments about women, including jokes pertaining to hormonal imbalances. This editor also openly expressed his belief that "women didn't deserve equal pay because they had husbands." Moreover, male coworkers were provided with equipment and business cards; however, Julie and other female employees were not. In a similar vein, for Tina, a new manager at a service station, disparate treatment included denial of training. Although new male managers were provided with on-site training, Tina's boss prevented the trainer from visiting Tina's location.

Like other women, Julie and Tina found their employment terminated while men in similar job locations were not. After almost four years with the newspaper, the editor fired Julie, citing personal phone use and performance problems. Yet, investigative documentation suggests male employees were permitted personal calls and had lower overall levels of productivity. Prior to terminating male employees, the editor also implemented progressive discipline; Julie was not afforded this treatment. Indeed, coworkers and others who testified before the (CRC) were shocked by Julie's sudden termination. According to one female coworker,

> He [the editor] wanted her terminated because he has a thing against women who are smarter than him, women with ideas. He frequently yelled and screamed if she challenged him with an idea that was better than his own.

Such tensions and the eventual firing outcome hold true in Tina's case as well. When an employee failed to refill a customer's oil, causing damage to the vehicle, the regional manager fired Tina and the employee directly involved. As in Julie's case, there was no progressive discipline. However, at least two male managers had been involved in similar instances—one of them twice—and had received *no* discipline. Upon firing Tina, the regional manager indicated that he would not hire any more women and that he would not allow other managers to hire women. In fact, he pressured another manager to fire another woman that he had recently hired in an effort to purge the company of women altogether.

While some employers, like those above, show outright hostility toward working women, some exhibit what appears to be benign paternalism—paternalism that ultimately leads to women's exit from paid employment. Betty, for instance, was discharged from her company where she worked in sales. Her manager had warned her previously that she could not survive at the company because she was not privy to the "good ole boys club." He suggested to her that leaving would be in her best interest. Notably, such paternalistic rationales for discrimination are most prevalent in cases of pregnancy, wherein employers often cite fear for safety and health of the mother and/or fetus in their decisions to terminate the pregnant woman's employment. We revisit this issue, of pregnancy and discrimination, in significant detail in chapters 5 and 7. Whether or not the intent is truly to protect the woman's best interest, the effect of this discrimination is the same: job loss for women—women who wish to remain employed.

Job Mobility and Sex Discrimination

Women who secure and maintain employment face other types of unequal treatment. Seven percent of women found themselves unfairly denied promotion or demoted on the basis on their sex. Blocked upward mobility is often referred to as the "glass ceiling," an invisible barrier in the employment hierarchy through which women cannot break. It also has been conceptualized as the "sticky floor," which impedes women from rising above their initial low-level positions (see, for instance, Padavic and Reskin 2002). Such discrimination for women appears to occur most commonly in the state sector, followed by core-sector jobs.

Two examples from women working in government positions illustrate how women are prevented from achieving upward mobility. These promotion discrimination cases reveal a pattern of less qualified men being promoted ahead of women with similar or better qualifications and longer tenure with the employing organization. Rachel's case is illustrative. Discussing her promotion denial, her personnel director describes the inequality in the applicants' qualifications.

> The candidate selected has been here only eighteen months, while Rachel has over 19½ years service. The candidate selected achieved his labor relations experience in the private sector which is quite different from the public sector. Rachel was/is very experienced and knowledgeable on the basis of interpreting our contract.

While the organization's cited reason for denying Rachel the promotion was a lack of experience with contract negotiations, the investigation revealed that she, in fact, had five years of contract experience with the firm. The man who was hired had, as a point of fact, less than one year of management experience with the firm and limited knowledge of contract negotiations.

Blocked upward mobility is seen as well in the case of Barbara, another state-sector employee. An employee with the agency for over a decade, Barbara was denied a promotion. The job was awarded to Jim, a man with less job experience and less experience with the specific duties of the job. Furthermore, documents suggest that at the time of the case, Jim continued in this position despite having a required licensure revoked. Barbara, on the other hand, met and continued to meet the stated job qualifications.

It appears that in mobility cases generally, informal mechanisms and criteria are used in a manner that favors male employees. In promotion cases, it is also common for employers to not formally post a position. For example, in Barbara's instance, she became aware of the position via a company memo announcing Jim's promotion. Since the position was listed as a temporary one, she fought to be considered for the position as it would be incorporated into the permanent job structure of the organization. By not advertising positions, employers can use much discretion in filling positions via informal networks. This works to the disadvantage of qualified women who may never have the opportunity to be considered. Given the bureaucratic procedures for formally posting jobs in many state-sector organizations, women may be more likely to know of open positions and feel unjustly disqualified when denied. This may help account for why discrimination in promotion is found more commonly in the state sector. Indeed, later in chapter 5 we find a similar pattern in the state sector for race discrimination cases as well, and we elaborate on how career ladders, bureaucratic procedure, and ongoing knowledge of other employees may be playing a role.

While we often think of mobility as being upward in nature, downward mobility is also reflected in the case material. Here, women are demoted on the basis of their sex. This appears to be most common in the core economic sector and, in many ways, the process of discriminatory demotion looks similar to patterns we witnessed with regard to firing. These women are generally held to different standards than men, experience unequal treatment, and/or receive unfair evaluations. The consequence is loss of their current job for one with lower rewards and status.

Susan's case from the freight industry exemplifies such processes. Prior to the demotion, she was given clerical responsibilities outside of the position requirements while a comparable male was provided ongoing clerical support. Although the company's policies mandated formal performance reviews, Susan was not formally evaluated throughout her employment. When she was demoted on the pretext of poor performance, she was replaced by a man with less seniority. Interestingly, and as noted in the opening quote to this chapter, even the man who replaced her saw the injustice in the situation and eventually served as a witness to the OCRC on her behalf.

Harassment of Women in the Workplace

While access to jobs and mobility are central discrimination issues for many women, not to mention issues of principal concern in most sociological scholarship on gender and labor market stratification, equally important are the day-to-day experiences women have on the job. For many women, these daily experiences and interactions often include ongoing harassment and degradation—something seldom accounted for in scholarship on gender stratification and employment. Notably, and across industries, harassment is the second most common type of sex discrimination that women face (see figure 3.1).

Harassment often precedes other discriminatory actions such as demotions and firings. At times these gender disparities may appear somewhat marginal, such as allowing men to make personal phone calls but reprimanding women for engaging in the same behavior. Yet, these behaviors tend to coincide with unequal treatment that may very well lead to more obvious and troubling consequences. For example, as part of a larger pattern of harassing behaviors, female law enforcement officers in one jurisdiction were not assigned bullet-proof vests, while the male officers were. One female officer reported that she was denied a properly functioning radio, a potentially dangerous situation given that she was assigned to foot patrol in large areas normally patrolled by car.

Many other cases denote ongoing and sometimes systematic antagonism and intimidation. Oftentimes in settings where women are the numerical minority—a point we return to in more detail in chapter 6—we find women subjected to significant hostility and resentment. For Rebecca, upward mobility within her company did not protect her from a hostile work environment. As a line supervisor, and by all indications, she was "sweared at and disrespected." She also was denied assistance with equipment, while male workers would assist each other. When she reported this behavior to her supervisor, she was told "if she wanted a man's job, she should buy tools and work on machines like a man does."

There is, in a significant portion of these cases, a sexualized component to the harassment, antagonism, and intimidation. Consider the case of Tammy, who encountered a hostile work environment since she began working in a health care related retail firm. In her four months of employment, she was subjected to "crude and graphic comments" by her supervisor. As she states, "on one occasion, he told me he was so mad he wouldn't even fuck me." And, notably, such harassment was not limited to this one supervisor. "At my 40 day review, Mike [the department manager] stared at my breast until I called him on it." When she complained of sexual harassment, management's response was, "it's not like anyone got raped." In fact, like many women, Tammy's situation worsened after she went to management for support.

> Following my complaint, Mike asked me out for drinks after work so we could "talk." After I refused, his attitude toward me became very hostile. He threw things at me and on many occasions became so threatening that I and other employees believed he was going to hit me.

Oftentimes, women are simply expected to endure a hostile work environment. Tammy was told during her meeting with management that "cursing does occur in the workplace," suggesting that the victim, not the harasser, needed to change. While supervisors are actively involved in harassment in half of our subsample of cases, employers and managers can and do support harassment in more subtle ways. For example, in Tammy's case, the OCRC concluded,

> There was apparently no recognition on the Respondent's part that the females were not complaining about the use of particular words, but about the sexual, and sometimes sadistic, comments directed toward women or related about women.

Employers, it seems, often fail to follow their own existing company policies against sexual harassment, do not investigate complaints, and/or do not take actions prescribed in their policies. For example, when a worker complained about sexually explicit graffiti drawn in a public work space, management, rather than investigating who did it and why, simply "took it upon themselves to clean the wall." Tammy's employer documented meetings concerning her incident, but interestingly she was never involved in or invited to any such meetings.

Such examples suggest how the lack of actual policy enforcement contributes to the persistence of harassment and targeted bullying toward women, but also sexual harassment in particular. Indeed, rather than helping resolve the issue, companies and managers in our data often direct their energies toward retaliating against the victim of harassment. As one employer stated, "if you go around looking for trouble, you are going to find it." In Tammy's case, company records show that her daily performance was scrutinized. The company copied documents showing a history of errors purportedly made by the victim; yet, on review, these documents were shown to be written in other employees' handwriting, and no other employees had their work documented in this manner.[4] As an interesting and pressing issue for many employed women, we return to the process of sexual harassment in detail in the next chapter. Specifically, we provide detailed analyses of how it unfolds, what it entails interpersonally and organizationally, and the serious consequences it holds for women as workers.

Conclusion

The consequences of sex discrimination are vast. Women who experience harassment are often emotionally drained by the experience and contemplate changing jobs, as Tammy's coworker discusses.

> At this point I feel it is pretty sad that I would rather work at customer service and have customers yell at me and "cuss me out" than work in [this department]. . . . It is to the point that Tammy and I don't want to come into work. I feel there is so much tension right now in the department as a whole that our business is beginning to suffer.

The pressure was too much for Tammy, who eventually left her job due to the stress. For other victims of harassment, the injuries can become physical, including attempted sexual assaults. These women often feel that they have no choice but to quit their jobs.

Victims of other types of sex discrimination describe the personal toll in emotional terms as well. As one victim writes after being fired, "I feel I've been slandered and I have been defamed as a woman." Importantly, these women also suffer a clear financial cost. Discrimination in hiring and firing costs women opportunities to earn a living and to gain job experience. Discrimination in promotion prevents women from moving into positions with greater financial benefits, authority, and power. Unfair demotions push women further into low-level job positions and send a message that this is where they belong. Combined, these dynamics operate to systematically exclude and disadvantage women.

Reskin (2003) calls on social scientists to develop a deeper understanding of the mechanisms through which advantage is preserved or challenged. The experiences of the women described in this chapter shed light on several forms of employment discrimination that women face and their consequences. Sex discrimination undoubtedly creates and reinforces occupational sex segregation and wage inequality (Tomaskovic-Devey 1993a; Reskin 1993, 2000). Employers' consideration of gender in decisions to fill and vacate positions has implications for gender-segregated workplaces. Workplace harassment can contribute to segregation as well by alienating women and pushing them out. Furthermore, by blocking women's job opportunities, sex discrimination in employment contributes to the gender gap in earnings. While there are cases of outright wage discrimination in our data, our analyses show how other forms of sex discrimination contribute to the gender wage gap. Indeed, the jobs into which discriminatory decision making practices force women tend to be positions that are less financially rewarding. These also are positions with less authority and autonomy.

Discriminatory actions on the part of employers and managers may also have the effect of depressing women's levels of job experience, particularly if women are being systematically pushed out of employment altogether, being blocked in the mobility process, or being steered into dead-end career ladders with little to no opportunity for further skill development and training. Unequal levels of support and training opportunities, seen in several of the cases presented, will certainly result in significant pay differentials for women and men across the life course.

Human capital theorists have traditionally asserted that much observed gender stratification in the labor market stems from personal preferences and skill investments. Our analyses of sex discrimination, while not denying the importance of preference or skill acquisition, suggest quite clearly that both actors and organizational processes often act to impede women's pursuit of skill, authority, and even their preferences for higher status jobs. For most of the women represented in our data, the preference is for equal treatment in access to jobs, opportunities for job retention and promotion, and equitable work conditions. It is time to recognize the influence of discriminatory actions and turn our attention towards eliminating these barriers. Only then will there be hope for gender inclusive workplaces and wage equality.

Notes

1. For a more comprehensive overview of occupational sex segregation, gender wage gaps, and gender and work, see Padavic and Reskin (2002).

2. For an overview of human capital theory and discrimination, see Cohn (2000).

3. See also Cohn (2000, 108–12) for an historical overview of sex discrimination in entry into medicine.

4. Company policies, including dress code and attendance policies, are often selectively enforced for women who complain about unfair treatment, discrimination, and harassment. For the officers who were denied bullet proof vests, the harasser compelled the male officers to watch the female officers and document any infractions. Such differential application of company policy is a consistent theme throughout the sex discrimination cases. For Tammy, this selective treatment resulted in her being placed on probation. Within two months, she began a medical leave from her job due to stress; she was unable to return to work.

4

How Sexual Harassment Happens

with Theresa Schmidt

It got to the point where James could not walk by Cynthia without touching her, putting his arm around her waist or on her shoulder, hugging her, or massaging her shoulders. he would do this in a suggestive manner. . . . Cynthia told me that she told James not to touch her all the time. . . . This was sexual harassment.

—witness testimony to the Ohio Civil Rights Commission

As THE PREVIOUS CHAPTER DEMONSTRATED, gender discrimination of various sorts continues to plague workplaces, even in the face of corporate policies pertaining to fairness in employment and affirmative action. One particularly insidious type that we have already mentioned is sexual harassment (MacKinnon 1979). Data from the 1996 General Social Survey finds 43 percent of adult females and 26 percent of adult males report experiencing sexual harassment, including "sexual advances, physical contact, and sexual conversations" (Uggen and Blackstone 2004). This astonishing prevalence has led many researchers to ask exactly what is happening in workplaces, to whom, and why.

In this chapter we examine the legal foundations of sexual harassment, and then turn attention to existing research on the topic—research much more focused on why sexual harassment happens rather than the ways it unfolds and its consequences. The process and implications of sexual harassment, while periodically addressed using retrospective accounts or survey techniques, have seldom been examined using corroborated accounts held to some legal standard. Moreover, analyses rarely speak to issues of workplace organizational response or culpability.[1] We are able to do so in this chapter by immersing into handful of sexual harassment cases, and the detailed information and accounts each provides.

What is Sexual Harassment?

Sexual harassment has been defined legally as "workplace sex discrimination" under the Civil Rights Act of 1964.[2] Law distinguishes between quid pro quo harassment, which makes tolerating or engaging in sexual behavior a condition of employment or advancement, and hostile environment harassment, in which an employee's ability to work is hampered by intimidating or offensive behaviors in the workplace. Such harassment can include verbal or nonverbal behaviors. Quid pro quo harassment may be less common (see especially MacKinnon 1979; Welsh 1999) and implies that the harasser is able to make employment decisions concerning the target. Coworkers, structural superiors, and structural inferiors can perpetrate hostile environment harassment. In trying cases of hostile environment sexual harassment, courts employ a "reasonable woman standard" that asks if a reasonable woman would find the behaviors severely pervasive or objectionable (Wiener et al. 1997).

Ohio has been quite consistent with federal protections in its definition, defining sexual harassment as "any unwanted attention of a sexual nature from someone in the workplace that creates discomfort and/or interferes with the job." Between 1988 and 2003, 4,748 people filed complaints in the state claiming sexual harassment as form of discrimination they had experienced. The overwhelming majority of these, 88.8 percent or 4,212 were women. During this same time period, the Equal Employment Opportunity Commission (EEOC) found almost identical results at the national level, with an average 88.2 percent of cases filed by women each year (EEOC 2005). The percentage of cases filed by men has, nevertheless, also increased during this time period from 9.1 percent in 1992 to 15.1 percent in 2004. Because sexual harassment disproportionately affects women, this chapter will centers on processes of harassment impacting women.

The Foundations of Sexual Harassment

High visibility cases of sexual harassment and high incidences have prompted researchers and legal theorists to provide theoretical explanations for why people harass or are harassed.[3] These explanations can be divided by their focus on interactional roots of the phenomena, organizational causes, or dimensions of sociocultural power that may be implicated.

Interaction

Early sexual harassment researchers focused on interactional processes and specifically "sex-role spillover" as the principal culprit. According to this work, male-on-female sexual harassment is driven by male expectations of feminine behavior that are carried into the workplace from the domestic sphere (Padavic and Orcutt 1997; see also Gutek and Cohen 1987). Consistent with this point, Rogers and Henson (1997) argue that sexual harassment is part of a broader process of "doing gender."

As most prominently discussed by West and Zimmermen (1987), doing gender is the process by which gender is (re)constructed through interactions based on behavioral expectations. Workplace interactions require low-status individuals, especially women, to defer to their superiors and display themselves as sexually available. Sexual harassment can thus be read as an enforcement of gender roles.

Quinn (2002) elaborates somewhat, discussing sexual harassment as also encompassing interactions among men. Here, she suggests, "girl watching" bonds men together in opposition to female "objects." Kimmel and Smith (2005) concur, viewing harassment as men "doing" masculinity for the acceptance/approval of other men. Harassment, in such a scenario, raises the social status of the male harasser in workplaces that value hegemonic masculinity. Conversely, the instilling of fear and discomfort lowers the power (or hierarchal position) of the feminized target.[4]

Organizational Foundations

The structure of workplaces themselves may be, in part, culpable for sexual harassment. Acker (1990) argues that gender and sexuality are mechanisms of control in organizations. Men and women hold different sorts of jobs in the workplace and those that require skills traditionally possessed by or attributed to men have more status and hierarchical power. Jobs held by women, on the other hand, implicitly include sexual availability and submission in their descriptions. Functionally, sexual harassment helps to reproduce these hierarchical power structures (see also MacKinnon 1979).

In addition to discussing who holds which jobs, theorists of organizations have examined workplace gender ratios, or numerical as possibly conducive to the emergence of sexual harassment. When the composition of a workplace is overwhelmingly male or female, harassment tends to occur "because skewed situations render 'femaleness' more salient and visible."[5]

Researchers find organizational foci, such as expectations of those in particular positions, sex ratios, and organizational climates that tolerate or rebuke employees who sexually harass, particularly appealing because they provide attendant solutions. Workplaces can use proactive tactics to reduce the incidence of harassment and create climates of nontolerance, as perceived by employees. Such conscientious strategies can indeed be effective (Gruber 1998; Richman et al. 2004).

Sociocultural Dimensions

Power relationships dictate behavior both inside and outside of the workplace. In addition to organizational power over women, men also have social power. One possible motive for sexual harassment is thus the enforcement of that power through domination: men harass to dominate and control women (Gruber 1998; Padavic and Orcutt 1997). When men have institutional power over women, domination is facilitated, but because men also have social power, they are able to harass women who are structural equals or superiors. Rospenda et al. (1998) read this "contrapower harassment" as reassertion of social power in the absence of institutional power. The sociocultural relationship therefore becomes reciprocal: Men use power to get sex (MacKinnon 1979), and sex to get power (Wise and Stanley 1987; Lee 2001).

Sociocultural power dynamics also emerge from, and are sometimes enabled by, workplace cultures. Male dominated workplace structures and a work culture that celebrates normative masculinity bring gender to the fore in interactions between workers (Acker 1990). In instances of normative dominance, women workers in traditionally male or female jobs are vulnerable, though women who fill "male" jobs may be perceived as especially threatening and targeted for harassment given what Stockdale (2005) refers to as "rejection" motives. Gruber (1998) finds that numerical dominance is a better predictor of harassment than normative dominance.

That the dynamics of sexual harassment about which we are speaking are harmful emotionally and economically for those targeted is well documented. This is by no means to suggest, however, that targets of sexual harassment are void of agency. Rather, they usually engage in a variety of coping techniques. Whether or not they officially report incidents of harassment, most women who are targeted engage in strategies of avoidance, diffusion, negation, and confrontation (Rogers and Henson 1997). Wasti and Cortina (2002) add negotiation, social coping, and denial to this list. Unfortunately, when targets do choose to report harassment to officials within the workplace, they are often dismissed or subjected to retaliation.[6]

How Sexual Harassment Unfolds

Despite valuable insights, the literature on sexual harassment remains remarkably fragmented across theoretical camps and academic disciplines.

Most perspectives, however, ultimately focus on the "whys" of harassment and structure and motive, respectively. We weave such foci together in the analyses that follow and address the process of harassment and how it unfolds in real workplaces.

Like some prior analyses, we employ self-reports. Yet, our reports have been substantiated to the point of probable cause by a neutral, third-party agency using legal criteria. Moreover, our qualitative data include sworn witness observations and information pertaining to workplace organizational response. Such organizational information is important because in many of the cases discussed, workplaces and workplace cultures are implicated in allowing and even encouraging sexual harassment.

Who Is Harassed?

Our data confirm that the vast majority, or 88.8 percent, of those filing sexual harassment charges are women. The mean age of complainants is 32.5 years old. Previous research has shown that women who are racial minorities are more likely to be harassed (Rundblad 2001; Murrell 1996). Of the filing sample, 69.8 percent is white, 22.9 percent black, 0.1 percent Latino, 0.4 percent Asian or Pacific Islander and 6.7 percent "other." When compared to census data from both 2000 and 1990, blacks file at higher rates than whites, whereas Asians and Latinos are slightly underrepresented in the sample.[7]

Of the content coded sample of approximately 850 randomly selected and serious cases of race and gender discrimination in employment, 70 represent serious cases of sexual harassment. One dimension of the content coding entailed the occupational status of the victim. Another indicator we coded was the workplace position of the harasser/discriminator. Coding on these dimensions helps reveal the power structures that render low status workers especially vulnerable to discrimination. It also implicates, in this chapter and chapters 7 and 8, the ways in which social class as a source of power plays out structurally as well as informally in the processes of inequality we describe.

There are several notable differences between the 70 sexual harassment cases and the other content coded "serious" cases of discrimination. Targets of sexual harassment have consistently lower occupational prestige than targets of other forms of discrimination ($r = -.101, p < .05$). This could be an indication that lower status workers are structurally vulnerable and thus more easily sexually harassed, or socially vulnerable because they are lower class (Rospenda et al. 1998).

The workplace position of the discriminator is also distinct (chi-squared = 105.27, $p < .01$), as shown in figure 4.1. More than 30 percent of sexual harassment complainants directly implicate the business owner, whereas this is only true in about 6 percent of other forms of discrimination cases. These may

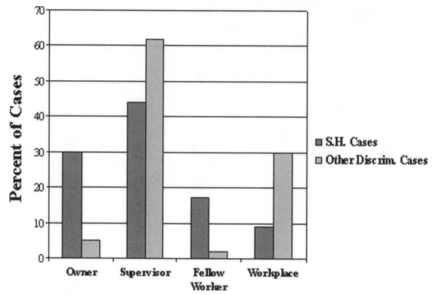

FIGURE 4.1
Case Type and Person Accused (content-coded subsample)

be cases of quid pro quo sexual harassment. The majority (almost 62 percent) of nonsexual harassment cases cite a manager or immediate supervisor as the alleged discriminator, whereas only 43.5 percent of sexual harassment cases do so. Only 1.3 percent of nonsexual harassment cases allege a fellow worker as the discriminator, but that percentage jumps to 15.9 percent in sexual harassment cases. These likely represent hostile environment cases. Workplace institutions are also the focus of charges in 29.0 percent of other discrimination cases, but only 8.7 percent of sexual harassment cases. It thus appears that sexual harassment may be more overtly interpersonal in nature than other forms of discrimination. These differences remain nearly constant when only women are considered ($n = 439$, chi-squared $= 83.7, p < .01$).

In the remainder of this chapter, we provide an in-depth analysis of sexual harassment. The case-specific data we employ allow us to isolate instances of sexual harassment that were defined as such subjectively by complainants, male and female, and also from the legal standpoint of civil rights investigators. These are, by no means, frivolous cases.

Following our review of case files—including statements from the men and women complaining of harassment, their workplaces/employers (or lawyers), witnesses, and sometimes harassers, as well as documents containing workplace composition statistics, and interoffice memos—we established general categories for claims and counterclaims (with reference to Stockdale's 2005 measures of the content of harassment). Following Richman et al. (2004), we coded specifically for:

The content of harassment
Whether content or severity of harassment changes over time
Number of harassers involved and their genders
Workplace position of harasser(s) vis-à-vis charging party
Charging party's responses to harassment
The workplace outcome of harassment
Responses to each of the charging party's grievances
Company actions and explanation for workplace outcomes

Our analyses thus provide detailed insight into the realities of the sexual harassment process as it unfolds within everyday workplaces.

The Process of Sexual Harassment

Of the seventy content-coded cases, sixty-seven reflect female targets of harassment and three are male targets. This is an indication of the rarity of male cases of sexual harassment. The women were between twenty-eight and forty-six years old when they filed. They held jobs as varied as secretary, waitress, seamstress, electrician, police officer, corrections officer, laborer, assembly line worker, and janitor.

The harassment we observe in the case material suggests three general sexual harassment categories: individual, collective, and pan-harassment. These categories are bred by different workplace contexts, lead to different responses by targets, and have different workplace outcomes. Additionally, the distinction between collective and individual captures the variation in harassment more accurately than traditional legal definitions of *quid pro quo* and *hostile environment*. Collective harassment is nevertheless most associated with a hostile environment, while more individualized cases can legally be either.

Notable is the fact that most incidents of sexual harassment begin almost immediately when the woman first enters the workplace. As a new employee, she is structurally vulnerable. In nearly all cases, the male harassers had been in the workplace longer than the female targets. This means they had higher social status as employees and as men.

Approximately half of all cases entail an individual's harassment by a superior or coworker. Such cases are consistent with Stockdale's (2005) model-of-approach-based sexual harassment, because targets experience unwanted sexual advances (i.e., requests for sex, pressure for dates, and/or groping/ touching), indicating sexual attraction on the part of the harasser. Women encountering such behavior, such as Denise, Eva, Cynthia, Lynn, and Kim, tend to hold a variety of jobs: secretary, janitor, assembly line worker, laborer, and waitress, respectively. Denise and Lynn were harassed by structural superiors, while Eva, Cynthia, and Kim were harassed by coworkers. Denise was the target in a classic case of sexual coercion by the president of her company:

> Mark asked me to come over and he rolled his desk chair over towards me, grabbed me by my hips and pushed me towards him. He put his legs around me and put his head on my breasts. He then said "I can make your job easy for you here." I became very upset and left the room.

When Denise refused his advances, Mark became aggressive and she was soon fired.

Collective harassment occurs when multiple people "team up" to harass one target. Two cases in point are Deirdre, a corrections officer, and Kay, an electrician. Both were employed in workplace environments and occupations that witness normative male dominance. This qualifies Gruber's (1998) finding that numerical dominance is more predictive than normative dominance for the prevalence of harassment, because different workplace contexts breed different forms of harassment. The harassers in both cases included both coworkers and supervisors. Such collective harassment more often than not contains behaviors that can be easily read as gender policing and enforcement of traditional gender roles (see also Stockdale 2005; Kimmel and Smith 2005; Lee 2000).

Kay was the only female electrician in her department and was subjected to numerous forms and instances of sexual harassment. She was shown pictures of nude women, was asked "seductively about a light bulb and [saw] a male co-worker have it between his legs," and had her face "pushed toward a male co-worker's crotch." She was also subjected to more generalized gender harassment. For example, one of her coworkers made comments about women working:

> [He said] in other countries the women know their place and that I was taking a good paying job away from a man and that I should be at home taking care of my kids. . . . He said maybe I should move to another "cunt'ry."

Contrapower harassment (Rospenda et al. 1998) also occurs in a collective harassing situations. Deirdre, the corrections officer, experienced sexual allegations by male prisoners (something common for female prison guards).

Though they lacked institutional power, the prisoners used their social power as men to harass Deirdre and undermine her position in the workplace.

Pan-harassment is an amorphous category that is defined by one individual who harasses multiple targets, sometimes both men and women. In all cases of pan-harassment, the harasser was a boss or supervisor. These situations of pan-harassment often lead to filing of claims by multiple charging parties. Deborah and Kay were both subjected to requests for sex, groping, lewd display, and sexual remarks by Lawrence, the male president of the manufacturing company where they worked. Many other women were also "victims of Lawrence Booth's unwelcome touching. . . . Testimony from witnesses . . . demonstrates a pattern of sexual harassment by Booth towards females in his company." Pan harassment is usually used for status maintenance—that is, to position the harasser as "alpha male" among fellow men by degrading and undermining female workers.

Reactions to Sexual Harassment

Targets of sexual harassment are not passive victims: they react in a variety of ways in an effort to stop the harassment and gain or regain respect in the workplace. In the cases we analyzed, the women tended to respond in a combination of three ways: ignoring or humoring the harasser, confronting the harasser, or complaining to an authority. Some also made their dissatisfaction with the situation known to their coworkers.

Williams (1999) suggests that many workplace environments are sexually charged, and workplaces in which the women in our sample are employed are no exception. This seems particularly true of food service establishments. Initial reactions in such environments might include ignoring the harassment or laughing it off. In some cases, the charging party attempts to diffuse the situation by participating in the joking. Such is the case with Kim, a waitress, who is harassed by coworker Duane Foster in a restaurant. According to a witness, the environment:

> Was junior high-ish . . . there was a lot of joking around and . . . sex was the center of a lot of the jokes. . . . Foster was probably the worst of the joke tellers.

However, as other witnesses and the respondent assert, Kim also engaged in joking. Yet, ignoring and humoring harassment are not effective strategies for stopping the behavior. More often, the harassment continues unchanged. As the charging party realizes that the harassment is more persistent and offensive than standard joking, or after the harasser makes sexual advances, the target will often refuse the advances and confront the harasser by saying that she

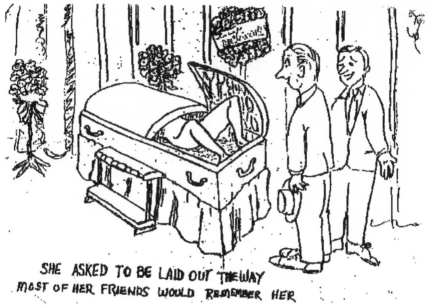

SHE ASKED TO BE LAID OUT THE WAY
MOST OF HER FRIENDS WOULD REMEMBER HER

FIGURE 4.2
Cartoon Placed on Desk of Sexual Harassment Victim

does not appreciate the behavior. It is at this point that the victim of harassment often complains to coworkers. This, however, is much less common in
cases of collective harassment, possibly because the charging party may fear
ridicule, retribution, or further isolation.

In cases of persistent and collective sexual harassment, women often are
pushed to lodge complaints with a manager or supervisor instead of confronting the harassers directly. Charging parties experiencing individual harassment may also be reluctant to confront their harassers. Eva, who worked
in a housekeeping department, frequently witnessed obscene sexual displays
from Ralph, who was in the habit of using a floor buffer to arouse himself to
the point of erection. According to Eva's female personnel director,

> I told her that if Ralph, or anyone else should make her feel uncomfortable with
> an action or verbal let the person know that you dislike it and it is unwelcomed
> then let your supervisor or me know. Eva was upset with this. She related it to a
> past experience in school. . . . I tried explaining that if it is not known that the
> action is disliked than nothing can be done. She left very upset.

While ignoring or humoring harassment has little effect, confronting the
harasser(s) or refusing advances tends to have three possible consequences
within the cases we observed: (1) Harassment continues unchanged; (2) Ha-

rassment changes from sexual to general workplace harassment and bullying, or; (3) Harassment escalates (in frequency or severity).

General workplace harassment is described as generalized workplace abuse by Richman et al. (2004). It is defined here as behaviors that are not explicitly sexual or gender demeaning, but are nonetheless part of a work environment that is hostile and disruptive to the charging party. Such activities represent an evolution or adjustment of sexual harassment and include staring, nongendered insults, sabotaging work, ignoring the charging party, or giving the charging party the "cold shoulder." This category also includes workplace retaliation (for complaining or refusing advances), including poor work assignments or denial of promotion or overtime. Lynn, a laborer, refused requests for dates by her male supervisor, and was repaid with poor work assignments and an environment that she describes as "a living hell." A witness supports this claim, saying:

> Andy was upset because she would not go out with him, and after she kept turning him down, he would punish her by giving her all of the dirty job assignments.

In cases of collective harassment, or after confronting the harasser results in continued, worsened, or changed harassment, the charging party often lodges an informal or formal internal complaint with a supervisor/manager/human resources person/employer. In cases where the harasser is also the boss, the charging party may have no other options in the workplace and will resign, legally considered "constructive discharge." Deborah and Kay, for example, resigned after the company president harassed them. For Kay, this resignation came after only eight days of employment.

Consequences of Sexual Harassment

Filing an internal complaint often leads the charging party down a road of embarrassment, accusations, and isolation. Workplace reactions to internal sexual harassment complaints, in contrast, are diverse in our data, although most are ineffective and fail to adequately address the concerns of the victim. Indeed, when internal claims are handled effectively, the case simply never reaches civil rights or EEOC investigators. Thus, effective and constructive organizational responses no doubt result in cases not appearing in data such as ours.

Workplaces, we found, sometimes react by counseling the harasser(s) that "if this is going on, it is inappropriate," or monitoring the harasser's behavior. They may dismiss the charging party by telling her not to "make waves" or "rock the boat." By intent or not, workplaces also tend to draw negative attention to the charging party by telling the harasser who complained, conducting an internal investigation that usually involves interviewing other employees, and holding meetings to discuss thinly veiled references to the charging party's complaints. Such was the case with Jenna, an electrician and target of insidious collective harassment. During an employee meeting, her female affirmative action officer delegitimized Jenna's complaint. Here, the officer:

> alleged those who find things offensive of having low self esteem, being on the edge mentally and not feeling good about themselves.

Kim, a waitress, also describes the actions of her female manager,

> I spoke to Stephanie directly after each of the three [3] incidences with De'wan asking for Stephanie's help in handling the situation. Stephanie did absolutely nothing to help the situation but what she did do is make fun of me and told everyone in the store what was going on. . . . I feel that as a manager your job is to manage people! It's important to listen and respect what an employee is saying.

As is evident in these scenarios, the actions (or inactions) of the workplace and its representatives can further amplify feelings of frustration for victims of sexual harassment. Victims come to feel that they are not being taken seriously and are, instead, now objects of workplace scrutiny. Internal company investigations (often provided to civil rights investigators by companies themselves) typically yield no corroborating evidence in support of victims' claims. Coworkers often take sides, further alienating the charging parties in cases of collective harassment or bitterly dividing the workforce in individual cases. In cases where the harasser is also a supervisor, the charging party is sometimes isolated out of fear of retaliation. Superiors and coworkers accuse her of lying or being overly sensitive and may make jokes about the situation. Cynthia's therapist describes the workplace consequences of complaining about being sexually harassed:

> [The foreman] treated it superficially, like a disagreement among co-workers, and did not reprimand or remove this employee. . . . The incident became the subject of jokes and Cynthia felt ridiculed and demeaned. . . . A human relations worker reportedly told her to simply drop the issue. . . . She reviewed Cynthia's record, learned that Cynthia had completed treatment for chemical dependency, and had decided Cynthia was part of the problem also.

Notable in many of our cases of individualized sexual harassment is that many of these cases often transition into generalized workplace harassment, or nonsexualized bullying, after the charging party files an internal complaint. Harassers, once under scrutiny, modify their behaviors in an equally aggressive, although less explicitly sexual, manner. This becomes particularly problematic when the harasser holds organizational power relative to the harassee and is informed of who lodged the initial sexual harassment complaint.

The transition from sexual to a more general form of workplace bullying for Jackie was also a transition from individual to collective harassment. She is a biracial woman who was fresh out of the police academy and still in her probationary period when her male trainer sexually harassed her. An internal investigation found this officer guilty and Jackie was transferred to another training officer. According to civil rights investigators, this male officer made racial remarks and, "would work crossword puzzles and read the newspaper as opposed to training her." Jackie again complained and was transferred to a female officer, who "scorned her for turning in a fellow officer and retaliated against her in the evaluation process."

Much collective sexual harassment seems to only escalate after internal complaints are made, often adding bullying that includes jokes about harassment. These collective situations prove especially frustrating when supervisors also participate. Deirdre, the corrections officer, was harassed by other officers and by a lieutenant and a captain. Kay, the electrician, was also harassed by her coworkers and supervisor. In one incident, a clay penis was left on Kay's workbench, as her attorney describes:

> She took this to her supervisor indicating her disgust. . . . Three employees were disciplined receiving only five days off. It is also my understanding that the supervisor may have been involved in this. This act was caught on videotape which is now in the possession of the police.

When targets fail to eliminate harassment, they continue to avoid antagonists and sometimes adopt personal coping strategies that, themselves, have negative workplace results. Some women within our data took time off work. Absenteeism, however, gave employers an excuse for disciplinary action. Ramona, for instance, worked as a secretary in a correctional institution and complained to multiple officials about sexual harassment "as far back as . . . several months before she became AWOL due to attendance. Ramona [also] sought professional help to cope with the problem of sexual harassment." Three other women also visited a mental heath professional or pastor.

As the cycle of harassment and complaints progresses, the charging party's tolerance with harassing and marginalizing behaviors wears thin. Case files are indeed replete with the reality that victims become filled with indignation at the procedural and interpersonal injustice of the situation (Richman et al. 2004). Internal grievance procedures are often exhausted while, simultaneously, employers question or dismiss claims or handles them superficially. Approximately 20 percent of the women were forced out of their workplaces altogether.

For their part, workplaces often respond to complaints of sexual harassment filed with the Ohio Civil Rights Commission or EEOC by suggesting that the alleged behaviors never occurred; that described actions occurred, but do not constitute harassment; that actual sexual harassment occurred, but the problems were solved internally; or that the charging party was engaging in (or initiating) the behaviors, and thus the alleged incidents do not constitute harassment.

Conclusions

This chapter has outlined processes of sexual harassment, moving us beyond simply content and motive. Individual and collective harassment are identified as distinct phenomena that occur in different contexts. What they all have in common, however, is that many employers seem incapable of or unwilling to adequately address sexual harassment in their workplaces.

Although we have focused on the experiences of women, men are also targets of sexual harassment and experience a different process as we discuss elsewhere. The statistical findings offer qualified support for Uggen and Blackstone's (2004) assertion that more vulnerable workers are harassed. Uggen and Blackstone use age as their measure of vulnerability and women filing for harassment are indeed younger than those filing for other forms of discrimination. Targets of harassment are also vulnerable in other ways, however. They have a lower occupational prestige than workers filing for other forms of discrimination and most often harassed by owners and supervisors. Harassers also tend to have more social status and seniority then their targets, and harassment usually begins when targets first enter a given workplace.

Although the structure of workplaces may be predictive of the frequency sexual harassment, workplace culture may ultimately determine the form harassment takes. Individual and pan-harassment often appear in sexualized workplace environments where sexuality is tolerated or built into the shop-floor culture. Although we can never truly know the motives of harassers, individual harassment and some instances of pan-harassment can be inferred as approach based (Stockdale 2005), since the content implies sexual attraction. However, individual and pan-harassment are also used to assert or reinforce power. As we have seen, individual harassment transitions to workplace harassment, or generalized bullying, after the charging party complains internally.

Collective harassment, our findings suggest, is fostered in workplaces and jobs that are both normatively and numerically dominated by men. Collective harassment, thus, tends to be rejection based and highly gender normative. Harassers target women as women and as workers, isolating them in their workplaces. Within many such cases, harassment escalates.[8] Though the power dynamic of being harassed by a superior certainly remains important, as Rospenda et al. (1998) argue, men retain social power over women who are structural equals or superiors. In male-dominated, hypermasculine shop situations, this social power is manifested as collective harassment.

General workplace harassment or bullying, as discussed in this chapter, has important legal implications. If harassment transitions from the explicitly sexual to a nonsexual environment that is nevertheless hostile, it must not be assumed that the workplace has effectively eliminated discrimination. A nonsexual hostile environment should still be considered an actionable form of gender discrimination as it consists of unequal terms and conditions of employment.

Sexual harassment is not confined to interactions between the harasser and target, nor is it something mapped on to innocent organizations. Women who experience sexual harassment are often systematically dismissed, exposed, and punished for their experiences in the cases we have discussed. Workplace responses to harassment are as much a part of the problem as the harassment itself. Because of this, workplace nontolerance (Mueller et al. 2001) would figure largely in a successful attempt to eliminate sexual harassment. Policies against sexual coercion must, of course, be strictly enforced, but the nontolerance should also extend to highly sexualized or gender normative workplace cultures. Sexual banter at work may be a harmless way to pass the time, but when participation becomes a requirement for employment, the behavior becomes offensive and harassing.

Notes

1. The exceptions include mostly high visibility cases and class-action suits filed against large corporations and/or the military.

2. See www.eeoc.gov.

3. Sociologists typically rely on self-reports through surveys to measure the prevalence of various harassing behaviors. Uggen and Blackstone (2004) analyzed data from the 1999 wave of the youth development study and found that out of 425 twenty-five- to twenty-six-year-old women, 42 percent experienced direct questioning about their private lives since high school. The next largest group, 35 percent, experienced offensive jokes, remarks, or gossip. Thirty-two percent experienced unwanted touching

(13 percent) or invasion of personal space (29 percent), while 2 percent were physically assaulted. Dubois et al. (1998) find that 99 percent of female targets of sexual harassment have male harassers. In their survey of military personnel, they find that the most common harassing behaviors were sexual jokes (64 percent), looks (49 percent), and touching (45 percent). Requests for sexual favors applied to 12 percent of the targets while 4.9 percent were raped. Such findings suggest that although the most severe forms of sexual harassment are relatively rare, they do happen and the prevalence of other harassing behaviors calls for exposition and explanation.

4. See Stockdale (2005) and Kimmel and Smith (2005). Those dealing with interactions pertaining to sexual harassment often consider the motives of the harasser. Stockdale, et al. offer a nuanced account of these motives by suggesting that they can be considered either approach based or rejection based. Approach-based harassment describes behaviors such as "unwanted sexual advances or sexual attention" that are motivated by attraction or sexual desire. Rejection-based harassment, on the other hand "consists of behaviors that imply a desire to humiliate, punish, and otherwise drive away the target" such as sexual insults

5. See Welsh (1999) for an overview on this point.

6. Richman et al. (2004) find that women who make unsuccessful internal complaints suffer from increased use of alcohol as a coping mechanism.

7. In 2000, the racial composition of Ohio was 84 percent white, not of Latino origin, 11.5 percent black, 1.9 percent Latino, 1.2 percent Asian or Pacific Islander, and .2 percent Native American (Ohio Quick Facts http://quickfacts.census.gov/qfd/states/39000.html).

8. These categories go beyond legal definitions of quid pro quo and hostile environment, for collective harassment can include both superiors and coworkers and the content of individual harassment is similar at a quid pro quo or hostile environment level.

5

Discrimination in Public
and Private Economic Sectors

with Reginald Byron

I have been employed by the Respondent for 12 years. . . . My evaluations
have all been excellent. . . . [Yet] in a letter I was informed that I was denied
the position of Traveling Supervisor. The letter indicated that I was denied
a promotion because Laura Wabash, White, graded out higher than I
graded out. . . . Ms. Wabash has only four years experience. [However], the
respondent promoted Ms.Wabash instead of me and another Black employee who has seven years experience.

—Linda Watkins, an African American public sector employee

RACE AND SEX DISCRIMINATION, as chapters 1 and 3 denoted, do not occur
in a contextual vacuum. There indeed appears to be industrial sectoral
differences in the occurrence and unfolding of various discriminatory forms
and experiences. These differences, while partially attributable to disparate
concentration of women and racial/ethnic minorities are, in all likelihood,
also tied to the organization of work itself within sectors. The public versus
private sector distinction reflects an added and important dimension of
context which likely affects the frequency and character of discrimination.
In this regard, the increasing representation of women and minorities in the
public sector (Crewson 1995) has fueled a popular assumption that discriminatory processes may be attenuated there. This attenuation is attributed to a more serious implementation of affirmative action law and greater
bureaucratic procedure and rules governing the terms of employment and
the treatment of employees.

This chapter expands our knowledge of discrimination and potential variations between public and private sector employment—variations that first became apparent in chapters 1 and 3. What we observed were a disparate number of cases of race and sex discrimination particularly on issues of mobility and harassment in the public sector versus particular labor market sectors in the private sphere. Here we focus on both race and sex discrimination, and what occurs in public and the private sectors broadly.

We begin by reviewing existing research and theorizing on race and gender inequality and public/private sectoral representation. This overview highlights countervailing expectations. While some (Reskin, McBrier, and Kmec 1999) suggest that formalized procedures should diminish public sector discrimination levels, others, drawing from the Becker (1971) hypothesis, believe that competition for services and workers should keep discrimination low in the private sector. Our analyses focus specifically on hiring, firing, and promotion discrimination across public and private spheres and arguably reflect the most in-depth analyses of private and public sector discrimination to date. Moreover, the rekindled focus on sectoral variations places many of the microlevel interactions highlighted within our examples presented thus far within structural context per figure I.1 in the introduction.

Inequality and Public Sector Formalization

All jobs in the federal, state, and local governments make up the public sector. Representing the practices of the U.S. government, the public sector is often viewed as a model of fair employment. Formalization is often described as the conduit through which antidiscriminatory practices are upheld (see Reskin, McBrier, and Kmec 1999). Entrance testing, performance evaluations, and job ladders all provide a structure for the decision making of public sector managers (Pfeffer and Cohen 1984; Diprete and Soule 1988; Dobbin et al.1993). Indeed, research shows that these formalized policies have reduced subjective bias in hiring practices (Konrad and Linnenhan 1995).

Public sector promotion policies have, nevertheless, been subject to an abundance of criticism. Women and minorities face glass ceilings in the public sector as they are relegated to low authority job ladders and are limited in their ability to transfer into higher tiered jobs (DiPrete and Soule 1988; Steinberg, Haignere, and Chertos 1990). Moreover, serious questions have been raised about the validity of tests designed to direct certain employees into managerial posts (Wallace 1973). Relatedly, the possibility of institutional discrimination in public sector employment, owing to dependence on seniority systems for promotion, remains. For instance, when seniority systems cause older employees to ascend the job ladder, new employees (disproportionately women and minorities) remain at the bottom of ladders because of past discriminatory processes and segregation (Riccucci 1990; see also Marini 1989).

Understanding the process of firing is more challenging. While some research has been devoted to voluntary quit rates (Zax 1989), there are few studies that have attempted to look at involuntary exits or firings by sector. Those studies that do exist suggest that both black and white men are less likely to be laid off in the public sector than the private sector (Wilson and McBrier 2005), but that blacks face increased rates of dismissal over whites within the same sector (Zwerling and Silver 1992). These patterns reveal a complexity to public sector exit processes. Employees may face lower exit rates than private sector employees. Yet, race remains quite salient.

Private Sector Competition and Discrimination

The private sector consists of all organizations not directed by a branch of the U.S. government, and is characterized by free market economic principles. Inherent in this classification is the idea of competing establishments. Companies often contend to make the least expensive product with the least expensive (yet productive) workers, thus increasing the profit margin. Competition is such an inherent part of private sector functioning that the government has historically enforced antimonopoly legislation to keep this competition alive.

Observing this social Darwinist environment, Gary Becker (1971), drawing largely from classical economic theory, has suggested that enhanced competition for inexpensive yet productive workers should keep discrimination low in the private sector. Ideally, fair personnel procedures should exist—personnel procedures wherein employers are simply interested in the most efficient workers, independent of race or sex.

A review of the literature suggests mixed evidence, at best, for Becker's argument. Some find that when public transit bus companies began privatizing through subcontracts, race and gender earnings gaps narrowed (Miller and Talley 2000; Peoples and Talley 2001, 2002). In other words, competition for private company workers and services inhibited wage discrimination. Yet, a significant amount of contradictory evidence exists. Wage analyses, using more representative data, seem to suggest that employers in the private sector discriminate more in wages than those in the public sector (Long 1975; Johnson 1978; Hoffnar and Greene 1996). Notably, however, and despite conclusions that have been drawn, few if any of the studies around which these debates revolve examine hiring, promotion, or firing directly (Petersen and Saporta 2004). Our analyses that follow do just that.

Public/Private Sector Discrimination at Work

Ohio had an average of 6.5 private sector employees to every 1 public sector employee from 1997 to 2000.[1] Of the 7,140 serious discrimination cases pertaining to hiring, promotion, and firing reported by black and white men and women to the Ohio Civil Rights Commission, 6,388 cases were in the private sector and only 752 cases were in the public sector, a ratio of 8.5:1 (private: public). One way to gauge the extent to which the prevalence of discrimination in one sector is disproportionate to the other, is to compare the overall employee ratio in the state to the representation of discrimination cases as we did earlier in chapters 1 and 3.

Figure 5.1 displays frequencies of established cases of race- and sex-based discrimination across public and private arenas relative to overall levels of em-

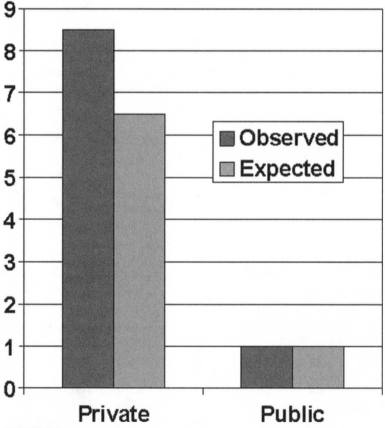

FIGURE 5.1
Private and Public Sector Discrimination Ratios

ployee representation statewide. Clearly, the private sector is overrepresented in the total of all hiring, promotion, and exit cases for blacks and whites during the period of observation. This difference between public and private sector discrimination is also statistically significant—a fact that offers some confidence that the differences reported are not merely a function of chance.

But where and how is race and sex discrimination taking place within these sectors? Prior stratification research has tended to highlight allocative discrimination (hiring, promotion, exits) as being central to this question (see Petersen and Saporta 2004). Within our data, hiring and promotion discrimination measures are direct. Exit discrimination, in contrast, is a bit more complex and includes cases of constructive discharge, outright discharge, and layoffs. We examine each independently and their sectoral variations.

Table 5.1 presents discrimination counts by sector. The results highlight significantly fewer cases of hiring, promotion, and exit discrimination in the public sector than in the private sector. However, differentials in the statewide representation of public and private sector employees make these comparisons alone insufficient. The problem of sectoral population unevenness can be accounted for by percentages of discrimination. The assumption behind this method is that hiring, promotion, and exit discrimination will all ideally be as likely to occur within individual sectors. Using these within-sector percentages reveals that exit discrimination takes the lion's share (over 87 percent) of all measured private-sector discrimination cases. On the other hand, public-sector discrimination is more evenly distributed across the three types, increasing from nearly 20 percent in hiring, to 32 percent in promotion and then again to 48 percent representing exit discrimination.

TABLE 5.1
Comparing Discrimination Counts by Sector

Type of Discrimination	Sector		Differences	
	Public	*Private*		
Hiring	148	399	Chi-Square	115.2***
Raw Score	*19.7%*	*6.2%*		
Within Sector %				
Promotion	244	401	Chi-Square	38.2***
Raw Score	*32.4%*	*6.3%*		
Within Sector %				
Exit	360	5588	Chi-Square	4595.2***
Raw Score	*47.9%*	*87.5%*		
Within Sector %				
Total	752	6388		
	100%	*100%*		

*** p < .01

According to these data, then, promotion-related discrimination is not the most problematic type of discrimination within the public sector (only 33 percent of cases). Instead, more energy, it seems, appears to be exerted into the expulsion of devalued employees regardless of sector. It would be hasty to conclude, however, that race and sex queuing are not significant in the public sector.

Table 5.2 presents counts of African Americans and Caucasians by sex and discrimination type. It is notable that, in total, African American women report the highest number of serious cases in the public sector, whereas Caucasian women report discrimination most often in the private sector. Again, these are just raw counts. The qualitative narratives, described next, shed light on these patterns.

The Discrimination Process and Sectoral Variations

On a general level, hiring discrimination appears to operate in a similar fashion across both sectors. That is, employers in both sectors require that employees "fit" within their firm as a condition of employment. This supports queuing theory as it relates to the hiring process. However, upon deeper examination, we find some variation in the process of hiring discrimination across sectors. While both public- and private-sector employers seek particularistic attributes (i.e., dependability) during interviews, some private sector employers (most often from small establishments) went further and overtly specified sex "appropriateness" as a prerequisite for hire (see examples in chapter 2).

These private sector employers impose preferences very early in the hiring process, often incorrectly believing that the civil rights commission has no jurisdiction over their employment practices. Public sector employers appear to use a more subtle process of filtering through applicants in the interview process. Notably, if the most covert preferences across sectors were captured, the relatively small number of serious hiring discrimination cases (see table 5.1) would increase. Overt comments during the hiring process, in contrast, may alert prospective employees of discriminatory intent and provide them with evidence to support their claim.

Promotion discrimination processes are even more distinct by sector. In the public sector, seniority attainment or "state time" is an important factor in determining promotion decisions. Thus public-sector employees, using their intimate knowledge of coworker qualifications and the seniority hierarchy, understand the "rules of promotion." When those rules are violated in a race- or gender-based manner, and a less qualified competitor obtains the position in

TABLE 5.2
Group Differences in Discrimination by Sector

	Public				Private			
	Hiring	Promotion	Exit	Totals	Hiring	Promotion	Exit	Totals
African American Female	38	94	127	259	145	176	1713	2034
African American Male	45	68	101	214	126	121	1628	1875
Caucasian Female	50	59	108	217	89	93	1988	2170
Caucasian Male	14	23	23	60	38	10	249	297
Totals	**147**	**244**	**359**	**750**	**398**	**400**	**5578**	**6376**

Note: There are 14 missing cases from the original sector comparison.

question, discrimination becomes obvious. For example, Joan, a public sector, white employee asserts,

> I bid on the position of Labor Relations Officer for which I am well qualified. A male less qualified, was selected. The individual also has less state time than I.

Despite the significance of seniority attainment in public sector promotion decisions, those employees who faced promotion discrimination were subject to additional obstacles that circumvented their seniority advantages. For example, Darlene, a black public-sector employee, and Mary, her white competitor, were given an impromptu test prior to selection for promotion. According to the employer, the test (which had never previously been used to assign the position) was an important factor in awarding Mary the position. A civil rights investigator notes,

> Darlene should have received the position based on her seniority and qualifications [in line with the union contract], and the employer did not need to give a test for the position. Darlene had the basic knowledge or skills to perform the basic functions of the job. Instead, the employer gave the position to Mary, a less senior Caucasian.

Likewise, Lisa, a public-sector black employee asserts,

> I believe that I was denied a promotion due to my race, Black and retaliation due to a previously filed charge. I put my bid in for the position and was the only in-house applicant. The assistant director interviewed me for the position. She told me and several employees that she recommended me for the position. Approximately an hour later Benjamin Larkin, [white director] came to me and asked me for all my classes that I had taken since high school. He requested transcripts and my University bulletin. He has never questioned any other in-house employee for such documentation when applying for the position. [Subsequently] Mr. Larkin put his wife in the position . . . and told me that I did not receive it because I was not qualified.

Upon investigation, evidence substantiates that Lisa met all of the minimum specifications for the job, although Mr. Larkin's wife did not. Furthermore, documentation of course work was not required of Mr. Larkin's wife, as it was for Lisa.

These narratives reveal seemingly neutral barriers (e.g, tests, credentials) that public-sector employers use to justify preferential treatment. The attempts to cover such preferences can be directly tied to public sector pressures to fit an antidiscriminatory mold (Dobbin, Sutton, Meyer, and Scott 1993). What is particularly notable as well is that seniority—something that has been documented to hamper minority and female access through institutional discrimination—is actually overlooked in many of these decisions and employer preferences prevail. Discriminatory race and gender preferences in public sector promotion practices may remain, even when women and minorities hold seniority advantages.

Minorities and women in the private sector also report differential treatment as they are consistently passed over for promotions. One emerging theme underlying this differential treatment explains how employees are already performing the duties of the position to which they wish to be promoted but without the associated authority and pay benefits. As Marcy, a white private-sector employee suggests,

> For approximately the last ten years, I have worked as a Credit Collections Clerk. During my employment in the Credit office, I performed the functions of the Credit Manager in his absence. I have always performed my duties well. The Vice President has stated that males are better qualified for the Credit Manager position. Although I had expressed my interest in being appointed to the position of Credit Manager, a less qualified and less experienced male who does not have a college degree was appointed to the position.

Renee, a black service-sector employee notes similar frustration.

> Previously on two occasions I was denied promotion to supervisor. . . . To date I have not been given any reason why I was not promoted. . . . When I questioned the Area Manager about this decision, he informed me that if I did not like it, I could quit. . . . I have an excellent work record as evidenced by the fact that I was selected to assist in the training of two Caucasian males placed in supervisory positions and also was placed in charge of all the company's temporaries.

Though not exclusive to the private sector, such accounts suggest a means through which the private sector maintains cheap labor. Employees are expected to perform managerial tasks without due recognition. The actual promotion, however, is reserved for employees higher on the job queue.

Even more compelling evidence of sectoral differences in process comes from cases pertaining to exit discrimination, or discrimination in firing. Such discrimination in the public sector is, by and large, based on differential enforcement of performance and alleged violations of procedure. Firm representatives complain that the employee in question is terminated, simply, for unsatisfactory performance. Interestingly, the workers themselves often corroborate these accounts, yet note (1) how the termination was unfair because the performance issues were out of their control and (2) that there was a similarly situated coworker who was not subject to the same standards of treatment. Public sector employers most often use seemingly meritocratic mechanisms, noted in some detail in chapter 2, to justify their actions and to arguably escape scrutiny if challenged on the decision. While holding one to performance standards is reasonable, doing so differentially based on race or sex is discrimination.

Private sector employees who are fired in a discriminatory manner suggest two principal reasons—two reasons that likely relate to the greater overall frequency of exit discrimination in the private sector (see table 5.1). The first, discussed to some extent in chapter 3, surrounds being fired or pushed out of a job due to pregnancy. As Jennifer, a pregnant white private-sector employee asserts, her employer took issue with her maternity leave.

> I was laid off from my position of Purchasing Agent. . . . Jim Warren [vice president] and Tom Lakey [manager] met with me to discuss my maternity leave. During the meeting Mr. Warren indicated that six weeks was too much time off for maternity leave. He further stated that I could have three weeks off and "don't expect this much time off for your next six kids."

Tom (a white mid-level manager) corroborates this unfair treatment through a signed affidavit. He states,

> When I told Jim that Jennifer was pregnant, he already knew. While I can't remember his exact words, it was something like—Oh my God, I told you not to put her in that position—now she is in a critical position and she is going to have a baby. . . . I can see 2–3 weeks maternity leave . . . [but he] privately read the riot act to me for my willingness to give her two weeks vacation on top of maternity leave. [And when termination was brought up] I told him that there were others I would prefer to lay off. . . . There were three less essential people with less seniority . . . [but Jim responded] "you have had your say. Larry (the owner) and I have reviewed your situation. These are your instructions and this is what I'm telling you to do" . . . I made up my mind then and there to leave the company because I was forced to lay-off two persons against my better judgment as a manager.

Such treatment, and the importance of pregnancy to the discrimination process in the private sector, clearly transcends the boundaries of race. Yvonne, an African American female, tells a similar story.

> I am a pregnant female who was discharged from my position as [a] Waitress. Peter Foster stated that I was discharged because I am pregnant and he couldn't afford another liability. My performance and attendance, as stated by Mr. Foster at the time, were not an issue. I believe that if I was not pregnant, I would still be employed.

Though many women were fired prior to leaving for pregnancy, a more subtle strategy of not rehiring women after they give birth is also pervasive. Sarah, a White employee in a sales department notes,

I am a female who gave birth on March 30, 1992. . . . On March 21, 1992 I informed my employer that I intended to take a six to eight week maternity leave from my admissions representative position. On April 5, 1992 I was informed that I would not be able to return to my position upon my physicians release to return to work. Janet (Agency Director) explained that the decision was in part based on my prior years sales statistics. . . . However, prior to my maternity leave, I was not warned that there was a problem with my sales statistics. In addition, when I asked Janet if my position would be there when I came back, she asked me if I could realistically see coming back after having a baby. She told me that I was not going to have the energy and I'm not going to want to work. Other admissions representatives [nonpregnant] were not fired or removed.

Termination following childbirth appears to occur for African American women as well.

[Less than one month after] I gave birth I was terminated [from my job as a Packer]. Joe Palowski, Attendance Director, was provided with a medical slip that my return to work would be 6 weeks after my delivery. I took maternity leave with the intent to return to work. [Instead] Mr. Palowski told me in a letter that unless I return to work [within three weeks] I would be terminated. My job was not held open unlike Respondent's past practice involving disability cases.

Overall, the data reveal a clear pattern of statistical discrimination in the private sector. Statistical discrimination is tied to the view that women are less useful, if not liabilities, once they become pregnant. They are also considered a financial drain to firms who have to pay for pregnancy leave. Such devaluation processes may manifest more obviously in the private sector given explicit productivity foci and related profit rationales in decision making. Formalization, affirmative action policies, and public scrutiny all likely work to prevent such blatant pregnancy discrimination from occurring in the public sector.

Another tendency among private-sector firms in particular is the arbitrary nature of firing, particularly for black men—an explicit focus of chapter 8. Analyses of the body of firing, constructive discharge, and layoff cases suggest that some private-sector firms differentially enforce company rules or police only certain segments of their workforces. One supervisor (white) admittedly told Jason, a black male employee, that

he had to cut me loose. He did not know why and said that I had to talk to the Manager [White]. The manager later told me that his supervisors said that I was not very good with my stacking of my paperwork. During my six days of employment, no one ever told me that there was anything wrong with my job performance. I never worked alone, but was teamed with a White employee each day. My initials are on each day's paperwork along with the White employees, but none of the White employees were terminated.

In a similar case an employer alleges that George was fired for

> "misusing, destroying, or damaging company property," when that employee "bumped into the guard on the motor of a press with a hilo." George stated that White employee "Bill" broke a water main causing severe flooding [in violation with another of the company's rules] but he received discipline of a written warning.

What appears to be an accident, in this case, resulted in termination from the job for a black male employee, yet a previous incident with a white employee (with arguably greater damage) resulted in a less serious penalty. Such examples indicate that black males are devalued within private-sector employment, and are arguably seen as easily replaceable. Private-sector managers, throughout the case material, often use company policies to build up fictive cases against black men to help justify their dismissal, or draw from company policies in an arbitrary manner, depending on who they want to get rid of. One can imagine how, in the aggregate, such patterns might contribute to the high unemployment rate of African American males.

Conclusions

Cumulatively, the analyses offered in this chapter suggest that there remains differential treatment based on race and sex in the public sector—differential treatment that somehow defies the protection of formalization and affirmative action policies. This fact sheds light on the differences in public sector black–white exit rates despite similar qualifications (Zwerling and Silver 1992).

Analyses of general patterns as well as case-specific qualitative material suggests that allocative discrimination may be more problematic overall as an issue in the private sector. This is more likely than not tied to less formalized procedure and greater employer latitude in how employees are treated. Findings indeed suggest a discriminatory tendency and threat to women who seek to keep their jobs after becoming pregnant. The fact that women of various occupational statuses are included among pregnancy cases suggests that these patterns are not specific to a certain job status or class position. Chapter 7 expands upon this heterogeneity of status among black and white women and the extent to which more prestigious occupational positions might provide certain protections for women, or simply convert discrimination from one form to another.

The somewhat unpredictable nature of discriminatory firing (or exit) for private-sector black males makes every day on the job threatening. It may emerge from their low status on the job queue—a low status that makes them especially vulnerable to differential and poor treatment—a theme that we elaborate on in chapter 8. Such "on the job" preferences against black men are consistent with many qualitative reports (Shih 2002). To the extent that policies are differentially enforced in the private sector in particular, or that black male employees are held to greater levels of scrutiny relative to white coworkers, is indicative of serious, problematic tendencies.

The qualitative narrative material from which we have drawn provides some understanding of the processes implicated in race- and gender-based hiring, promotion, and exit discrimination. Employers in the public sector still discriminate, despite the historical stronghold of affirmative action policies within this sector. Both pregnant women and black men in the private sector experience pronounced and disproportionate discrimination in firing. The private sector pregnancy penalty denotes a key processual difference in exits between women and men. And, the differential treatment experienced by minorities suggests the continuing significance of race in the contemporary world of both private and public sector work.

Note

1. U.S. Bureau of Labor Statistics. Quarterly Census of Employment and Wages.

6

Competitive Threat and Isolation at Work

with Marguerite Hernandez

When Jonesfield Auto has or anticipates an opening for mechanics, they post the job and select the class based on seniority. But they have to pass the class. Passing is somewhat subjective. It depends on who you know rather than what you know. Those who know the foremen and spend time with them are given more of a chance. Delores was not well liked; she was not part of the "in-the-office" crowd. Everyone who would hang out in the office is a white male. Delores was not popular, but she was very capable of doing a mechanic's job.

—witness testimony to Ohio Civil Rights Commission

PROCESSES OF DISCRIMINATION, as noted in the prior chapters, are patterned to some degree by the organization of work across industrial sectors generally, as well as formalization and bureaucratic variations between public- and private-sector industries. Yet, more proximate workplace-level dynamics pertaining to race and gender composition may matter as well. In this regard, segregation remains a key feature of many U.S. workplaces—a fact denoted by much classic (e.g., Bielby and Baron 1986; Kanter 1993; England 1981; Reskin and Roos 1987) and contemporary research (e.g., Maume 1999b; Tomaskovic-Devey 1993a; Huffman and Cohen 2004; Robinson et al. 2005; Stainback et al. 2005).

Sex segregation in employment remains common, while racial segregation is even more obvious (Tomaskovic-Devey 1993a; Padavic and Reskin 2002). Such segregation is a result of broader social processes wherein women and people of color remain disadvantaged even in the face of historical changes—historical changes including but not limited to decreases in race and sex gaps in education and the implementation of federal and state protections against discriminatory treatment.

Despite several trends toward sex parity, patriarchal tendencies persist in workplaces and men consequently continue to enjoy better access to jobs and promotions, and higher wages and benefits (see Acker 1990; Martin 2004; Padavic and Reskin 2002). Moreover, as revealed in chapters 3, 4, and 5, women often face unique discriminatory obstacles both in the aggregate and in terms of interactional workplace encounters. Discrimination and its associations with sex segregation remain problematic.

Racial segregation similarly serves to protect white privilege at the cost of closing off jobs, opportunities, and benefits for people of color (Blalock 1967). For those minorities not segregated into low status, low-wage service sector jobs, the possibility of social and interactional isolation in predominantly white workplaces remains very real—isolation that may have consequences for targeted bullying by supervisors or exclusionary and harassing behaviors by coworkers. Empirical evidence concurs on these points, suggesting women and people of color face general disadvantages due to segregation, and within segregated workplaces (Reskin 2000; Reskin, McBrier, and Kmec 1999).

Our knowledge of the relationship between segregation and discrimination, however, is elementary and relatively speculative owing to lack of useful data on arguably relevant processes.[1] This chapter contributes to our prior findings on the interactional nature of disadvantage as well as the broader race and sex stratification literatures by examining the relationship between workplace composition and discrimination. Specifically, we ask whether there are variations in discrimination generally, and in forms of discrimination, depending on the compositional contexts within which people work. Is discrimination more problematic where female and/or minority isolation prevails? Or, is discrimination more likely in balanced workplaces—workplaces wherein competitive pressures and opportunities to discriminate are arguably more prevalent? Theory and research on processes of social closure and inequality suggest that contexts of isolation and competition both likely matter, albeit in distinct ways.

Why Gender and Racial Compositions Matter

Workplace composition reflects an everyday context in which individuals interact with people of similar and different sexes and races (Reskin, McBrier, and Kmec 1999). Correspondingly, looking at the actual number of people on the job belonging to specific racial and gender groups can provide some clarity on the types of settings that trigger discrimination, how discrimination unfolds, and perhaps even why (Kanter 1993; Yoder 1991, 1994; Tomaskovic-Devey 1993b). It can also speak to possible "consequences of diversity" for workers within their current job settings. The workplace compositional data we employ in this chapter, which parallels that usually collected by the Equal Employment Opportunity Commission (EEOC), provides us the unique opportunity to analyze if and how the workplace matters when understanding people's experiences of discrimination and inequality. Unlike more commonly used EEOC data, however, ours includes both large and small establishments as well as those in private and public sectors.

If employers hire workers without consideration of race and gender, we would anticipate that the composition of establishments would reflect the availability of qualified workers in the labor pool. It remains clear, however, given prior literature as well as evidence presented in prior chapters, that employers and establishments still use gender and race as proxies for worker skill, productivity, and potential costs to the establishment (Tomaskovic-Devey 1993a, 1993b; Kirschenman and Neckerman 1991; Moss and Tilly 2001). Indeed, several prior qualitative examples of the discrimination process suggest that employers may perceive women and people of color who apply for jobs as fundamentally different and, thus, a "poor fit" relative to their current workforce. Others, employing equal employment or affirmative action criteria in their hiring protocol, may effectively create more integrated work environments. As chapter 5 revealed, though, even such policies do not necessarily protect women and minorities from differential treatment and harassment once on the job.

As women and racial/ethnic minorities gain representation in the workplace, their ability to challenge white male overrepresentation in good jobs increases (Tienda and Lii 1987; Kanter 1993). Yet, as noted in both Blalock's (1967) predictions derived from competition theory—which suggest that greater subordinate representation can induce a threat for those in advantaged positions—and actual historical cases within white male dominated sectors of employment, there lies potential for backlash against those who are perceived as intruders into the arena of white male employment. Herein lies the possibility for both workplace exclusion and discriminatory treatment by coworkers. In contrast, isolation may make visibility and "difference" all the more obvious to potential discriminators.

Competitive Threat and Isolation

How people interact on the job is not merely shaped by personal attitudes about "others," but also by relative representation within the workplace itself.

Where one falls in the composition of a workplace impacts whether and how one interacts with others of similar or different racial and gender groups (Kanter 1993).

Although researchers suspect that workplace composition matters in how workers are treated and relate to one another, they tend to disagree over when and why majority groups and individuals in a given workplace context may respond. Indeed, one line of research focuses on the negative consequences for minorities working within relatively isolated contexts. Numerical minorities within an establishment may, of course, be token representatives and experience rapid access and promotion into visible positions within an organization.[2] Conversely, they may be on the losing end of differential treatment, may be scrutinized more closely, and enjoy less in the way of promotions, pay raises, and other benefits relative to their majority counterparts. This may be driven, at least in part, by explicit and implicit employer and coworker biases, not to mention an already existent workplace culture that privileges whites and males generally (Kanter 1993).

Majority group members usually possess more power over workplace operations and occupy higher status jobs. Given power in numbers, dominant group members are also more often insiders within social networks. Those not belonging to these networks are considered, and often treated as outsiders. This implies not merely numerical isolation, but workplace social isolation as well. Isolation itself is double-edged in so much as it entails limited information and networks, but also greater visibility and possible scrutiny in job performance. Indeed, as denoted by examples in prior chapters, being a minority makes one subject to stereotypes. Workers may not be accurately judged on the quality of their work, but rather treated according to the majority group's perceptions and expectations for minority group members (see Kanter 1993; Tomaskovic-Devey 1993b; Moss and Tilly 1996).

Kanter (1993), observing women in corporate workplaces, concurs on the points above, suggesting that people of color and women generally often share the common experience of performing their jobs "under public and symbolic conditions different from those of dominants." In response, they often work harder than what is expected of others in an effort to prove their worthiness and to gain positive notice and recognition. Given their outsider status, however, they nevertheless experience stress, alienation, and anxiety.[3]

As an alternative to predictions pertaining to isolation, competition theory would suggest rather straightforwardly that discrimination toward women and racial/ethnic minorities will manifest more commonly within integrated contexts wherein female or minority representation reaches a point or threshold of "threat" from the viewpoint of current workers. The threat itself may be driven by preconceptions and biases of dominant group workers toward the subordinate group, or by a more general fear that the status and rewards of the work itself might be diminished as a consequence of female and/or minority presence. In either case, one is likely to witness a triggering of social closure and discrimination.

Applications of competition theory to the study of inequality and discrimination are most often found in historical analyses of violence directed toward minorities and immigrants (for examples, see Boswell 1986; Olzak 1990), backlash directed toward women in cultural and political arenas, and unrest pertaining to female and minority integration in education. Some recent research on inequality and employment similarly has found utility in such a conception of discrimination potential. Cohen (1998), for instance, predicts levels of female and minority wage inequality across labor market sectors varying by race and gender compositions. He finds negative effects of composition, generally, which are partially attributed to discrimination. Tomaskovic-Devey and Roscigno (1996) similarly find heightened racial inequality in the southern United States within more integrated contexts and conclude that unmeasured discriminatory practices are likely playing a part in these relations.

If integration invokes threat in some fashion, dominant groups (be they men or whites) may invoke a host of defensive and discriminatory strategies both to preserve tangible, objective privileges and to reinforce prevailing societal hierarchies of race and sex within their particular workplaces. While prior work is certainly suggestive in these regards, data pertaining to compositional context, concrete workplace interactions surrounding race and gender inequality, and discriminatory treatment are rare. Below we analyze 292 such cases, derived from our content-coded subsample.[4]

Workplace Composition and Discrimination

The 292 cases included in these analyses are drawn from the original, randomly selected and content-coded subsample, and include those cases wherein workplace racial and gender composition were available. Notably, the 292 cases reveal quite significant heterogeneity across labor market sector, by organizational size (range: 3–1, 743) and by racial minority and gender compositions (ranges: 1–87 percent, and 1–90 percent, respectively).

The larger graph in figure 6.1 presents the distribution of serious sex discrimination cases for women generally across gender compositional contexts, while the smaller graphs in this figure break down the more general distribution for Caucasian and African American women. While isolation is obviously meaningful in some of the case material presented thus far, it is not the typical scenario for women who experience sex discrimination. Indeed, less than

Chapter 6

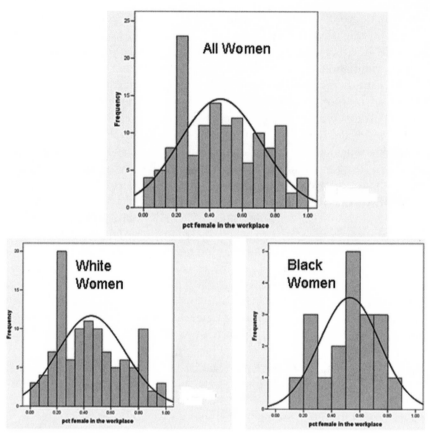

FIGURE 6.1
Distribution of Serious Sex Discrimination Cases for All Women (upper graph), and then for White Women (lower, left) and African American Women (lower, right) by Sex Composition of the Workplace (*n* = 136)

15 percent of the women reporting sex discrimination in this subsample report working in a workplace that is less than 20 percent female. This suggests that for women generally, the more common scenario and point of interest has to do with what occurs in somewhat integrated places.

There is, however, a notable difference in the distribution of sex discrimination cases for African American and Caucasian women. For Caucasian women, there is a heightened likelihood of discrimination when workplace sex composition reaches around 20 percent. This very likely reflects movement into traditionally white male jobs, and potential backlash with increasing female numbers. For African American women, in contrast, the discriminatory experience is more normally distributed. Such a normal distribution implies that sex discrimination for African American females occurs straight-forwardly in increasingly integrated contexts (at least until women become the majority). The same holds for Caucasian women, with the exception that a tipping point or competitive threshold with male coworkers occurs at or just under 20 percent female representation.

Figure 6.2 presents a parallel figure, but in relation to race discrimination cases and workplace racial compositions. Looking at the composition of these workplaces by race, and for African American males and females separately, we find discrimination cases falling overwhelmingly in contexts wherein race/ethnic minorities are numerical minorities in their workplaces. This may reflect several things. First, it may be a function of simple demographics; that

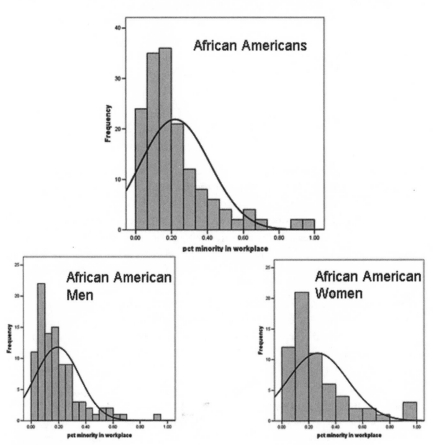

FIGURE 6.2
Distribution of Serious Race Discrimination Cases for African Americans (upper graph), and then for African American Men (lower, left) and African American Women (lower, right) by Racial Composition of the Workplace (*n* = 156)

is, unlike women, who comprise 50 percent of the population, African Americans constitute about 18 percent of the state's population. As such, and based on numerical ratios, most African Americans in the state will be working in workplaces where whites are, by and far, the numerical majority.

Another, equally plausible and important possibility exists as well—that race/ethnic workplace segregation in the current era is substantially higher than workplace sex segregation. As such, workplace contexts within which whites and nonwhites interact will be disproportionately laden with white numerical dominance. Here, minorities working in relatively isolated employment contexts prevail. Indeed, as these data show, the majority of black males and females work in contexts that are no more than 20 percent minority (and 80 percent white). Ninety percent of the black women represented here work in jobs where few other minorities work. For black men, 93 percent are in the numerical minority at their jobs. Six percent work in jobs where around half of the other workers were also black men. Only 1 percent of black men work in jobs where they are part of the numerical majority. Like black women, these men, all of whom experienced racial employment discrimination, work in largely white, segregated workplaces.

The Experiences and Costs of Gender Competition and Isolation

The findings above—particularly the rather high level of isolation of racial minorities, and the possibility of a competitive threat dynamic especially for white women experiencing sex discrimination, raise some interesting questions. But how might competition or isolation breed particular forms of discrimination? To address this, we examine variations in discrimination types reported across relatively isolated and integrated workplace contexts. We also draw from case materials themselves to highlight how compositional contexts may matter.

Drawing from figure 6.3, we report prevalent discriminatory forms across contexts. As noted previously, only a small proportion of women in the sample work in isolated contexts (where female representation is less than 20 percent). Such jobs largely reflect traditionally male occupations, such as a truck loader, steel worker, car dealer, assembly line worker, security guard, and so on.

As the reader will note in the figure, there are subtle variations depending on compositional context. While discriminatory expulsion, or firing, prevails most often in each scenario, ongoing harassment and mobility processes are more pronounced in integrated and competitive environments. Here, harassing behaviors—behaviors that are either broadly sexist in tone, or clearly sexually harassing in nature—are more obvious. Also more apparent are dis-

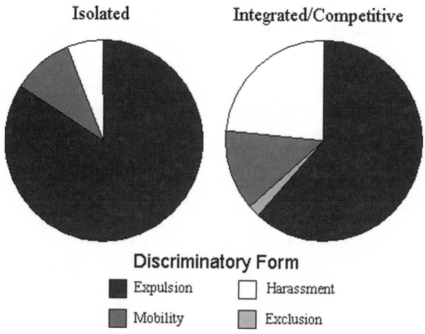

Isolated

Integrated/Competitive

Discriminatory Form

■ Expulsion	□ Harassment
■ Mobility	▨ Exclusion

FIGURE 6.3
Forms of Sex Discrimination by Compositional Context

criminatory mobility processes, and, importantly, differential treatment toward women due to maternity or pregnancy. Employers within integrated settings, it appears, are willing to hire women but reserve suspicion that maternity or pregnancy reflect a liability especially when female employees are assessed relative to male coworkers. Women in this situation, as revealed by qualitative material already presented in chapters 3 and 5, are sometimes explicitly (and illegally) dismissed from employment. At other times, their mobility within a company is halted, they are demoted, or are pressured to resign. One such example is that of Joan Williams, a white female, who describes what happened in her particular case, and the immediate and long-term consequences.

> He [manager] told me that the facility was merging with Office Services and that . . . I was laid-off indefinitely, effective immediately. George LeFranc, who was given my position, had formerly worked as manager of facility services and did not even know what the duties of my job consisted of. . . . They recreated it [my position] and gave it to a male employee. . . . I must have looked pretty bad because a female employee from another group followed me upstairs to my office. Two of my employees helped me pack up my personal items. Word of my layoff

got around the office very fast and several people were coming into my office in shock and disbelief. . . . I was still white and not breathing very well. I still felt like I was going to pass out. Even though I was insisting that I could drive home on my own, two of my close friends and fellow employees insisted that they were taking me home. . . . Both my physical and mental health have been damaged by this whole ordeal.

Whether mobility or expulsion, we find in the case material that within integrated and competitive workplace environments, males are typically the beneficiaries of employer decision making when it comes to layoffs and/or promotional practices. Subjective assessments of females as less dependable, or less suited for managerial responsibilities, clearly play a role. Examples presented in the preceding chapters consistently refer to these dynamics, and "dependability," as part of employers' evaluative criteria. Stereotypical assumptions regarding lack of dependability, owing to maternity or pregnancy, seem especially clear. This is captured in a statement by a female worker in sales, who was denied several promotions over time and then eventually laid off.

> After my layoff, Tom Himmelstein was offered a sales position. . . . Sales Manager Jim Henrickson told another sales person that he did not feel that I would be able to perform my job as well since having a baby. He believed I would concentrate more on family and less on my job.

The fact that women facing discrimination are more often in integrated and competitive environments should not detract from the fact that isolated contexts pertaining to sex composition also hold unique implications for the discrimination experience. Indeed, it is precisely within these workplace environments that women may be especially vulnerable to systematic targeting either by individuals or male workers, collectively. The case of Danielle Rinaldi is informative in these regards. Not only was she the victim of collective sanctioning by males in her job as car salesperson, but it is also evident in her account that, when on the job, she was sexualized by her coworkers and at least one supervisor.

> My termination was generated when I became involved in a dispute over splitting a commission with Paul Hirschman. The company's decision makers [all of whom are male] took his side and I got discharged. . . . I am here to sell cars. That's all I care to sell and pardon my French, but I'm not here to fuck your team so leave me alone. . . . I'm not here for the guys. . . . I'm not interested in anybody. I—you know. I just told him I'm not interested in anybody. I'm married. I want to be left alone. I come here to sell cars, that's all I care to sell.

Another clear possibility in largely segregated male contexts is one wherein the female employee is relegated to traditionally female work tasks—tasks not in her job description, or tasks that similarly situated males are not asked or pressed to undertake. Take the following two cases in point. The first pertains to differential employment expectations.

> I was the only female salesperson and the only salesperson required to fill in for the sales secretary and on the switchboard. Males did inside and outside sales, but I was never given outside sales.

This alternative case pertains more directly to blocked and "gendered" mobility within a traditionally and nearly all male workplace.

> On or about June 24th, I asked to be transferred to auto parts clerk. . . . I was told that as soon as the bookkeeper learned her job, I would start as auto parts clerk. I was to start on September 9th, however, on September 6th Ed Mershon was brought in to be trained as auto parts clerk. On or about June 6th, I was asked to transfer to be an auto parts clerk and I said "yes." Then on or about June 15th Dan Schreider was brought in to fill the position.

Based on these analyses and qualitative materials, it is apparent that sex discrimination occurs within and across a wide array of compositional contexts for both white and minority women. Precisely how it manifests, however, appears to be conditioned to some degree by compositional dynamics. While women in isolated and competitive, integrated environments disproportionately experience discriminatory firing—firing often rooted in managerial perceptions of dependability within their workforce—mobility processes seem more distinct. In integrated work settings, soft skill criteria are often invoked to the detriment of women—women who are more openly and directly competing with males for the same jobs. Where females are isolated, in contrast, they seem to be relegated to "female jobs" within the particular organization, oftentimes despite the obvious desire to obtain a higher status position. Harassment, either general or sexualized, exists in both contexts. Although harassment does manifest more obviously in integrated settings, where opportunities to harass are arguably greater, one can easily imagine the very real vulnerability experienced by isolated female targets.

The Experience and Costs of Racial Competition and Isolation

Discrimination for African American women and men is most commonly occurring in jobs where they are either the only person of their race and/or gender or one of the few. As prior research indicates, this may lead to individuals feeling isolated and alienated from their coworkers. The isolation itself, as noted by Marvin Coldridge, a black male sales worker, invokes a sense that something is wrong. Coupled with unique and differential treatment, discrimination becomes all the more obvious to the victim.

> My employer has five locations. However, I was the only Black person employed by [him]. I was the only person laid off.

Figure 6.4 reports forms of discrimination for African American charging parties for serious cases of employment discrimination across isolated and competitive contexts. As was the case for women generally and sex discrimination, African Americans facing race discrimination in employment are, by and large, most likely to be victims of discriminatory firing according to these data. Although this pattern is more obvious in isolated workplaces—workplaces where minority composition is very low to begin with—the risk of being fired in a discriminatory manner is also quite high within integrated settings (nearly 60 percent of all race discrimination cases). Not surprisingly,

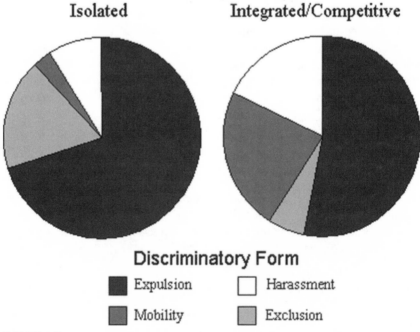

FIGURE 6.4
Forms of Racial Discrimination by Compositional Context

workplaces with few to no minority employees are charged most frequently with exclusionary practices pertaining to hiring—perhaps the most difficult form of discrimination to observe or demonstrate legally.

The fact that discriminatory hiring and especially firing exist today to the extent they do helps explain why black unemployment is consistently double that of white unemployment. While part of this is a function of straightforward differentials in human capital, including education and workplace skills, our analyses thus far suggest that differential treatment by employers in both workplace entry and exit are also most assuredly playing a role.

Beyond expulsion and exclusion, African Americans also continue to experience significant harassment on the job and blocked mobility, more commonly in integrated, competitive environments. Sometimes, as in the case of Laura Wilson, differential wages and the differential application of leave policies are most poignant.

> I was not being paid at the same rate of pay as other Customer Service Representatives. Caucasians [Marsha] and [Louise] were hired as Customer Service Representatives in 1991 and started at a higher rate of pay than I was currently earning after serving one year in the position. . . . I was on disability leave due to having chicken pox. Upon my return to work, I was informed that I was discharged due to absenteeism. [Jeremy], Caucasian, has taken a disability leave every year since 1987 for a period up to three months and has not been disciplined or discharged.

A coworker of Laura's further explains that Laura had the "most difficult accounts and heaviest workload," and that this coworker was forbidden to help Laura while allowed to help others. As another coworker of Laura's states:

> White employees have been in violation of the [same] rules without being terminated. [The company] enforces the rules to the letter of the law only when they want to get rid of someone.

At Sarah Gillis' workplace, over half of the other workers are also African American. Sarah was twice denied a promotion that went to white women instead. As Sarah explains:

> I had more seniority, education, experience and I was better qualified to fill the Floor Manager's position than [Brenda]. I had more seniority and was better qualified to fill the [second] position than [Claire].

As a coworker of Sarah describes, and as confirmed by the Ohio Civil Rights Commission investigator, "Only white nurses got the promotions." In addition to being passed up for promotions without an explanation, her immediate supervisor, a white woman, also made the comment in front of Sarah and other employees that "this place would be better run without all the niggers and fags." Working in this hostile environment, Sarah felt like she had no other option than to quit her job.

Numerous other cases attest to an unwillingness to promote African American employees in integrated contexts—employees that have more seniority and better objective qualifications. As prior chapters revealed, the invoking of subjective criteria, including a desire for particular soft skills, by gatekeeping actors seem to be especially pronounced. As revealed in Michael Smith's statement below, blacks on the job become aware of such differential mobility particularly when whites are visibly reaping the rewards.

> [My employer] has not upgraded or promoted any Blacks while Whites, who are no more qualified, are promoted with the result that there are no Black management on staff.

As noted at the outset, the more typical employment situation for African Americans is one of relative isolation; that is, being employed where one is both numerically and socially in the numerical minority. One's visibility in such a context is more pronounced, and targeted differential treatment may indeed be more commonplace as some prior examples suggest—examples including the lone black police officer taunted with racial slurs by a supervisor; the black male sales employee inundated with racial epithets and jokes; and the many examples of singular black employees disciplined or fired in a targeted way for violations of company policy when whites, in fact, commonly violate such policy without sanction. Targeted harassment and differential application of policy and rules is very apparent in isolated environments for both black males and females. And, although sometimes coworkers are culpable, differential treatment and policing often lie in the hands of immediate supervisors, as in Dorothy Rutledge's experience (as reported by a witness).

> [The foreman] frequently spoke to Dorothy in an abusive manner, but did not speak to white employees in the same way. [The foreman] wrote [Dorothy] up for reading a newspaper when she was not reading the newspaper, but white employees were reading newspapers and books, and they were not written up. . . . He [the foreman] observed white employees at the same time doing the same thing . . . but did not say the same thing to them.

Although this supervisor "never made a racial statement" according to Dorothy, it was his "everyday exchange" with black workers wherein he was "just plain watching and looking" that was problematic. The "just plain watching and looking" to which she refers is particularly problematic throughout the case materials, impacting disparate punishment and firing, but also mobility prospects in isolated contexts. Melvin Palmer's discrimination experience highlights this fact.

> I have been discriminated against, harassed, and excluded for overseas assignments due to consideration of my race because Mrs. Jessup has given me two poor evaluations in the past two years and after consulting with her supervisor she was told to change the evaluations to reflect my accomplishments. I was the only Black in the Overseas Training Program. I was replaced on the Taiwan assignment by Greg White who is Caucasian. White has two years of experience compared to my twenty five years of experience.

Conclusion

The composition of workplaces matters in the discrimination experience, albeit in relatively subtle ways. Most workplaces have some level of sex integration, and the majority of women found in our data are indeed employed in relatively integrated contexts. Racial diversity in contemporary workplaces is clearly more limited, at least numerically, as most minority individuals work in isolated environments—environments wherein they are the lone minority employee or part of a quite small handful.

The prevalence or likelihood of discrimination, at least as captured by these data—data that no doubt underestimate the occurrence of discrimination—is relatively normally distributed across sex and race compositional contexts. What this means, rather straightforwardly, is that discrimination occurs across a wide variety of workplace contexts, including both those that are highly integrated and those wherein women and blacks represent a very small fraction of the workplace population. For white women, there appears to be a compositional threshold, or a peak in discrimination occurrence, around 20 percent female. This, combined with the fact that such workplaces in our data tend to be engaged in traditionally male work, suggests some process of competitive threat for women.

Beyond the issue of discrimination occurrence is the more interesting fact that the unfolding of discrimination occurs in unique ways depending on levels of integration and isolation. In the case of sex-integrated and competitive environments, women are often competing with men for job promotions. Supervisors, for their part, invoke soft skill criteria and perhaps even more poignantly, the subjective criteria of dependability, when trying to decide who to promote. Sometimes implicit and sometimes explicit, issues of maternity and pregnancy become important to gatekeepers and, more often than not, work to the disadvantage of hardworking women.

Within isolated contexts—contexts that tend to embody traditional male work—women may also face the dependability issue, yet our data reveal that they tend to be excluded from male networks and often funneled into what is deemed female work. This proves to be especially problematic, as there is little protection in these environments. Lodging a complaint, in fact, is tantamount to further isolation from coworkers. Correspondingly, it is especially within these isolated contexts that we see women displaying amazing patience in terms of promotional opportunities, or in efforts to rectify the discrimination themselves. As one woman notes:

> I wanted to just try to handle things on my own . . . that if I was responsible for getting anybody fired, that a lot of the guys may make things harder for me than what they were.

Nevertheless, and despite efforts over time to resolve the situation on their own, these women are eventually forced to lodge a formal discrimination suit, often because the discrimination intensifies, because supervisors and human resource personnel ignore what is going on, or because the female employee is eventually fired for causing trouble despite her best efforts to resolve the situation quietly.

For African Americans, the more typical scenario is one of relative isolation at work—isolation numerically but also socially. Here, problems pertaining to discrimination often relate to being watched, disparately policed relative to company rules and policies, and sanctioned for violations when whites are not. Again, and as in the case of women, isolated individuals are not in a position to, nor do they wish to, "make waves." Indeed, discriminatory treatment is often internalized. Periodically, however, as some of our case materials reveal, the cost becomes too high, including but not limited to losing one's job. It is often at this final point that a complaint of discrimination is waged with an external body.

Race-integrated workplace environments—a byproduct of civil rights law and a history of discrimination suits and victories—are certainly more commonplace in the contemporary era. Integration in itself, however, as a measure or barometer of equality, can only reveal the extent to which exclusionary and expulsive dimensions of discrimination continue to manifest. As the distribution of discrimination types across race-isolated and competitive workplace contexts and our case material reveal, discrimination is still a factor in integrated settings. Differential policing and sanctioning of white and minority employees still occurs, and disparate mobility prospects owing to supervisory use of soft skill criteria seem to matter as our examples in this and prior chapters make clear.

Workplace race and gender composition are by no means the underlying forces behind discrimination. Instead they represent structural contexts that condition interactions within workplaces, and that define the extent to which broader beliefs regarding race and gender differences are dealt with. The history and culture within a given workplace organization no doubt play a role in how compositional dynamics play out. Workplace organizations can either mitigate racist and sexist tendencies through policy, clear procedure, and managerial constraint, or reproduce larger societal disparities by allowing preconceptions, biases, and behaviors to intrude on internal processes of inclusion, equal and fair treatment, and mobility. We acknowledge that there are likely numerous workplaces—workplaces not represented in these data—that represent the former. As suggested throughout this chapter, however, there remain plenty of workplaces in Ohio and in the United States more generally wherein workplace enforcement of civil rights remains lacking, where integration remains problematic, and where isolation prevails.

Notes

1. On this point, see Reskin, McBrier, and Kmec (1999), Sorenson (2004), and Yoder (1994). While certainly useful and suggestive, much of the empirical literature relates, at an aggregate level, how female and minority populations segregated at the workplace level tend to be paid and valued less occupationally relative to those who are not. This implies either a general and even historical devaluation of female and minority work, or active preference for female and minority employees who are cheaper. Cross-sectional work, which sometimes control for human capital of employees (e.g., education, skills, etc.) but also race and gender composition of either the labor market sector or workplace-level composition, similarly reveals a devaluative tendency—a devaluative tendency which is often interpreted as unmeasured, active discrimination in processes of employment, promotion, and pay. For recent work in this regard, see Cohen and Huffman (2003), England et al. (1994), and Kmec (2003).

2. This seems to be especially true, however, for white males within largely female-segregated work contexts, such as teachers or nurses, and driven by perceptions that male employees have managerial and bureaucratic skills more suitable for advancement (Kadushin 1976; Floge and Merrill 1986).

3. Other scholars, such as Yoder (1991, 1994), propose that understanding numerical proportions of a group at a workplace is not enough to fully understand the discrimination people face. The effects of being a numerical minority, as described by Kanter, may actually have more to do with the status afforded to women within a broader patriarchal society.

4. Of the 850 randomly selected content-coded cases, only 297 had available data on the race and sex composition of the workplace in question. The 292 cases, however, reveal quite significant heterogeneity in terms of labor market sector, race and sex composition, and organizational size. We discuss this heterogeneity momentarily.

7

The Experiences of Black and White and High- and Low-Status Women

with Susan Ortiz

Defense Attorney: Do you know why he was treating you differently than other employees?

Dolores Williams: I think . . . because I am a Black female and that John Dixon has a problem with females. . . . He also has a problem with Blacks. He just had a problem with me being on the job.

DESPITE POLITICAL CHANGES and protections occurring since the late 1960s, most notably implemented in the public employment sector, there remain discrepancies in what is stated by law and the actual treatment and opportunities available to women on the job. Progress has certainly been made in areas such as wage inequality. Yet, the sex-based division of paid and unpaid work, sex segregation across industry and occupation, sexual harassment, gender labeling of jobs, and sex-based earnings inequalities remain relatively commonplace as noted in chapters 3 through 6 (Marini 1989; Kilbourne et al. 1994; Padavic and Reskin 2002). Such disparities may not only be about sex, or about race, but rather intersections of sex, race, and social-class status.

Here we address how race and class confound broader patterns of sex discrimination as established earlier, and the types of social closure women of distinct race and class backgrounds experience. We specifically compare the forms and experiences of labor market discrimination of black and white women in various occupational positions. Notable are high levels of discriminatory firing among both, and higher instances of promotional discrimination directed toward black women—patterns partially attributable to their disparate concentration in positions of lower occupational prestige. Our qualitative immersion reveals some underlying mechanisms.

Race and Class Variations in Discrimination

As the body of research on gender-based labor market discrimination has grown, so has research on race-based oppression and discrimination. As with gender discrimination, race-based labor market discrimination as noted in chapters 1, 2 and 5 has been linked to segregation across occupation and industry (Becker 1980; Davis 1995; Bertrand and Mullainathan 2004). Findings, including some presented earlier, moreover suggest that race is closely tied to promotion and discharge (Baldi and McBrier 1997; Greenhaus, Parasuraman, and Wormley 1990; James 2000; Zwerling and Silver 1992; Elvira and Zatzick 2002).

Black women have been and continue to be quite poorly represented when it comes to structural opportunities, hiring practices, and promotional opportunities including positions of high authority and wages. They also tend to leave full-time work sooner than their white counterparts due to layoffs, firing, or other forced exits. Although human capital, structural location, and occupational segregation matter (Reid 2002; McGuire 2002), inequalities persist even with these factors accounted for. This leaves open the possibility that the employment and discrimination experiences of minority women are distinct relative to majority women and that different types of closure may be playing a role.

Finding discrimination variations for minority relative to majority women should come as no surprise, really. African American women have historically been treated differently than their white counterparts. Anderson (1982) addresses this specifically in her historically grounded examination of black women's status in the U.S. economy. Racial gaps for women become especially obvious during war years when the demand for workers, particularly female workers, increases dramatically. For their part, white women have historically opposed or refused to work alongside black women.

In the early 1940s black women were almost solely employed in lower-prestige jobs, such as unskilled blue-collar jobs. White women, in comparison, were principally employed in pink- or white-collar jobs (Cunningham and Zalokar 1992). By the 1970s black women had moved into almost every occupational realm, yet were still experiencing race and sex discrimination. In 1980, black women mostly occupied jobs as clerical workers (29.0 percent) followed closely by jobs as service workers (25.6 percent). During the same period, the majority of white women (36.5 percent) were also clerical workers, but 20.1 percent had moved into the ranks of professional and technical work. Only 16.1 percent of black women were in the professional/technical category (Cunningham and Zalokar 1992).

Occupational differentiation now has changed very little from previous decades. Black women with degrees remain concentrated in teaching and nursing, but even without a degree many are working in the public sector. Black women also continue to find themselves in service positions (27 percent) and sales/clerical positions (26 percent). White women also remain disparately concentrated in clerical occupations, yet discrepancies remain between professional/technical occupations for white women (19 percent) and professional/technical occupations for black women (14 percent) (King 1995).

Current research, particularly that grounded in feminist theorizing, has witnessed a shift in orientation toward understanding these persistent inequalities—a shift highlighting the need to consider the connections across and between various statuses. Although many studies include some aspect of social stratification, few highlight interconnections. When race and class are examined with gender, discrimination can no longer be relegated into separate spheres. Discrimination has and does occur differently for people of different gender, race, and social-class backgrounds, and as such, race, gender, and class should be examined in a conjoined fashion if empirically possible.

Theories of "gendered" organizations provide a valuable starting point (Acker 1990; Britton 2000), yet questions remain about the role of race and class. Indeed, according to recent developments in feminist theory, gender, race, and class stand in relation to each other through a system of domination and subordination. Gender, race, and class "intersect to create unique constellations of disadvantage and privilege in all institutions" (Browne and Misra 2005).

We take the issue of intersections of race, social class, and gender to heart in this chapter. We draw from all serious race/sex employment discrimination cases filed by black and white women ($n = 8,412$) to examine discriminatory experiences. We then turn to the smaller content-coded sample of women ($n = 388$), which provides unique occupational information including occupational title and prestige and, thus, an indicator of class status.

To determine how race and class shape the prevalence and experience of gender discrimination, we filtered the data to look specifically at discrimination encountered by females in the labor market. Like all materials presented in this book, these are "probable cause" and "settled" discrimination cases which women filed on issues of hiring, firing, promotion, demotion, and general harassment.[1] A combination of each woman's occupational prestige score was compared and cross-referenced with the Equal Employment Opportunity Commission's (EEOC) Job Classification Guide to gauge social class position. Occupation is often used in research as an indicator of class, and it is frequently seen as the best indicator. Women's class status is, admittedly, difficult to operationalize given its relation to marital status. Yet, recent work concurs that class status remains important when trying to understand women's relative status, and the inequalities that women face (Browne and Misra 2005).

Discrimination against Women and Racial Variations

Women traditionally find work in female-dominated occupations, and they tend to work in part-time jobs more often than men. Whether or not these differences can be explained by human capital differences or discrimination is subject to dispute. We know that men have a labor market advantage over women generally, but do white women have an advantage over black women? And, if so, does this pattern play out in terms of the types of discrimination that black and white women experience?

In 1990, almost 55 percent of women over the age of sixteen in the state of Ohio were actively in the labor market. Whites comprised 88.2 percent of the total labor force while blacks comprised 10.4 percent. Yet, as reported in earlier chapters, black women are most highly represented among victims of discrimination. Does this mean that they are more likely to be fired? Who, among the women represented in these cases, is stuck below the "glass ceiling?" What types of injuries are black women sustaining, and are their charges significantly different from those of white women?

Figure 7.1 shows the injuries filed by black and white women, broken down by percentage within the charging party's own race/ethnicity in each of the following injury categories: hiring, firing, promotion, demotion, and general harassment. Notable is the high representation of firing cases (57 percent) and general harassment (29 percent) cases for both black and white women. General harassment cases include those where the employer or fellow employees are doing something to make the work environment intolerable for the charging party. It can take on many forms, including sexual harassment, differential treatment due to pregnancy, antagonism, exclusion from opportunities given to other employees, and so on. The basic premise of general harassment is to make the charging party feel unwelcome and uncomfortable.

When examining breakdowns of the injury claims, both black and white women have high and relatively similar rates of discriminatory firing. Yet, in-

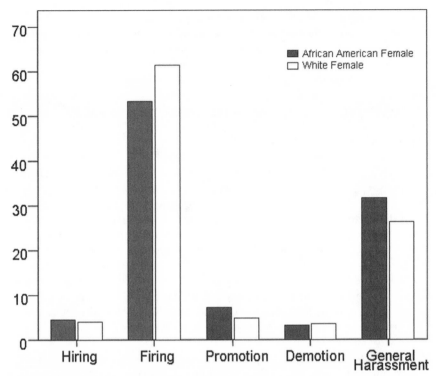

FIGURE 7.1
Percent of Cases Filed by Women, by Race for Each Injury

depth analyses of qualitative case material suggests that the experience of discriminatory firing itself does indeed vary. Many more white women are unjustly fired, it appears, owing to pregnancy and maternity related issues—a result consistent with findings reported in chapter 3 and variations between the public and private sectors reported in chapter 5. Black women, in comparison, tend to define their discriminatory treatment in terms of differential treatment or unequal terms and conditions relative to other, white employees. For example, as Regina Smith, a medical biller, states:

> On September 21, 1999, Adrianne Moss, White, Manager, gave me a letter that stated that they would no longer be needing my services due to excessive absences and my inability to take direction and work the hours I was hired to work. . . . I believe that I was discharged due to considerations of my race, Black, because Martha Gregory, White, Medical Biller, had excessive absences and was not discharged. I only missed two days while employed by Respondent

and I successfully completed my probationary period. Between September and December, Moss called me an asshole, referred to me as a child and called me out by my name, but Moss never treated White employees this way. Two days after my discharge, Respondent replaced me with a White person. Prior to my discharge, I was never given an oral or written warning or a suspension.

On the other hand, several comments taken directly from charges filed by white women for discriminatory firing often referenced pregnancy. As a white female credit manager relates:

> On April, 3, 1992, I was advised by Samantha Jacoby, female, Office Manger, that I was being let go because I was no longer dependable. I believe that I have been discriminated against because of my sex [pregnancy] for the following reasons. I had a doctor's appointment on April 1, 1992 at which time it was confirmed that I was pregnant. On April 2, 1992 I went to work and told everyone in the office that I was pregnant. The Owner's wife, Sue McGrady, was visiting the office when I was telling everyone of my news. Ms. McGrady asked me if it was a planned pregnancy. She told me I should deal with Sam about it. On April 3, 1992, my supervisor, Samantha Jacoby and Sue McGrady . . . were in a meeting for the majority of the morning. At approximately 5:15 p.m. that same day, Samantha told me that I was let go because I was no longer dependable. . . . My doctor did not place any restrictions on me and I am able to perform my job as Credit Manager. I am aware that the Respondent employs approximately two hundred [200] employees and only approximately ten [10] of them are females. I am also aware that a pregnant employee, Kate Flounder, was discharged while out on leave after giving birth. The Respondent does not have a maternity leave or disability leave policy.

Although our data reveal no statistically significant differences in levels of discriminatory firing between black and white women, underlying reasons for discriminatory firing can be completely unrelated. Indeed, the weight of the qualitative material available to us suggests differences in process. White women are often fired around gender-based issues. The discharge of black women appears to be much more commonly related to their race status.

Unlike discriminatory firing, there are statistically significant associations between race and women filing discrimination charges for hiring, promotion, and general harassment (see table 7.1).[2] Black women file more charges of discrimination in hiring. This is obviously one of the most difficult areas to ascertain whether or not discrimination has occurred, yet within the context of these cases, civil rights investigators have managed to collect enough evidence that it likely did. And, notably, black women also appear to be denied promotions and harassed more frequently relative to white women once in the door.

TABLE 7.1
Comparison of Black and White Women, by Discrimination Type

	Black Women	White Women	Chi-square
Hiring	192	144	6.857*
	4.6%	4.0%	
Firing	2,247	2189	.758
	53.4%	61.3%	
Promotion	305	171	37.723*
	7.2%	4.8%	
Demotion	136	124	.554
	3.2%	3.5%	
General Harassment	1,332	941	67.260*
	31.6%	26.4%	
Total	4212	3569	

* denotes statistically significant difference below .01

Social Class and Workplace Discrimination for Women

Black women, as we noted at the outset, typically earn less and are in lower-prestige jobs than white women. Black women mostly occupy jobs as clerical workers (29.0 percent) followed closely by jobs as service workers (25.6 percent). The majority of white women (36.5 percent) are also clerical workers, but 20.1 percent are professional and technical workers, while only 16.1 percent of black women are professional and technical workers (Cunningham and Zalokar 1992).

Perhaps it is the case that differential location in the occupational hierarchy may be playing a part in the differences previously reported. Indeed, there is good reason to suspect that levels of formal organization and bureaucratic prudence (often characteristic of high-status jobs) and/or unfettered managerial discretion and arbitrary decision making (often prevalent in low-status, service-oriented jobs), may shape discrimination likelihood and the discrimination experience generally, and even the differentials between white and black females previously reported.

If black women are segregated into certain occupations, they may be filing more discrimination claims because of their location within particularly vulnerable, lower-status occupations. When taking into consideration the sex-based segregation of occupations between women and men in general, black women still traditionally hold lower-status jobs as compared to white women. Looking at the cases from the content-coded sample, figure 7.2 shows the occupational distribution of serious cases filed by black and white women. Notably, the majority of both black and white women who file

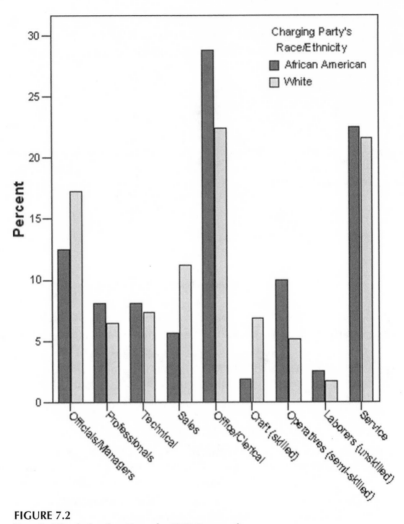

FIGURE 7.2
Female Discrimination Cases by EEO Occupation

charges are located in office/clerical positions (25 percent) and service occupations (21.9 percent).

This pattern is quite similar to the more general sex-based segregation of
occupations. Especially notable, however, is the higher percentage of white
women filing charges in official/manager positions as well as in sales and craft
(skilled) positions. This is a reflection of Black women's low representation in
these higher-status occupational categories and possible male resistance to
white women entering traditionally male work sites.

Breakdowns by each job classification in figure 7.2 reveal that there are some (statistically) significant differences between the proportions of black and white women filing charges in various occupational categories. The percentage of white women filing serious discrimination charges within official/manager, sales, and craft (skilled) occupations is significantly different and higher than that of black females. Again, we interpret this as being largely due to the difference between black and white women's representation in these particular occupational ranks.

Do we find variations in rates of discriminatory claims and even forms of discrimination by occupational prestige? Absolutely. Using standard occupational prestige scores cross-referenced with the EEOC Job Classification Guide as a proxy for class, figure 7.3 shows the breakdown of serious discrimination cases by low-, medium-, and high-occupational status and race for our content-coded subsample.

The majority of serious discrimination cases are made by women with medium occupational prestige. Nonetheless, the gap between middle class and

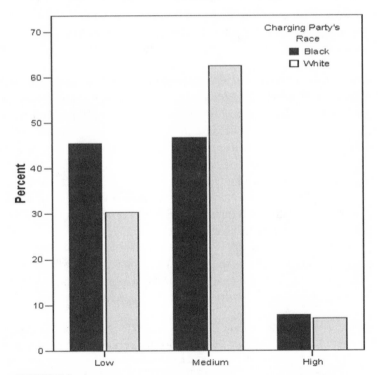

FIGURE 7.3
Breakdown of Serious Discrimination Cases for Females by Race and Occupational Status

working class closes dramatically for black women whereas it increases for white women. Working-class and middle-class black women filed almost exactly the same number of charges, 45.5 percent and 46.8 percent, respectively, yet there is a large difference between the percentage of working-class white women versus middle-class white women, 30.4 percent and 62.6 percent, respectively. High-status women filed the fewest number of cases regardless of race. This may be due to the limited number of women in high-status positions or other structural differences.

The question remains as to whether or not there is a relationship between the forms of discrimination one is likely to experience as social-class status. Does firing remain the most visible form of discrimination for each class? As noted previously, firing is the most frequently recorded injury for both black and white women. Supplementary analyses shows us that when examining only the percentage of charges based on unlawful firing practices and general harassment, the highest percentages of cases are filed by white women within the middle class. Why are middle-class white women filing more firing and harassment charges than middle-class black women? Middle-class white women were leading the charge in the feminist movement, and this may be continuing with the white women represented in this sample.

Of all women, middle-class women in general are filing the most charges, suggesting that these women may feel more empowered than their working-class counterparts. This may also be a product of sociodemographic factors, such as education. Women with advanced education may know more about how and where to file charges, where to find information about filing, or may have access to other resources such as attorneys. They may also be cushioned against potential job loss by a well-earning spouse and/or savings. There are very few cases for upper-class women. This corresponds to the few women in occupations with high prestige, or perhaps the fact that women in high-prestige positions also have more to lose by filing discrimination charges. Yet, even with small numbers we find women within high-prestige occupations experiencing discrimination.

The rich qualitative data allows for a more detailed understanding of the process of discrimination for women of similar status. The following quotes were taken from the separate charge forms from a black woman and a white woman, both secretaries but working for two different companies.

I received a letter of termination from Lucy Marks, white, Regional Supervisor, stating that I had not fulfilled my probationary period standards within the thirty days. I believe I was discriminated against and terminated due to my race, black, because I was the only Black employee at this location. Lucy Marks did not give me the necessary training for the position. On many occasions I asked another secretary for the procedures that were used, such as, giving clients particular information or giving providers information concerning clients benefits status. I was not allowed computer training in June 1992 with other secretaries [white]. Lucy Marks told me I would not be paid for attending staff meetings. Other employees attending the meetings were paid. After attending several meetings, I was excluded from two and then invited back. Other secretaries' work was not scrutinized in the same manner mine was.

Obviously, this woman was not given the same terms and conditions as other white female secretaries. The following quote is from a white woman working in a similar position. Similar to the case above, she also was not given the same terms and conditions as other employees, yet differences are apparent.

Shortly after I notified Respondent of my pregnancy I began being treated less favorably than my non-pregnant co-workers and on June 20, 1990, Respondent attempted to force me to sign a warning letter/agreement regarding my attendance. When I would not sign the agreement, he suspended me. On June 20, 1990, Ed Sawyer, male President, informed me that my attendance was unacceptable. I believe that I have been unlawfully discriminated against in being treated less favorably and suspended because of my sex, female/pregnancy, for the following reasons: 1) My attendance is comparable to that of my non-pregnant co-workers. 2) Mr. Sawyer expects me to lift heavy boxes. Since I notified Mr. Sawyer of my pregnancy he has required me to do the work of two people. On the attendance warning/agreement Mr. Sawyer wants me to sign, it is stated that if I miss one day, I'm suspended and at three days missed, I am terminated. The warning/agreement also states that I will have a designated break and lunchtime. No one else has these stipulations nor were they required to sign such an agreement. The women in Respondent's office are disallowed from wearing pants in the office.

Such comparisons between white and black women of similar status are interesting. Once again we see that relevant issues for white women often concern pregnancy and maternity related issues. For black women, differential treatment and unfair treatment with regard to terms of employment seem more paramount, and race prevails, across the cases.

As revealed earlier in figure 7.3, working-class and middle-class black women file almost an equal number of charges. Middle-class white women in contrast, file more serious charges compared to white women of other statuses. Social class, or occupational status, when taken in the aggregate, seems to matter less in the discrimination experiences of black females. In these data, black women often report and experience differential treatment from their coworkers—*coworkers who also tend to be female*. White middle-class women, however, are filing many more charges due to pregnancy or maternity. For them, employment discrimination seems more intimately tied to gendered notions and, specifically, the view that white women cannot be good workers and good mothers at the same time. Not only do the data, and particularly the qualitative data, show that these women were unlawfully fired, but it also appears that the injury claims themselves vary by class and race.

Examining how employment discrimination differs by race and class provides a deeper sense of how inequality unfolds depending on various statuses. There are, in fact, different types and processes of discrimination that occur across industry and occupation. Women experience discrimination associated with equal treatment, mobility, maternity and pregnancy leave, and sexual harassment in both the private and public sector. Black women, however, due to perception or actual experience, see discrimination more so as related to their race and less to their gender. The discriminatory experience of white women, in contrast, is more closely associated with others' preconceptions of motherhood and work.

Conclusions

Race and class remain salient issues when it comes to understanding gender inequalities in the labor market, and discrimination specifically in the arena of work. Discrimination, as our analyses reveal, is to some degree a subjective experience. Both black and white women continue to view and experience discriminatory firing as the most salient reason for filing a discrimination charge. Black women, by all indications, are more likely to experience discrimination in hiring, promotion, and general harassment, and such discrimination seems to be largely race based.

Whether this is the objective reality or whether African American women are simply more sensitive to race as a salient identity and issue in their lives, however, remains an open question. Women may be experiencing discrimination through a combination of stratification systems, but are only reporting what seems to be the most obvious form. Even if black women are experiencing discrimination based on their sex, for instance, it may be perceived as a function of differential racial treatment. Most white women, in contrast, clearly interpret discrimination as being based on their sex, despite the objective importance of social class in shaping discrimination prevalence and form. Regardless, there is good reason to believe and make explicit that discrimination faced by women in the contemporary workplace has some racial and social-class character. Individuals correspondingly can experience simultaneous advantage and disadvantage, but may attribute their experiences of inequality to a singular dimension.

Previous research has shown that gaps in wage inequality between women and men from working-class backgrounds are less significant than the differences found among other classes. Our results reveal that there are differential experiences between middle- and working-class white women. As for black women, there appears to be little in the way of social-class differences in their discriminatory experiences. Both working-class and middle-class black women file an almost equal number of cases, and with little variation in discriminatory form.

Black women have historically been more concerned with discharge because they were often the "last hired and the first fired," but as our results show firing is not just a problem for black women. White women also file significantly more firing charges than any other type of injury. Although there are no major differences between working-class black and working-class white women for any injury, there are arguably important differences between middle-class black and middle-class white women in discriminatory firing, demotion, and general harassment. Specifically, working-class black and white women and middle-class black women file more charges based on unequal treatment compared to their middle-class, white peers. Middle-class white women file more charges based on pregnancy and maternity related issues. At least for middle-class white women and/or their employers, a disjuncture seems to remain about their roles as mothers versus their roles as full-time workers; whereas most black women and working-class white women experience discrimination based on unequal treatment, which may include a combination of factors pertaining to race and class.

It is certainly conceivable that many employees do not report discrimination out of fear of retaliation. Or, if they are victims of discrimination, they may simply quit or transfer from their current job instead of filing charges and seeking compensation. This would arguably hold more true for working-class women—women who, lacking safety nets, need these jobs to survive. They are also in a disadvantaged position relative to collecting evidence, knowing what their rights are, or understanding how to most effectively follow through on grievances. This will affect both the total number of discrimination cases as well as the number of cases involving women in situations of promotion, demotion, or discharge. We thus temper our interpretation of findings with acknowledgment that the realities of discrimination are much more prevalent than can be captured in any single data set, and that there may be some systematic (and sociologically interesting) biases in cases that end up in data such as ours.

Admittedly, we only examine the discrimination experienced by black and white women. Discrimination certainly may occur, and perhaps even differentially, for women of other races and ethnicities—a fact that we hope future research will consider. Although the population of Ohio is not representative of the population of the United States in many respects, it should be noted that according to the U.S. Bureau of the Census (2000b), the participation of white and black women in Ohio's labor force is quite generalizable relative to national patterns. Thus, although our data and findings may not be nationally representative in terms of racial/ethnic heterogeneity of the country as a whole, our analyses and results nevertheless do tackle explicitly, like few studies have, how discrimination unfolds for black and white women in actual workplaces. There is little reason to believe that the patterns revealed—specifically the high rates of discriminatory firing and harassment, the race or gender-based nature of the discrimination experience, and the social-class variations we have uncovered—should not be of relevance to most analyses of discrimination and inequality, regardless of region, state, or maybe even nation.

Notes

1. General harassment includes sexual harassment, exclusion, antagonism, and intimidation.

2. We ran nonparametric chi-square tests to compare the significance of the differences between the types of discrimination reported by black women versus the type of discrimination reported by white women ($p < .01$)

8

Discrimination and African American Men: A Precarious Historical Legacy

with Sherry Mong

I asked him about the criteria . . . and, how did he get the position over me or any other blacks in the company who had been there much longer than him. . . . His comment was, in effect was . . . that remark about laying his wallet down and it being there when he get back and . . . I said, "Do you know what you're saying? Like you're laying your wallet down, say like, like blacks are going to steal from you or something?" I said, "do you know what you're saying?" He said it was his prerogative or at his discretion to make what promotions that he wanted to and the way he sees fit, it was best for the department or something to that effect.

—black male security guard, relating an incident with his supervisor.

JUST AS WHITE AND BLACK WOMEN experience inequality uniquely, so do African American men—men that have long held a tenuous and vulnerable place in American society. Beginning with slavery and continuing through the Jim Crow era, they have struggled for their very *lives*. Migration to northern and Midwestern urban industrial areas from the 1920s into the 1950s raised new issues. Encountering more subtle, but nevertheless important, forms of de facto segregation and discrimination, they were barred from unions, relegated to unskilled jobs, and shut out of manufacturing positions by whites (Roediger 1991; Landry 2000). Such workplace exclusion, including alienation from coworkers, has made for a unique cultural and economic history.

The economic marginalization of African American men has continued into the present era. Although black men traditionally found employment in agriculture, industrial transitions in the mid-twentieth century caused significant reductions in the labor force; and in the years following World War II, black men experienced high rates of unemployment, earning less than half the wages of their white counterparts (Blankenship 1993). The Civil Rights Act of 1964 ushered in a period of reform, and significant gains were realized in both education and employment. Black earnings, however, slowed in the 1980s relative to white earnings, and intergenerational improvement in income stagnated (Blau and Beller 1992). Using the 1972–1989 General Social Survey, and comparing white father–son and black father–son pairs, Davis (1995) found that black men were more downwardly mobile than white men and that black fathers' occupations did not protect their sons from falling, as did white fathers' occupations. Moreover, there is evidence that black men still tend to have the lowest mean occupational prestige of white, black, and Hispanic men and women, and have not fared as well as black women in closing the earnings gap with white males (Xu and Leffler 1992; Blau and Beller 1992).

Research on labor market inequality continues to suggest a unique and vulnerable role for black males—that of a reserve, low-wage, labor force whose rate of unemployment is consistently double that of whites. Sociologists have indeed documented persistent disparities in employment (Wilson, Tienda, and Wu 1995; Cohn and Fossett 1995), income and wages (Tomaskovic-Devey 1993a; Smith 1997; Grodsky and Pager 2001; Coleman 2003), and promotion/authority attainment (Baldi and McBrier 1997; Wilson 1997; Wilson, Sakura-Lemessy, and West 1999; Smith 2001, 2002). African Americans generally, as noted in the chapters 1 and 5, are disproportionately represented in occupations that pay less, and there is much evidence of race-based queuing into less desirable jobs (Lieberson 1980; Reskin and Roos 1990; Kaufman 2002). Black workers are more likely to be in jobs with poor work environments (Moss and Tilly 2001), and are more closely supervised and hold jobs with less task complexity than whites (Tomaskovic-Devey 1993a; Kaufman 1986). There is evidence, however, that even middle-class status does not offer them protection against inequalities (Feagin 1991; Anderson 2001). Black managers may feel isolated, have more difficulty obtaining career support (Thomas 1990; Jackson, Thoits, and Taylor 1995), or lack vital upper management contacts (Friedman, Kane, and Cornfield 1998).

Recent work has begun to shift attention to active exclusion and discrimination directed toward black males by employers. Using both audit (i.e., racial testing) and employer interview methodologies, researchers such as Feagin (1991), Moss and Tilly (2001), and Pager and Quillian (2005), have begun to effectively denote how and why discrimination continues to be uniquely relevant to the black male employment experience. We elaborate on these themes in this chapter by first examining how and why labor market inequalities may be linked to cultural stereotypes of black men. We then turn to the ways in which this might trigger discrimination among gatekeeping actors in the contemporary world of work. Our analyses, which draw on the subsample of African American males who experienced workplace discrimination, reveal the processes involved and the various labor market and personal consequences of the discrimination that they experience.

Cultural Stereotypes and African American Men

The stereotyping of African American men in popular culture, something historically tied to their low status and to broader historical and cultural processes of racial competitive threat, remains problematic. Current portrayals of black men in public media as dangerous and violent criminals are disturbing, not to mention potentially problematic for employers and managers. Cultural scholars, such as Glassner (1999), have indeed argued that there is a profound fear of black men within American society. In expressing their own discrimination experiences in public life, black men have indicated that they sense that others perceive them as a threat (in this regard, see Feagin 1991).

Cultural preconceptions are problematic for day-to-day experiences and encounters, but also for the direct treatment of black males by institutional gatekeepers (for recent, well-known examples, see Kirschenman and Neckerman 1991; Moss and Tilly 1996, 2001; Shih 2002). Relative to employment specifically, Moss and Tilly (2001) find that employers hold negative views of both the hard and soft skills of black men in entry-level jobs. Black men are also often categorized as "defensive" or "overly sensitive" to racism. Moreover, some managers express fear of black male employees, often believing them to be violent and "difficult to control."

Such stereotypes certainly hold consequences for hiring and mobility prospects, given the autonomy most business owners and managers express when making decisions about who to hire, fire, and promote. Recent audit test analyses concur on this point. A study of matched black and white male job applicants for entry-level jobs in Milwaukee, for instance, revealed that black males who did not have an incarceration record did not fare as well as white males who did (Pager 2003).

Discrimination Potential

Whether black men are in working-class or menial jobs in which they are tightly controlled, or in middle-class jobs where they are left out of informal networks, there is much reason to suspect that discrimination is pervasive and occurs across a wide variety of occupations. Although prior studies have provided strong inferential support that occupational mobility differences are, in part, due to discrimination processes, very little remains known about the mechanisms—or how such inequalities are produced in actual workplaces (Reskin 2003; Vallas 2003). Moreover, while scholars have made great strides in studying inner-city male joblessness, little is known about the day-to-day experiences of black men who are employed in formal economic sectors (see Royster 2003 for an important exception).

Prior research into occupational mobility for both black men and women, has focused on significant work-related events such as hiring, promotion, and firing, and has given us important clues as to where discrimination might occur. Audit studies have generally shown that blacks were less likely to be hired and receive call backs (Fix and Struyk 1993; Bendick, Jackson, and Reinoso 1994; Pager 2003; Bertrand and Mullainathan 2004). Generally, more formal recruiting procedures result in more blacks being employed. Yet, there is also evidence that employers are able to get around formal hiring procedures, and that nepotism still plays a role (Moss and Tilly 2001; Royster 2003).

Studies designed to detect racial discrimination in promotions have shown that blacks are less likely to be promoted, or are promoted at slower rates than whites, even after controlling for individual and firm characteristics (Baldi and McBrier 1997). Interestingly, using separate waves of PSID data, Maume (1999a) found that while race has no influence on the likelihood of being promoted to manager for women, black men are 52 percent less likely to be promoted after controlling for personal and job characteristics. Moreover, James' (2000) cross-sectional management survey in a financial services firm reveals that black managers are not only promoted at slower rates than whites, but also receive less psychosocial support.

Scholars have focused on promotion due to the inherent problem of subjectivity and supervisor bias in the evaluation process, and a number of studies have indeed shown that blacks are rated lower than whites in performance evaluations (Greenhaus, Parasuraman, and Wormley 1990; Sackett, DuBois, and Noe 1991; Elvira and Zatzick 2002). Expanding on Kluegel's (1978) concept of particularistic manipulation, in which employers base promotion decisions on subjective and often, vague, personal measures, a line of research also supports a "particularistic mobility thesis." Here, blacks must follow more narrow and restricted mobility paths than whites (Mueller, Parcel, and Tanaka 1989; Wilson 1997; Wilson, Sakura-Lemessy and West 1999; Smith 2001). Wilson, Sakura-Lemessy, and West (1999) have maintained that due to factors such as segregation in job networks and training and internship programs,

African Americans have less opportunity to prove themselves in informal ways. As a result, human capital variables such as educational attainment and work experience with the same employer matter more for blacks than whites in receiving promotions (see also Wilson 1997; Wilson, Sakura-Lemessy, and West 1999; Fernandez 1975, 1981).

Employer subjectivity may also affect layoff decisions; and a number of studies, including some of our prior chapters, have shown that blacks are significantly more likely than whites to be laid off, after controlling for on-the-job absenteeism, injuries, and/or disciplinary actions (Elvira and Zatzick 2002; Park and Sandefur 2003). Employer impetus to layoff workers may be exacerbated in times of economic downturns. McBrier and Wilson (2004) find that African American white-collar workers were disproportionately displaced into lower-level white-collar and, particularly, blue-collar jobs as corporations experienced downsizing in the 1990s. Importantly, while whites benefited from traditional protective factors such as higher SES, professional or technical employment, union membership, and firm tenure, blacks received no protection from downward mobility on these counts. Consequently, McBrier and Wilson (2004) have proposed a "minority vulnerability thesis"— a flip side to the particularistic mobility thesis—in which downward mobility is more general, less circumscribed, and less predicted by traditional protective factors for African Americans.

Thus, whether they are queued into positions for which they are overqualified, struggling to push through glass ceilings, or riding the escalator "down" the occupational ladder, there is clear evidence that race matters for black men. Although some have argued that black men may become "honorary whites" through their sharing of male common interests (Vallas 2003), there is a long history of exclusion of black men, which may be based on perceived threat (Lynn and Mau 2002). The analyses that follow provide both quantitative and qualitative insight into these various discrimination potentials, how they unfold, and what the consequences are for black men.

African American Men and Discrimination at Work

In the 2000 census, 11.5 percent of Ohio's population reported being black or African American, which is lower but quite comparable to the 12.4 percent rate for the United States. Notably, the employment statistics for black men in Ohio are also very comparable with those of the nation. In 1999, African American men made up 5.26 percent and 6.41 percent of private industry employees in Ohio, and the United States, respectively (EEOC 2004a). As

TABLE 8.1
Occupational Employment of Black Men in Private Industry, 1999

	United States		Ohio	
	Number Employed	Percentage in EEO Group	Number Employed	Percentage in EEO Group
Officials/Managers	153,320	5.55	5,904	5.29
Professionals	159,235	5.76	5.571	5.00
Technicians	122,848	4.44	4,212	3.78
Sales Workers	263,840	9.54	8,701	7.80
Office/Clerical	198,463	7.18	6,730	6.04
Craft Workers	271,378	9.82	9,935	8.91
Operatives	669,306	24.21	28,708	25.75
Laborers	439,005	15.88	20,118	18.04
Service Workers	486,980	17.62	21,628	19.40

Source: 1999 EEO-1 Aggregate Report for United States and Ohio (EEOC 2004a).

reported in table 8.1, the distribution of these men among occupations is quite similar in Ohio and the United States. Both nationally and in Ohio, most are employed as operatives (i.e. truck drivers, and equipment operators), general laborers, and service workers.

There are 3,164 serious cases of discrimination for African American men in our data. Of these, 134 were present in our random, content-coded sample. Additional data was thus available to us, including the open-ended claims made by the employee and employer as to what transpired as well as the employee's occupation.

Figure 8.1 reports the distribution of the injuries for all serious claims for African American men ($n = 3,164$). Notably, and consistent with results in prior chapters, hiring comprises the fewest claims. Of course, those who have not been hired for a position may not realize that they have been discriminated against. Conversely, it is likely that employees who are already familiar with the workplace would have greater knowledge of potential job openings, including which jobs are filled, and by whom.

Mobility, which consists of both promotion denials and demotions, represents approximately 8.2 percent of total claims, which is almost two times the number of claims as hiring. Firing makes up the overwhelming majority of claims, comprising 56 percent of all serious cases. Firing includes discharge, constructive discharge, layoffs, and involuntary retirement, as well as other employer acts which effectively encourage the employee to quit, such as suspensions or failure to recall. The overt nature of firing, as well as its emotional and financial ramifications creates, no doubt, a powerful sense of being wronged.

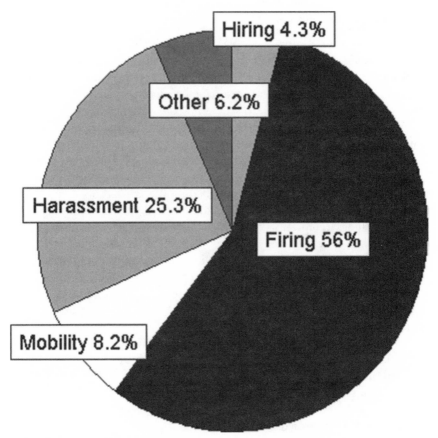

FIGURE 8.1
Distribution of Serious Claims and Injuries for African American Males

One of the most striking findings throughout the preceding chapters has been the prevalence of harassment claims. As we see in the figure, general racial harassment on the job is a principal form of discrimination for African American men. Comprising such injuries as disparate discipline, antagonism, and differential treatment, harassment makes up over 25 percent of the claims filed. Not only does the prevalence of harassment attest to the day-to-day experiences of discrimination and the emotional stress it can cause, it may also greatly impact occupational mobility by affecting victims' abilities to perform their jobs. Other differential treatment—which represents 6 percent of claims—involves perceived inequities in other key job measures such as benefits and seniority.

Occupational Differences and Discrimination

Ten cases of the 134 subsample cases represent incidents of hiring discrimination. The remainder, or 124, are serious cases of discrimination in mobility, firing, or harassment. We focus mainly on these issues. The distribution of the mean occupational prestige scores (total socioeconomic index) for these men is fairly normal with a mean score of 31.06, which is relatively low, and consistent with literature regarding the occupational status of most African American men.

Occupational prestige scores and EEO 1 job classifications were used to construct a three-point occupational scale. Category 1 represents laborers, entry-level service workers, and those in unskilled positions. Category 2 consists of occupations that require greater skill or training and demand better pay. This category includes technicians, craft workers, operators, and those in pink-collar or other skilled or semi-skilled positions. Category 3 represents managers and other professionals. These jobs generally require a college education or command greater authority, such as the ability to manage others and to hire or fire.

Figure 8.2 reports the percentages of major discriminatory injuries relative to total claims for each occupational category. As noted, firing represents the greatest percentage of claims across all occupations, and is highest for laborers and unskilled workers. Perhaps more interestingly, harassment is most obvious in skilled and semi-skilled positions where black men arguably compete in traditionally white male work settings. Discrimination in the mobility process is most apparent in the managerial and professional ranks.

Firing—Black Men Pushed Out

As was the case with black females, discussed in the previous chapter, discriminatory firing represents the greatest claim for black men across all three occupational categories and is most pronounced among laborers and unskilled workers. Certainly, the financial and emotional consequences of firing invoke strong feelings for action if one feels that he has been treated unjustly. Firing cases for unskilled workers often reveal workplace dynamics that are contentious and volatile. In such positions, men seem to have heightened anxiety about their work situations. A stock room clerk and a tire technician, for example, both filed charges against their work places because they were laid off and not rehired, while witnessing their employers hire white employees at approximately the same time.

Some of the men report unfair work conditions such as receiving less pay than white workers, or being forced to work in racially hostile environments, which included racial slurs by their supervisors. A telephone solicitation worker says he was always given the "cold calls" while white employees were

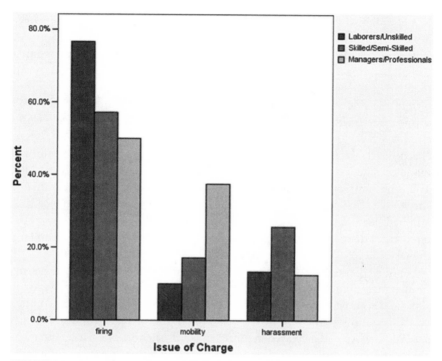

FIGURE 8.2
Discrimination Injury by Occupational Status, Black Male Content-Coded Subsample.

given "returning customers" to contact. Several of the men relate how they were dismissed for infractions, such as absences, that similarly situated white employees were not sanctioned for. One construction laborer was given permission to take the day off and was then fired for it. Ted Hunt, a waiter, was discharged from his position due to "low ratings from customers." The investigation, however, found that a white waiter with much lower customer ratings was retained.

Such seemingly arbitrary decisions attest to the relative powerlessness and vulnerability of men on the lower rungs of the occupational ladder, and may be indicative of the lack of coherent organization and procedure in the workplaces in which they are employed. Indeed, many jobs of this nature are characterized by high turnover rates and frustrating working conditions. Bill Howard, an order-puller in a low-wage services business, was employed for only five days before being discharged from a warehouse job. He states, "I have two years of similar previous warehouse experience. In one week's time I was not afforded the opportunity to learn all of . . . [the] procedures."

A number of the men admit to fights or other altercations in the workplace, yet evidence indicates culpable whites were not similarly disciplined. Brad Hill, for instance, a crater for an industrial company, was involved in a verbal dispute with a white maintenance worker after entering a bathroom that had just been cleaned. According to Hill, the maintenance worker poked him in the side and told him to get out of the restroom, and that he wasn't supposed to be in there. The worker, however, did not similarly warn a white employee who was also in the restroom. Hill told the white coworker to "keep his damn hands off of him." The worker filed a report and Hill was made to take a drug test and was suspended while waiting for the results. The other employees involved were not made to take the test and were not suspended. The test results were negative, and there was no evidence that Hill had been under the influence of drugs or alcohol. The employer countered Hill's discrimination claim, saying he was suspended and made to take the test due to his "aberrant behavior."

For skilled and semi-skilled workers the workplace is also contentious, although men in such positions are in more stable occupations requiring greater skills and technical knowledge. Notably, a fair amount of employers' counter claims contain statements that the person fired had "a bad attitude," was "insubordinate," or had displayed inappropriate, threatening or even criminal behavior in the workplace. Such responses were given in 30 percent of the cases for unskilled men and 40 percent of the cases of skilled/semi-skilled men (relative to 25 percent of the cases for managers/professionals).

Rule breaking and its relation with disparate policing and sanctioning appear to be used as mechanisms to fire black skilled and semiskilled men. Some were terminated due to mistakes or their involvement in work-related accidents, but evidence substantiates that similarly situated whites were not sanctioned. Ed Taylor, a hi-lo driver in a manufacturing business was terminated after damaging some equipment while driving. He suggests that whites had caused much worse damage including breaking a water main, yet they were merely given verbal warnings or allowed to change jobs.

Ben Goodwell, an operator in a manufacturing business, was fired by his supervisor for "improper conduct" when he failed to properly "report off" when leaving his equipment, and for taking a break in a restricted area. Civil rights investigators determined that employees routinely took breaks in this area and that the supervisor was using this excuse to fire Mr. Goodwell. Indeed, the case file substantiated that there was a racially hostile environment, that only 4 of the 105 employees were black, and that Goodwell's supervisor had used racial slurs toward him. When Goodwell had taken off a day for personal reasons, his supervisor had joked to other employees that he was "probably selling watermelons."

There is also evidence that lack of training may have contributed to some of the firings. Jake, a truck driver employed by a company that had no written personnel policy and no progressive discipline policy, was one of only two black employees, and was fired after only two weeks on the job. Jake maintains he was never even shown how to operate the truck:

> Nobody showed me how to drive the truck, nobody never got into the truck with me and said, here, we're going to see whatever . . . this is that. They didn't even let me see how the gears work, I went out and checked myself.

Although he was discharged for poor work performance and taking too long on runs, Jake tells a different story—he was harassed, and "forced to drive a truck that was unsafe." Coworker witnesses testified that they had overheard members of management make "derogatory racial remarks" about Jake, and that they, too, had previously had trouble with the truck. Jake believes that management was upset with him for speaking up about the safety problems.

African American men who are in management positions may experience discrimination through exclusion from networks, withholding of information, and the undermining of their authority. Brad, the general manager of a retail franchise, was discharged even though he had never been warned and had never been written up for disciplinary reasons. The employer alleges that there were customer complaints against him, yet he was never told about them. During his employment, he was left out of networks, and was not allowed the same authority and decision making ability as white general managers:

> On several occasions, I was made to travel to Corporate Headquarters . . . just to find out the meeting was canceled. *Everyone* [charging party's emphasis] else was notified. Upon my hiring I was told I could hire and fire. I was told I would have my own [new] store. I was not allowed to hire *anyone* [charging party's emphasis] and was told by . . . [the District Manager] that I didn't need to hire anyone. I began with a staff of three, when one quit, I couldn't hire anyone. Immediately after I received the old store they changed the hours of operating. About two week[s] later, Stan [an employee] quit. This forced me to work a 7-day work schedule. . . . I was finally allowed to take applications, I was not allowed to hire however. I had to call Corporate Headquarters to set up an appointment for them to come down and interview. . . . No other manager was told that they could not hire! The general manager before me was afforded a staff of three. Not I!

Holding black men to higher performance standards than their white counterparts and punishing them more harshly for policy violations is also evidenced in several of the cases. Phil Simpson, a store manager notes that he was fired by a racist district manager for low sales performance, but that a white store manager who had worse performance was retained. Phil also claimed that the district manager falsely accused him of stealing cash and store merchandise. A chief of police was fired for failure to follow company policy to purchase a home within the city limits of his community, but there is evidence that other city administrators had lived outside the city limits, and not been sanctioned. A boy's head basketball coach for a state school filed a claim because his contract was not renewed, despite favorable recommendations by the (white) school principal and (white) superintendent. He states, "I was not advised of any shortcomings on my part nor was I given an opportunity to correct any problems of which I was not aware." Although the school board claimed that it had received complaints regarding the coach's "bench demeanor and treatment of players," several witnesses, including one school board member praised his performance. The school board member claimed that other board members offered only "vague accounts" of who had complained. According to a local sports editor although the coach "demands a lot from his players and asks that they work hard. . . . He does not yell at players or officials any more than most coaches, and other coaches are not criticized." Cases such as these speak to the strong role of subjective, particularistic criteria in decision making.

Discriminatory Mobility Processes

Some of the claims relate to mobility issues wherein either the charging party was not promoted, or was demoted from a current position. Interestingly, mobility charges make up a greater percentage of claims for those in upper positions (managers and professionals) than they do in the lower and middle occupational categories. It seems likely that mobility may become more of an issue as those who are upwardly mobile run into "glass ceilings," or ride escalators down the occupational ladder (McBrier and Wilson 2004). As one might expect, mobility is not a large issue for the laborers and unskilled workers.

It is interesting in cases of mobility discrimination that the employee in question is, more often than not, not aware of any problems with his performance and knows of no reason why he should not be promoted. Civil rights investigators examine internal documents such as personnel evaluations in such cases. Because many of these men are equally qualified, at least according to evaluations, it is likely that particularistic or subjective criteria are playing a role. Indeed, and as revealed in prior chapters, many of these cases suggest that the employers have stereotypical views of hard or soft work skills.

As a case in point, a probation officer was denied promotion to supervisor because he "didn't interview well," while a white applicant without the necessary job qualifications was given the position. A lieutenant for a county park district was denied promotion due to his "poor writing skills," yet suggests that his regular evaluations never reflected this critique. A state rehabilitation specialist was denied a promotion given to a less-qualified white applicant because he ranked fifth in the oral interview and could not "provide proof" of his technical degree. This is particularly noteworthy because the employee had left the technical college twenty-seven years before, and the employer had accepted the credential for the past twenty-three years.

There is other evidence that "particularistic criteria" may play a role in prioritizing informal work relations over objective criteria in promotion decisions. Marvin Smith, a police officer, was denied reassignment to zone car patrol because he "could not find two other officers who would work with him." A further analysis of this case, however, reveals a story very different from a typical worker who had problems relating to others. The officer had been continually harassed by coworkers for an earlier charge of indecent exposure, for which he had been acquitted. Despite his acquittal, some of the officers posted lurid cartoons of him in sexual situations. Smith subsequently was treated for significant anxiety and depression. Although Smith filed his case for discrimination in promotion rather than racial harassment, this case speaks to how harassment may interfere with promotion potential, and may even affect the employee's ability to perform his job.

African American men who are managers and professionals also suggest that less qualified employees or those with less experience received the promotions. Even in state positions, as chapter 5 revealed, this pattern is prevalent. In management cases, issues of authority may also come into play. Shawn Sullivan, for instance, applied for a position as district field service manager for his current employer—a mail shipping company—and was temporarily filling the position until someone was hired. He was not even allowed to interview for the position and notes that he had "more seniority, experience and qualifications" than the white employee who was transferred from another facility and hired. A letter from the former district field service manger substantiated that Sullivan had a superior rating, but he was not given the job due to his lack of management "authority." Letters from fellow employees disputed this claim, stating that Sullivan had an effective management style, and that he reprimanded employees when necessary, but did so with compassion. Wrote one employee:

> He was wonderful to work for. I could talk to him as an equal. He treated you as a human being and didn't just tell you what to do. He would do as much work as you. Shawn was most definitely qualified for the promotion to manager. He had the leadership skills. People would work for him because he could ask you to do something without making it a command.

Notably, Sullivan worked under the new district field manger, but was terminated within a few months because the new manger believed he "undermined his authority." A white employee wrote that the new manager was "out to get" Sullivan and was "nitpicking on a lot of little things."

Such "nitpicking" provides support for the possibility that black men are often judged based on subjective criteria and are held to higher standards. Discriminatory demotion cases highlight this. Craig Benham, a sales manager in the retail industry, was demoted and later discharged for "poor performance" by Jones, his white regional manger. He had not, however, been previously notified of any performance problems. Benham notes that:

> I was the only Black Store Manager and Sales Manager employed by the Respondent. . . . I am aware that Jones set my sales goals much higher than the previous Sales Manager's at the same location. Respondent immediately replaced me with Tim Smith, White, who had much lower performance reviews than I. I became aware from co-workers that Jones was trying to fire me prior to my discharge.

If black men are held to higher standards than white men, conversely, a black employee who breaks company rules or commits minor infractions may be sanctioned much more severely than a similarly situated white employee. These dynamics may become particularly acute as black men reach management ranks. Consider, for instance, Joe Thompson, a superintendent of manufacturing who was demoted due to the improper use of a company vehicle. Not only did the company sanction him for this "offense," but there is also evidence that they harassed Mr. Thompson and his family by sending a surveillance crew to stake out his house. Crew members banged on the windows and questioned his children as they arrived home from school. Thompson, who suffered a nervous breakdown after his demotion, explained:

> Throughout my tenure with the company, my work record has been excellent. . . . During the course of my employment, it became more and more apparent to me that Respondent just did not want me to continue in its employ. Guthrie, Vice President of Operations, advised me of this fact when I inquired of him exactly why I was being demoted. In my twenty years with the Respondent, I know of no one else to be demoted for a disciplinary infraction. . . . I followed the same procedure for signing out a vehicle, as did all other salaried employees, yet I was the only employee disciplined. To this day, Caucasians sign out vehicles in an identical manner, without being disciplined. I believe that the vehicle issue was merely a ruse to humiliate me into resigning my position, because Respondent was uncomfortable with a Black in its highest salaried position.

McBrier and Wilson's (2004) minority vulnerability thesis should be considered here in relation to downward occupational mobility. They contend that minorities are especially vulnerable to lay off—or presumably demotion decisions—because they are not as protected as whites. It is quite likely that rule violations and minor infractions may indeed serve as the mechanisms that facilitate the demotion or firing of otherwise qualified African American men from management positions.

Harassment of Black Men at Work

As seen from these cases, harassment is woven throughout the claims, and is a mechanism for decreasing job mobility, even when the charging party did not specifically file on harassment issues. Harassment, no doubt, entails large psychological disadvantages which may impede job performance, even beyond our ability to measure.

General laborers and unskilled workers who filed harassment charges report differential treatment such as being passed over for overtime, or being subjected to racial slurs. It may be that these workers, although especially vulnerable to harassment due to their relative lack of power, may be more likely to file on other charges such as firing due to their reduced sense of agency or expectations of fairness. The case of Michael, a custodian in a state agency, however, shows how severe such harassment can be and how it may interfere with carrying out one's job duties. After being harassed and experiencing racial slurs by coworkers and a supervisor, he believes his written reprimand for failure to dispose of trash was racially motivated:

> In order to get to the dumpster, I am required to go the long way around, even though there is a shorter route through the gate. . . . [The Caucasian Coordinator and Caucasian Supervisor] . . . have refused to unlock the gate in order to allow me to dump trash. They have, however, unlocked the gate for Caucasian employees when they required access to complete their job duties. Additionally, Caucasians have missed trash barrels and have not been reprimanded.

Harassment represents a greater percentage of charges for semi-skilled and skilled employees than for unskilled workers or managers and professionals. The majority of these men are in traditionally white-male-dominated jobs, and many of them are in trades where there has been a history of exclusion, competition, and racial antagonism. Some were given unfair negative evaluations and others were asked to perform jobs that others weren't or were given unfair workloads. John Mullins, a diesinker in the metal industry, filed harassment charges because unfair, negative job evaluations kept him from the apprentice program. Bill Smith, a mechanic, suffered racist comments from coworkers and managers, was denied training, left out of meetings, and had his lunch time changed so he would have to eat alone. Matthew Montgomery, a grounds maintenance foreman for a landscaping company, believes he was laid off due to his race while white employees with less seniority were allowed to work during the slow season. He also suggests that he was "forced to do more work than whites" and was denied raises that white coworkers with his same seniority received. Other skilled and semi-skilled black men were paid less than whites, were not granted the same opportunities for overtime, or were not properly trained.

Approximately one-quarter of these men report the use of racial slurs by coworkers, and there are cases of extreme public harassment and humiliation, as reported in the preceding chapters. Take, for instance, the case of Tim Hughes, a computer operator for a state government facility. He was given a verbal reprimand for failure of good behavior because he was on a different floor than where he usually worked and was not wearing a badge. Security was notified that "a black man was causing a problem." Another case involved a foreman who was placed on probation because his supervisor did not approve of his relationship with a white female.

Although it appears that harassment charges are less often filed by those in higher-status occupational positions, it may be the case that harassment simply manifests distinctly and less overtly given the nature of their positions. Chet Watkins, a senior product training specialist in the communications industry, was denied overseas assignment and replaced by a white employee. Dan Jones, a tax examiner for a government agency, claims that he was given low evaluations and denied training. He also claims that blacks were consistently passed over for promotion and that errors were placed in his personnel file.

The data examined reveal that harassment is intricately woven into the discrimination experience, regardless if the employee made charges on that specific basis. This speaks to some degree to costs associated with discrimination that are not so neatly captured by the modeling of objective job outcomes. As in the case of the security guard quoted at the beginning of this chapter who filed on a promotion issue, analyses of case material revealed he was being intimidated routinely. He was eventually transferred to another district, where it was necessary to catch "two to three buses" to get to work.

Conclusions

African American men have historically experienced serious inequalities in employment opportunities and job mobility, as well as exclusion from primary labor market positions, but broad debates about the nature and causes of such inequalities remain. Prior research has included strong inferential support that stereotyping by employers and employer bias may be intensifying these disparities. Largely due to data limitations, however, we have known little about how such processes may play out in formal work settings, and even less about how they may vary by occupation.

Our analyses confirm that some employers and managers engage in processes of racial stereotyping when relating to African American men. Firing is the largest issue across all occupations, but notable also is how harassment is interwoven with claims of all natures. Harassment is a strong mechanism impeding job mobility, even for those who do not specifically file a harassment charge. Many of the men were also denied promotions or were fired when they had no reason to believe their performance was substandard. This highlights the strong role of particularistic criteria in differential treatment. In general, African American men appear to be held to higher performance standards than their white coworkers, and are more harshly sanctioned for rule breaking or even for work place accidents.

The contentious and volatile nature of the work environments of the men in unskilled positions may have some bearing on the form of discrimination they experience. Firing, in particular, was an issue for them. As Shih (2002) maintains, to the extent that supervisors expect compliance, black men may be disadvantaged by employers who have stereotypical attitudes of them as "insubordinate" or "hard to control." In such occupational positions, it is also likely that these men are subject to work environments that are unorganized or characterized by lack of appropriate supervision or arbitrary decision making. Here employees are more likely to engage in various resistance strategies, including absenteeism and in-fighting (Hodson 2001; Roscigno and Hodson 2004) and these processes, as they interact with employer bias, may mean that black men are more harshly disciplined for infractions that are also committed by white workers.

Skilled and semi-skilled men are also often in contentious work environments. Many of these men are in traditional white-male-dominated jobs, which are marked by a history of exclusion and competition. Harassment is a real issue for these men, including racial slurs by coworkers. In issues of mobility, seemingly well-qualified men are passed over for promotion, in part due to employer bias and perceptions of both hard and soft skills.

Issues of mobility are of greater concern for those in higher status positions. Here, African American men are sometimes held to higher standards, are denied authority, are "nitpicked," and are periodically more harshly sanctioned. Indeed, for both skilled/semi-skilled men and managers and professionals, rule breaking seems to be a mechanism that fuels what McBrier and Wilson (2004) call "minority vulnerability." While black men have a tough climb up the occupational ladder, they appear also to occupy a "slippery rung," and may be only one violation, one mistake, or one accident away from demotion or firing.

Overall, this chapter provides valuable insights as to how discriminatory practices block the mobility of African American men. Although such processes seem to manifest in unique ways, depending on occupational status or class position, the bottom line is that these men have to work much harder to prove themselves in the workplace. As one victim of discrimination so simply, yet eloquently relates, "I am required to go the long way around, even though there is a shorter route through the gate."

9

Race and the Process of
Housing Discrimination

with Diana Karafin and Griff Tester

The property manager charged me for routine repairs that were performed
in my unit (parts and labor) while not charging the White tenants for similar repairs. The complex is predominately white, with only a few African-
Americans. I was also written up and threatened with eviction for loud
noises in my unit at times when I was at work and no one was in my unit.

—David McGinnis, African American male.

TO THE EXTENT THAT DISCRIMINATION continues to play out in contemporary workplaces, there is every reason to believe that it occurs in other
societal arenas, including but not limited to housing. As noted at the outset,
stratification hierarchies and related social closure processes within a society tend to permeate most, if not all, institutional, organizational, and cultural spheres of social life. Housing, the focus of this and the following two
chapters, is no exception. In fact, racial segregation remains a persistent social phenomenon and problem in the United States (Charles 2003; Massey
and Denton 1993), despite the fact that a majority of white Americans en-
dorse the principle of racial residential equality (Farley et al. 1994; Schuman
et al. 1997) and that there has been a narrowing of the black–white income
gap in recent years (Logan et. al. 2004; Farley and Frey 1994). Several explanations have been posited, ranging from persistent economic disparities to
race-specific housing preferences, yet the most convincing analytical evidence points to the prevalence of discrimination in housing markets (Ross
and Turner 2005; Massey and Lundy 2001; Yinger 1995).

As with employment, a comprehensive understanding of residential inequality will incorporate potentially influential dimensions of action and the ways in which it reinforces and/or conditions structure (see Giddens 1984; Lawler, Ridgeway, and Markovsky 1993). This entails, for our purposes, consideration of prior research but also serious attention and theoretical development pertaining to the very social processes that create and reinforce housing inequalities. We do so in this chapter by focusing briefly on current gaps in the research literature, and then turning attention to important dimensions and processes of housing discrimination. Our analyses, which draw on unique quantitative and qualitative data from approximately 750 verified housing discrimination suits themselves, provide valuable insight into the various discriminatory forms that exist as well as the social-interactional processes and actors that are implicated.

Racial Residential Inequality and Discrimination

The 2000 U.S. Census reveals that blacks, compared to Hispanics and Asians, continue to experience significantly higher levels of residential segregation. How does one make sense of high and persistent segregation levels, even forty years after passage of the Fair Housing Act? As noted in the introduction, the most obvious possibilities revolve around economic differentials or racial residential preferences, but these explanations have only received limited support. Housing audits, instead, point to the continuing importance of discrimination.

Housing audit (or racial testing) studies have been used for some time by fair-housing groups as a systematic means of uncovering actual discrimination. Since the large-scale study of discrimination by HUD in 1977, numerous other housing market audit studies have also been conducted in individual cities.[1] They reveal that most blacks and Hispanics encounter discrimination revolving around housing availability and access to the housing sales and rental markets (Ondrich, Stricker, and Yinger 1999; Yinger 1991, 1995). Clearly, the audit methodology is a useful method for assessing levels of discrimination faced by potential residents. It also addresses some of the very actions and human culpability that scholars such as Gotham (2002b) suggest we should be focusing on. As noted in the introduction, however, there are obvious methodological disadvantages, not the least of which are the nearly singular focus on exclusion, as opposed to discrimination once housed, and limited attention to federal protections based on gender and family status—issues that, given complexities of family poverty, single parenthood, and preexistent racial stereotypes, may be especially pronounced for African

American women.[2] We address these specific gaps in the remainder of this chapter, and in chapters 10 and 11.

Notable in the social science literature on housing is the nearly singular focus on exclusion. Although exclusion from social institutions (including housing) is undoubtedly central to stratification maintenance within society at large, equally important are the ways in which inequality is activated and carried out on a day-to-day, interactional level for the purpose of status hierarchy maintenance. As vividly depicted in the play *A Raisin in the Sun*, such was the case in the 1940s through 1960s, where minority families, viewed as a threat to the established status and history of a neighborhood, were harassed and threatened by neighbors—neighbors without exclusionary institutional power, but who nevertheless attempted to reify the social status hierarchy in a manner that shaped the day-to-day experiences, comfort level, and overall sense of safety for minority families. And, as we have seen in the case of employment discrimination, exclusion plays a relatively minor role in minority perceptions and charges of discrimination. Rather, what happens *within* a given social or institutional environment seems to generate a greater sense of injustice and indignity.

Parallel arguments having to do with the day-to-day potentials for nonexclusionary discrimination, with the intent or outcome of hierarchy maintenance, can be found across a wide body of stratification scholarship, including that pertaining to "doing gender" (West and Zimmerman 1987; see also Martin 2004), social-class activation of cultural capital (Bourdieu and Passeron 1977; Roscigno and Ainsworth-Darnell 1999), and interactional dimensions and experiences of race and ethnic inequality in public spaces (Feagin 1991). Indeed, many of our prior chapters revealed such hierarchy maintenance with regard to race and gender harassment in employment by supervisors and coworkers. While perhaps not as profound as overall exclusion in terms of objective outcomes, nonexclusionary and often informal dimensions of discrimination, particularly if ongoing and intrusive, can have devastating consequences for mental and even physiological health (Krieger et al. 1993; Williams 1995; Williams and Collins 1995).

Our extended focus on nonexclusionary forms of discrimination, although quite unique in terms of prior housing research specifically, parallels our prior foci on employment and the ways in which social groups may be either excluded outright or treated differently within a given institutional context. Although possibly mutually reinforcing, we treat exclusionary and nonexclusionary forms of discrimination as they apply to housing as analytically distinct for several reasons. First, few if any analyses of housing discrimination have considered nonexclusionary, including more informal, forms of housing discrimination that occur once minorities are actually housed. This deserves attention in its own right. Attention to exclusion, in contrast, speaks more directly to prior literature and insights on segregation.

The actors implicated in exclusionary and nonexclusionary forms of housing discrimination may also differ, particularly in terms of institutional power, and the consequences for victims may be unique. For instance, mortgage brokers, with significant institutional power, can shape exclusion in profound ways for minority groups in general, whether or not minority group members are aware of such effects. Residential neighbors, in contrast, can harass and intimidate despite a lack of institutionalized exclusionary power. Although such action may not be systematic or aggregate in its consequences, it certainly may have important implications for the day-to-day experiences and even sociopsychological well-being of minorities on the receiving end. Residential landlords are likely an interesting case in point, with some institutional power to exclude, yet proximate enough to also engage in nonexclusionary forms of discrimination (i.e., differential treatment or harassment once the victim of discrimination is actually housed).

Patterns of Racial Discrimination in Housing

Between 1988 and 2003, 2,176 cases of racial discrimination in housing were filed that provide adequate data for analytic purposes. Of these, and using the criteria outlined in the introduction, 757, or approximately 35 percent, were deemed serious. Figure 9.1 presents breakdowns by race/ethnicity and gender. This distributional pattern remains relatively consistent between unverified and serious cases, with African American men and women making up the preponderance of all cases. As such, and since housing discrimination against African American men, women, and families accounts for between 80 and 90 percent of all serious discrimination claims over the fifteen-year period, our qualitative focus centers largely on the processes, actors, and consequences within these cases.

Qualitative material for these cases was content coded specifically on the type of discrimination and injury that occurred, and who the perpetrator was. Many forms of housing discrimination are noted in the case material. These include exclusion and efforts toward exclusion, unfair practices in lending and insuring, and various forms of harassment, differential treatment, and intimidation. Notably, approximately 50 percent of these reflect some dimension of discriminatory exclusion, while the remaining half capture nonexclusionary forms of discrimination. Key actors include banks, insurance companies, realtors, landlords, building complex owners, and neighbors.

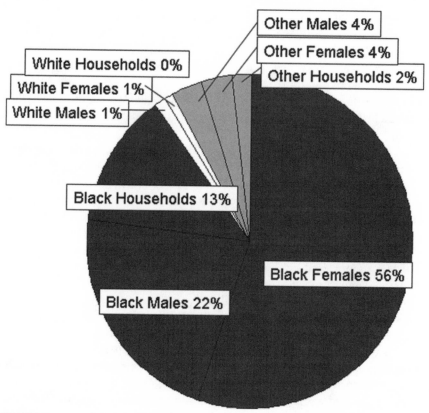

FIGURE 9.1
Distribution of Serious Race Housing Cases

Exclusionary Dimensions of Housing Discrimination

Much like the distribution of all serious cases, African Americans are impacted most by exclusion. African American women, men, and households represent 90 percent of these cases. This is particularly noteworthy, given that African Americans constitute only about 18 percent of the entire population of the state.

Consistent with Massey and Lundy's (2001) finding, derived from a housing search telephone audit, black women appear to be especially vulnerable to exclusion, representing 56 percent of the total number of these cases. Black males constitute 22 percent and other minorities represent 8 percent, while whites represent just 2 percent of verified cases of exclusionary discrimination.

One benefit of having access to case-specific data is that it allows for deeper inspection of the processes involved. In this regard, the majority of serious cases of exclusion (82 percent) entail various forms of outright exclusion, such as a direct refusal to rent or even negotiate a rental with a prospective tenant, refusal to sell or negotiate the sale of a property, or the false denial or representation of apartments or homes actually available for rent or sale. Outright exclusion is sometimes characterized by the use of overt racial slurs and verbal refusal to rent out an apartment, yet more often, consists of subtle actions, such as lying about apartment availability, or relaying differential standards for rental qualification that immediately disqualify certain individuals.

An additional 17 percent of exclusionary cases reflect discriminatory terms and conditions pertaining to the rental or sale of a home, in which the final outcome is a denial of access. Such discrimination, which prevents minority home seekers from obtaining housing, includes unfair financing or loan qualifications or terms, steering or restricting the choices of home seekers, differential terms and conditions to qualify to rent a home, and refusing to provide insurance which prevents the acquisition of a home. Perpetrators of these forms of discrimination typically utilize legitimate appearing processes to exclude minorities from gaining access to housing. Applicants may go through several steps of the rental or sales process and spend significant time and resources with the hopes of gaining housing. Yet, they are participating in a false process, tainted with discriminatory practices and conditions, that ultimately result in exclusion.

We speculated earlier that the principal perpetrators of exclusion would largely be institutional actors—actors with the institutional power to impede or who can employ discretionary powers to exclude. Notably, landlords and owners are most likely to exclude individuals from housing, comprising 84 percent of the exclusionary cases. Other actors or institutions responsible for exclusionary forms of discrimination include real estate agents or institutions (6 percent), banking/lending agents or institutions (4 percent), and insurance agents or institutions (4 percent). Whereas owners and landlords tend to exclude outright, banks are largely implicated in exclusion by refusal to provide loans. For their part, insurance agents can reject applications for homeowners insurance, while realtors in our data either steer or refuse service to potential African American clients. City and metropolitan housing authorities are the perpetrator in only 2 percent of cases. Neighbors, who have no real institutional power to exclude, are predictably absent in terms of exclusionary discrimination.

That landlords and complex owners are, by and far, most often implicated in exclusionary discrimination should not come as a surprise.[3] These agents are often the most proximate to potential tenants. Indeed, they may act in a manner that signals to prospective tenants that there may be biases, and that discrimination is occurring.[4]

While the numbers presented above provide insight into the barriers African Americans and other minorities disproportionately face when attempting to gain access to various housing markets—and a picture that is quite consistent with findings from audit studies—much about the actual process of exclusionary discrimination remains unexplored. How and why are African American women so vulnerable to exclusion? What are landlords/ owners and other actors doing specifically to prevent African Americans from gaining access to housing. And, finally, what are the consequences of these actions for African Americans in their quest to obtain housing?

Qualitative analyses highlight that the over-representation of African American women among victims of exclusionary discrimination is, to a considerable extent, a function of the intersections of family status, race, and sex. Take, for instance, the case of Susan, an African American female with children. She entered the office of a small apartment complex to inquire about an available apartment, and was told that she had too many kids and to "get your black ass out." Her deposition with the attorney general, and what is revealed, suggests that the problem may be quite widespread rather than case-specific.

Q: Tell me about your efforts to look for another place to live?

A: Every time I tried to find a place, they would tell me I had too many children.

Q: Okay.

A: And that being a single mother and having all those children I was not accepted anywhere.

Q: What type of place were you looking to move to?

A: A three bedroom home or apartment or whatever, in a decent area for what income I could afford to pay.

Q: Okay, what was your reaction after hearing that news?

A: I got off the phone and I cried to my mom because I couldn't find a home for my children. I was afraid I was going to end up homeless with four children, all because of my husband beating me up. I'm—nobody would take me because I didn't have a husband.

In this case, Susan repeatedly was denied the opportunity to rent an apartment when prospective landlords learned that she had children. She had reasonable hope that she would find a place "in a decent area for what income I could afford to pay," yet the investigation revealed that she was still illegally denied access as a result of her status as an African American mother with "too many children." This was all the more troublesome, given her efforts to escape an abusive situation. The tremendous stress and psychological turmoil she experienced as a result of this process is evident in her stated fear of becoming homeless.

Discriminatory exclusion on the basis of family status—the presence of children under eighteen years of age—is related to stereotypes about single women, especially single African American mothers, and may be impacting these larger patterns. Indeed, a significant amount of case materials reveal a similar tendency. For example, in one case, a sales agent asked an African American woman with children if she "was going to operate a day care center from her home," despite the fact that the woman had never operated a day care center before and said nothing to infer she would if the apartment was rented to her. In other cases, the roots of exclusion and its relation to family status, are explicit.

Anna Miller, a black female with children, was told by the landlord that he would not rent to her because "there were too many in my family." A witness in this particular case, who is also a black female with one child, testified that when she asked the landlord if she could have pets he said no. When she asked why, the landlord told her that she had no business taking care of pets when she had her hands full taking care of her child. The case investigator interviewed other residents and found that white tenants with children were permitted to have pets. Margaret Sims, a white female tenant, told the investigator that it was her fault that the landlord did not rent to Anna Miller because she (Sims) had asked him "not to rent the downstairs unit to anymore niggers" because the black family that lived there previously "were terrible." The landlord told Margaret Sims that he "would do his best to find her a good neighbor." Here, the landlord is certainly the culpable party, although a white neighbor is also partially to blame.

Exclusion of African Americans occurs not only in rental markets, but also in sales markets, as is evidenced by 14 percent of the exclusionary cases. Here, the perpetrator is an agent within a real estate, insurance, or banking/lending institution. Although discrimination in these arenas tends to be characterized by subtle and difficult to detect processes, such as application of differential criteria to qualify for loans or for a low interest rate, more blatant actions are also evident. Take, for instance, the case of Patricia, an African American female attempting to purchase a home. When initially meeting with her realtor to discuss qualifying for an apartment, the realtor "asked me what made me think I could afford a home costing $190,000." When Patricia complained to the company, she was assigned a new agent, who asked her similar questions. Patricia then directly complained to the new agent that such behavior was inappropriate, yet was told "It's you people who get on my nerves." The investigation revealed that white housing seekers were not subject to such rude, blatant questions in their intake meetings. Instead of moving forward with her housing search by viewing homes in her price range, Patricia's housing search was delayed and she was forced to find a new company.

In a somewhat similar case, a real estate agent told the sellers that they were wasting their time selling to Tawana Johnson, an African American female, because, according to the agent, she did not "have her priorities straight." This same realtor told Tawana Johnson that she was "tired of you all, young black girls, not having their credit together." Notably, Tawana Johnson was pre-approved for a loan prior to this interaction with the real estate agent, and prior to the agent's conversation with the sellers.

African American couples are clearly vulnerable to exclusionary treatment as well. Michael and Patricia, for instance, were continually asked to verify their income and the source of their income because the lending agent stated that he had to "make sure that their money was not made illegally or from drugs." Like the prior cases discussed, the lending agent here delayed the application process by subjecting the couple to more stringent screening standards than similarly situated white loan applicants, due to stereotypes about their race. The dearth of qualitative case materials, including but not limited to the examples reported here, demonstrate delays in the loan application process—delays resulting in the loss of loan closing "specials" and lower interest rates. Case material also demonstrates that some lenders target African American borrowers with "teaser rates which allow people on fixed incomes to borrow more money than they can afford to pay back." Such practices, as revealed in chapter 10, may be especially pronounced in segregated and poor minority neighborhoods.

A somewhat unexpected and emergent dimension of housing exclusion is the denial of housing to interracial couples. Indeed, immersion into the case material wherein the charging party is either white or African American revealed that the discrimination often centers around disapproval of interracial coupling. Baxter, an African American male, for instance, notes that:

> I was approved to rent on Feb. 22, 1996 a two bedroom apartment. However, when management found out that Teresa Landon, Caucasian female, was moving in with me we were both denied occupancy. We were denied occupancy due to being perceived as an interracial couple.

What is particularly interesting here is that the African American charging party (Baxter) was not excluded until after management identified him as part of an interracial couple. Also notable is the subtle and legitimate-appearing means by which the discrimination was carried out—that is, claiming that Teresa did not qualify to rent the apartment. The investigation, however, revealed that this standard of qualification was not utilized for other white tenants in the complex. Baxter and Teresa were both placed in the uncomfortable position of having to find a new place to live on short notice despite their prior understanding of having secured a place to live. Other cases of exclusionary discrimination, filed by white males and females, similarly revealed that the foundations of the discriminatory treatment revolved around interracial coupling.

Exclusionary discrimination remains an important part of contemporary stratification, with implications for housing segregation patterns highlighted in much prior work. As our data reveal, African Americans, and especially African American women, are highly represented among the victims of such exclusion. Landlords seem to be on the front line of the exclusionary process, although we suspect that their representation among discriminators is heavily weighted by their proximity to potential clients and corresponding auxiliary information garnered by those who are being discriminated against.

African American women seem to be especially vulnerable in the arena of housing searches due to their sex and especially their family status—statuses that may be providing institutional actors, such as landlords, with shorthand information that can be enacted in discriminatory ways. We revisit the issue of sex and family status in relation to race in detail in chapter 11. The qualitative material on exclusion also reveals that the costs of exclusion do not revolve solely around housing access. Rather, exclusion has multiple costs. Most obviously, individuals are denied access to housing options of choice and must spend significantly more time in housing searches. Such exclusion also often reflects an affront to the victim's dignity, not to mention an assault on their sense of security and opportunity.

Nonexclusionary Discrimination in Housing

Racial discrimination in housing functions not only to discourage attempts to obtain housing. It also often generates distress for the victim. This is perhaps even more evident in instances of nonexclusionary housing discrimination, wherein an individual, couple, or family who are already housed experience ongoing differential treatment, harassment, and intimidation. Such discrimination is especially problematic given that the residential victim is more often than not legally bound to a rental agreement or lease, and likely in interactional contact with the perpetrator on an ongoing basis, especially in the case of neighbors and landlords.

Figure 9.2 reports victim breakdowns relating to cases of nonexclusionary racial discrimination in housing. As with exclusionary forms, blacks (females, males, and households) are most highly represented. Black women are, again,

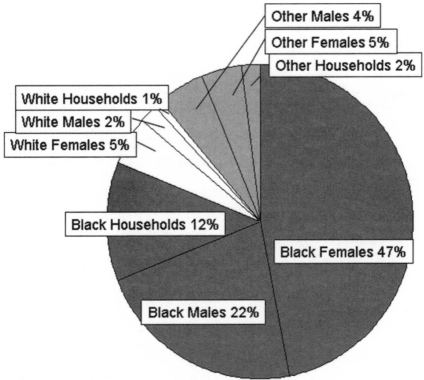

FIGURE 9.2
Serious Cases of Non-Exclusionary Racial Discrimination in Housing

the most likely to be victimized. Other minorities (11 percent) and whites (8 percent) make up a slightly higher percentage of the total number of cases (19 percent compared to only 10 percent for exclusionary forms). Again, in-depth examination of qualitative material reveals that much of these discriminatory actions are triggered by disapproval of interracial coupling.

Nonexclusionary discrimination entails unfair or differential terms and conditions pertaining to rentals or sales. Indeed, 84 percent involve the application of discriminatory terms and conditions within the current residential setting, most often on a rental property. Examples include differential enforcement of pet policies within a rental complex, unfairly raising the rent of a select group of tenants, or only allowing certain tenants privileges such as using the pool after hours or having parties on the lawn. Others involve failure to provide equal access to services and facilities. This manifestation of discrimination is typically characterized by purposeful neglect of service needs, such as refusing to fix a leaking bathtub or broken water heater.

Terms and conditions cases are largely characterized by discriminatory financing, loans, and appraisals, but also failure to provide homeowners insurance. In these cases, perpetrators often utilize subtle, financially lucrative, tactics that take advantage of minority home owners in predominantly African American neighborhoods. Finally, it is important to note that approximately 16 percent of nonexclusionary cases in our data reflect the direct use of harassment, intimidation, and coercion toward blacks and other minorities. Examples include racial slurs toward black residents in an apartment complex, or personal racial threats of violence, rape, or even death. Also illegal, such antagonism creates a racially tainted environment that victims are forced to navigate, sometimes on a daily basis.

Who is doing such discriminating? As with exclusionary forms of discrimination, landlords and owners are the largest group of perpetrators represented (67 percent). Notably, though, they are responsible for 17 percent less of the nonexclusionary discriminatory actions relative to exclusion. Through coercion or intimidation, neighbors represent 3 percent of the perpetrators of nonexclusionary discrimination cases. Interestingly, actors embedded in more formal institutions, such as banks or insurance agencies, also find means to discriminate in a nonexclusionary manner toward African Americans and others. Banking and insurance institutions are the perpetrator in 16 and 7 percent of the cases, respectively. These cases, as revealed by the qualitative data, tend to be characterized by differential and/or unfavorable terms and conditions in the refinancing of an individual's current home, or the refusal to provide or renew home owner's insurance for individuals living in predominantly African American neighborhoods. Hence, while these victims are not directly excluded from housing, they often suffer financial loss and/or excessive anxiety and stress as a result of illegal actions of the perpetrator. Finally, actors from city or metropolitan housing authorities and real estate companies represent 5 and 3 percent of cases, respectively.

Qualitative case analyses reveal the interactional nature of nonexclusionary discrimination and its sociopsychological consequences. Such discrimination ranges from the use of racial slurs to responding differently or more quickly to whites who report maintenance problems. And, as denoted by the example below, the same individual may experience multiple forms simultaneously. Alvin, an African American male, was subject to housing discrimination by the owner, Gordon, of the boarding house in which he lived. Specifically, he notes how the owner of the house raised his rent, but not the rent of white tenants.

> Since my first day at respondent's facility I have been subject to racial slurs and different rules not imposed on other white tenants. . . . Gordon said he was

raising my rent because I was the only one who cooked, and this was causing the electric bill to go up. I informed Gordon that the electric was going up because other white tenants were using space saver heaters. Gordon said, "You lying nigger." After I could not use the cooking facility, Gordon gave me permission to cook on a grill. I came home and discovered that Steve (a white manager) threw my grill away. Steve has been known on numerous occasions to refer to me as "nigger."

Evidence collected by the civil rights investigators substantiated the charging party's claim. Indeed, after interviewing the manager, the investigator notes that:

> The manager admits to using derogatory racial slurs while in the complainant's presence, but he claims that he used such words "in fun," and that he did not mean it derogatorily.

In addition, numerous witnesses provided statements stating that Alvin, the only black resident, was treated differently than other residents and that white residents who interacted with Alvin were also sometimes treated differently. One witness stated that the owner told him that, "we get this nigger out of here and we'll be back to an all-white building." Thus, although Alvin successfully acquired housing at a point in the past, the antagonistic racial slurs and differential treatment he was subject to within this setting resulted in a less than ideal, safe, or secure situation. Undoubtedly, the impact of this experience on the victim's sense of well-being and security is as consequential, if not more, than that which might have been caused had he been excluded from the housing initially.

As with exclusionary cases of discrimination, the breadth of discriminatory processes—namely how actors discriminate and the consequences of these actions—is extensive. Bertha and Howard, an African American couple renting an apartment in one of the state's largest cities, filed a charge of discrimination based on repeated harassment from their neighbor who also happened to be the complex's rental agent. They describe what occurred, as well as their interpretation of it as being racially motivated.

> Since the time of October 1, 2001 and continuing, we have been subject to ongoing harassment from our next door neighbor, and rental agent Julia Wright. An example of this harassment includes Ms. Wright placing trash on our property. We have complained about this harassment to Brian Anderson, Ms. Wright's supervisor, however, no action has been taken to address our concerns. The neighbor who lives on the other side of Ms. Wright is White and has not been subject to such harassment.

A neutral investigation by the Ohio Civil Rights Commission (OCRC) found probable cause that the harassment experienced by Bertha and Howard was racially motivated. Though one might conclude this to be a less severe case of discrimination, the mental anxiety, stress, and compromised aesthetic enjoyment of their property over a long period of time, in this case by a neighbor, was quite consequential for this couple.

Many cases of nonexclusionary discrimination do take on an even more severe form, such as intimidation and physical threat. Such was the experience of Alicia, an African American mother renting an apartment in a large complex. After several altercations, the boyfriend (Brian) of her white neighbor (Betty) made several threats. According to investigative documents:

> Brian Southgate, who is Betty's boyfriend and who is moving on to the property, has harassed Complainant and has threatened to kill Complainant, Complainant's boyfriend, and their "Nigger" baby because of their allegations against Betty. The property manager, Jason Short, has been aware of the harassment and threats since April, and is still allowing Brian Southgate to move on to the property. Jason Short is good friends with Betty.

Though not all cases are this extreme, the powerlessness and lack of ability to get help from legitimate individuals who hold authority (i.e., the landlord/manager) is common among non-exclusionary discrimination cases. Indeed, in many of the cases, if the harassment does not cease to exist, the victim must either move (exclude her- or himself) or seek outside assistance (i.e., from the OCRC, an attorney, or a fair housing group). For example, Sandy, a Caucasian female, states that:

> she and her children, four white and one bi-racial, have been subjected to harassment, racial slurs and physical confrontations by other, Caucasian, residents. Sandy states that the landlord has failed to take any action to stop the harassment. Evidence indicates that Sandy, her children, and other African American residents and their children were subjected to a racially charged, tainted environment.

Cases, such as these, suggest quite clearly that conceptualization of housing discrimination can be broadened to include discriminatory acts that occur within residential settings. Indeed, in many cases minorities may gain access to housing, yet their daily experiences are far from comfortable. Thus, one cannot assume that if exclusionary discrimination ended, minorities would no longer be discriminated in the housing market. Clearly, housing discrimination is a multidimensional phenomenon characterized by dynamic and interactional processes between multiple actors. Moreover, while certainly a large portion of discriminatory actions are aimed at institutional exclusion altogether, others seem more geared toward preserving status and maintaining racial hierarchy.

Finally, there may be a connection between the prevalence of nonexclusionary discrimination in the housing arena, in the form of differential treatment, intimidation and harassment, and persistent patterns of residential segregation or the avoidance of certain neighborhoods, areas, and complexes. It is certainly plausible that nonexclusionary forms of housing discrimination, such as in the cases reported above, either through personal experience or through communication within the broader minority community, may push individuals, families, and interracial couples to seek housing in predominately minority neighborhoods. We found numerous and quite complex cases which provide an initial glimpse of this process. The following case in point revolves around a Jamaican immigrant who experiences various nonexclusionary forms of discrimination and who is clearly embedded in the broader immigrant community where housing information and experiences are exchanged.

> This new manager does not welcome Jamaican citizens to this property. I am here as a student and I have friends who are Jamaican who were told nothing was available. Other persons not of Jamaican origin called and were told there were units available. Jamaican residents who live here are moving out because of the lack of services. The most recent incident occurred when I reported I had no hot water in my shower. I called both offices and was assured the repair would be made. When I called the main office, I could never speak to the person in charge. . . . I spoke to a white resident who told me he is not having a problem with his hot water and he has had no problem with repairs being made.

Such a case—and this is but one among many—demonstrates the complex, and perhaps interconnected, nature of nonexclusionary and exclusionary forms of discrimination. Indeed, to the extent that nonexclusionary discrimination is ongoing at a particular location, impacting several minority residents over time, it may very well lead to information sharing and, correspondingly, avoidance by the minority community generally. In essence, persistent harassment, intimidation, or differential treatment may, by default or design, very well impact exclusion and segregation levels.

Conclusions

The segregation of minorities within and across U.S. cities has been a focal point for much analyses of inequality over the last two decades. This literature speaks to segregation's persistence and to the aggregate and historical nature of inequalities and housing. What has been less explicit, perhaps with the exception of auditing studies conducted largely by fair housing groups or a few case analyses of mortgage and lending practices within a particular city, has been explicit discussion of the mechanisms and processes whereby such outcomes in housing continue to manifest.[5]

Our findings, which draw on truly unique qualitative and quantitative data to the field, highlight aggregate patterns pertaining to both victims and perpetrators and revealed the sometimes complex, sometimes explicit, and sometimes more subtle forms of racial discrimination that minorities may encounter. African American women are most likely to face both exclusionary and nonexclusionary forms of housing discrimination—a pattern that we interpret to be a function of several factors, including their gender and class status, as well as their status as mothers. It is no doubt the case that stereotypical notions of single black mothers are playing part in these relations, shaping landlords' willingness to rent, banks' willingness to provide mortgages, and neighbors' levels of civility. Chapter 11 addresses this possibility in detail.

Exclusionary processes uncovered speak to, and indeed inform, the large body of prior literature on housing segregation by revealing the ways in which institutional actors play a role from a distance, in the case of mortgage companies and banks for instance, or on a face-to-face and quite interactional level. With regard to the latter, it is quite clear that landlords and owners of housing units are on the front line, accounting for over 80 percent of all exclusionary discrimination cases in our data. We expect that this is actually an overestimate, given that discriminatory actions in lending and insurance are more covert in nature and possibly even unintended. Nevertheless, the institutional power of landlords and owners—power to allow access or not—combined with the face-to-face interactions they have with prospective tenants, sets up the most prevalent situation in which discrimination is both explicit and experienced by minorities. This parallels, to a significant degree, our earlier findings regarding employers and, more specifically, direct supervisors in employment—supervisors who hold institutional power to exclude if they chose, but that can also use discretion in targeted ways that work to the systematic disadvantage of particular individuals and groups.

The consequences, as witnessed in some of the exemplary material reported, are similar to those reported with regard to employment discrimination. Aside from outright exclusion and its objective consequences, victims of discrimination in housing clearly experience stress, anxiety, anger, and despair. Other analyses pertaining to the day-to-day experiences of African Americans and other minorities have similarly revealed the enactment of racial hierarchies in everyday life, and the toll it takes on its victims (e.g., Feagin 1991).

Seldom studied or considered in the housing inequality and racial segregation literatures are forms of discrimination that occur once minorities are actually housed, something we have referred to throughout as nonexclusionary discrimination. Such discrimination entails, most generally, differential treatment, harassment, and intimidation and has as its explicit intent not of exclusion, but rather the expression of intolerance, the reification of status on an social-interactional level, and even psychological and physical intimidation. Neighbors sometime play a part, as revealed in our examples of biracial couples and families with biracial children, wherein the victims were harassed, threatened, and in some cases eventually evicted from their dwellings.

Interestingly, and somewhat contrary to expectations, institutional actors (i.e., again, disproportionately, landlords) continue to play a quite obvious role in this form of discrimination, most often by denying equal treatment to minority persons who are already residing in housing units. Massey (2005, 149) argues that discrimination is a moving target; as "federal anti-discrimination policies become more effective in overcoming certain forms of racial bias in housing, new forms have emerged to perpetuate residential segregation." While we are not suggesting that nonexclusionary forms of discrimination are necessarily "new," this form of discrimination may become more prevalent as awareness and enforcement about what Massey (2005, 149) calls "the classic discriminatory mechanisms" (i.e., exclusion) increases. Housing providers, out of fear of prosecution, may allow minorities access to housing but that does not necessarily mean that they will be treated fairly.

Housing discrimination continues to be a social problem in the United States for racial minorities. We have argued in this chapter that while the current body of research into housing discrimination has articulated well the potential consequences of exclusion for segregation, it seldom examines the interactional nature of this phenomena. The focus on aggregate patterns of inequality, including segregation, has been and continues to be vital. Yet, sociological theorizing and analyses of stratification that go a step further, incorporating process-oriented foci and acknowledging the active nature of human agents in the inequality we are investigating, would add significantly to both our knowledge and efforts toward social justice.

Notes

1. E.g., Yinger (1998); Galster (1990a, 1990b). Black and Hispanic home buyers can expect to encounter approximately one act of discrimination every time they interact with a real estate broker (Yinger 1991). Similar evidence is reported from analyses of rental inquiries by phone (Massey and Lundy 2001) and interactions with mortgage

lenders and homeowner's insurance agents (Squires 2003; Smith and Cloud 1996; Squires and Velez 1988).

2. Indeed, evidence suggests that black and Hispanic couples with children face more discrimination than minorities without children (Yinger 1995; Page 1995). Other work has found that whites oppose school integration more than residential integration (Simpson and Yinger 1985) and that white resistance is even more pronounced among white families with children under eighteen (Emerson, Chai, and Yancey 2001)—two findings that perhaps explain why minorities with children face more discrimination that those without.

3. Consistent with this point, research in the sociology of grievance framing and resistance suggests grievance formation that invokes action often requires an understanding and interpretation that puts a malicious face on the inequality that is occurring. Such a causal interpretation provides those experiencing inequality with not only a more concrete target, but also an essentially moral justification for acts of contention. In this regard, see Gamson (1995); Roscigno and Danaher (2001); Roscigno and Hodson (2004); Snow and Benford (1992).

4. Such is likely the case here, as denoted by the qualitative data reported momentarily. One important implication, however, is that exclusionary actions undertaken by institutional actors not so proximate to the targets are less often observed, felt, or challenged. Correspondingly, although much of discriminatory exclusion is likely to be undertaken by landlords and owners, exclusion enacted by other, more distant institutional agents (e.g., banks, insurance companies, etc.) will often be unrealized and, thus, significantly underreported. See also Massey (2005).

5. Drawing on broader stratification theory pertaining to social closure, as well as the recent calls among stratification and housing scholars for explication of inequality processes, this chapter has attempted to fill this void in the literature. Specifically, we have (1) denoted the exclusionary and nonexclusionary ways that discrimination as a manifestation of social closure may be playing a role in inequality reproduction specific to minorities in the arena of housing; (2) highlighted why one might expect variations in the actors involved, depending upon the form of discrimination and role of institutional power; and (3) emphasized the interactional nature of such social closure as well as its consequences for victims beyond exclusion.

10

The Contexts of Housing Discrimination

with Diana Karafin

I was told, "We don't want them blacks in here."

> —white male, evicted after landlord
> discovered his live-in girlfriend is black

The house appears to be located on a street equally occupied by blacks and whites.

> —civil rights investigator notes on the above case

DO PROCESSES OF RACIAL RESIDENTIAL EXCLUSION, not to mention discrimination against minorities that are already housed, vary by neighborhood context? Much like our prior expectation that employment discrimination will differ in degree and form by labor market context and compositional dynamics, there is good reason to believe that housing discrimination too will manifest uniquely in certain neighborhoods. In this chapter, we draw from racial stratification theory, particularly that emphasizing the spatial nature of racial competition and threat, and delineate how neighborhood context may matter for the processes already described in chapter 9. Our analyses link discrimination data to information pertaining to neighborhood context, and then highlight how and why processes of housing discrimination differentially unfold in segregated white areas, segregated black areas, and somewhat integrated neighborhoods.

The Contexts of Housing Discrimination

Important to our objectives is the explicit premise that housing discrimination is not merely a function of individual actors with biased perceptions of minorities. Rather, discretionary decision making by key actors at the microinteractional level is more likely than not tied to the racial context and compositional attributes of local areas and neighborhoods. A case of discrimination in a white-dominated neighborhood, for instance, may represent the preservation of "white only" space. On the other hand, in areas experiencing an influx of blacks, discrimination could be tied to ongoing territorial competition and reflect broader patterns of threat and competition in U.S. society. Although one might not expect discrimination to appear in areas that are already largely minority in their compositional makeup, practices aimed at exploiting the economic disadvantage of vulnerable populations (e.g., predatory lending and mortgage practices) may be more commonplace in such areas. Each scenario described above represents discrimination, yet the intent, actors, and processes arguably differ at some fundamental sociological level.

Why are these differences important? Aside from the obvious fact that such actions are illegal, many scholars believe that racial discrimination in the rental, sales, and lending industry is a key mechanism in reproducing residential segregation in the United States (Massey and Denton 1993; Yinger 1995; Smith and Cloud 1996). Many speculate (and audit studies confirm) that housing discrimination constricts the housing choices of blacks (of all income levels) and other minorities. It is plausible that African Americans and other minorities are often forced, via outright exclusion or harassment, to reside in more segregated areas—segregated areas oftentimes characterized by physical and social disorder. Hence, the first step in untangling this complicated social process is to understand how discrimination unfolds not only within but across localities.

Stratification researchers have developed useful theories for unpackaging these complex processes. Blumer (1958), in particular, contends that levels of racial antagonism are directly linked to the degree to which a dominant group perceives that an outside racial group is threatening dominant group interests. Racial tension will thus increase as the majority group develops feelings of superiority, ethnocentric views toward the minority group, a sense of ownership and privilege over certain areas, and especially fear that the minority group will somehow destroy existing privileges. In other words, the potential for discrimination manifests as a function of group position, and is impacted by historical and contemporary struggles.

What causes perceptions of threat to emerge and/or intensify? According to the now classic work of Blalock (1967), a positive relationship exists between prejudice/discrimination and minority group size; as minority group representation increases within an area, feelings of prejudice and acts of discrimination by the majority group members will tend to increase (Blalock 1967). Blalock suggests that this relationship exists for two reasons. First, as a minority group increases in size, competition for scarce resources (real or perceived) intensify. Such resources may include jobs and housing, but may also reflect neighborhood boundaries and the use of public space (in these regards, see Lieberson 1980; Wilson 1978; Roscigno and Tomaskovic-Devey 1994; Tomaskovic-Devey and Roscigno 1996). Second, and relatedly, dominant group members may begin to fear that if the minority group becomes too large, dominant group employment, political, educational, and safety interests will be directly threatened.

Consistent with these points, the history of U.S. race relations is replete with examples of white mobilization and/or backlash against a sizeable or growing minority community and individuals within that community. Such cases include urban white riots in the face of minority influx (e.g., Olzak 1990; Lieberson 1980), significant unrest and violence during efforts to integrate school systems (e.g., Olzak, Shanahan, and West 1994), white voting polarization against minority candidates (e.g., Roscigno and Tomaskovic-Devey 1994), as well as lynching, violence, and social control generally aimed at minority populations (Tolnay and Beck 1995; Soule 1992; Jacobs and O'Brien 1998).

The implications of racial competition and what it means across unique residential contexts and for housing discrimination specifically warrants further elaboration. Below we address three types of residential settings in which housing discrimination might occur; segregated white areas, areas undergoing racial transition and integration, and segregated black neighborhoods. The tenets of racial competition and threat perspectives inform us as to how discriminatory forms and actors involved may vary across these three basic residential contexts.

Segregated White Space

Many areas of the United States are characterized by their relative homogeneity—that is, they are entirely or nearly entirely white in racial makeup. Housing discrimination, however, may still unfold in such localities as dominant group actors engage in the "protection of white space." Minorities who enter such space are all the more notable given their (visible) minority status (in this regard, see Roscigno and Anderson 1995; Pinderhughes 1993). More privileged white areas, with institutionalized actors who have the power to exclude and who may be more privy to fair housing laws, will arguably resort to the use of subtle and legitimate-appearing forms of discrimination to keep racial/ethnic minorities out. The use of economic criteria, differentially applied, may be especially key in this regard.

White areas, however, are by no means all advantaged. In moderate income and more disadvantaged white settings, where there is no clear-cut white economic advantage that can be drawn upon for exclusionary purposes, informal, blatant, or even more threatening tactics may be used. Indeed, and as witnessed in some of the examples provided in the prior chapter, there may be less overall knowledge or understanding of fair housing laws and procedures on the part of landlords especially in such a context.

The intent in white spaces of mid-to-low socioeconomic background would be to preserve some racial advantage in terms of space (or territory if you prefer), despite limited or nonexistent social class differences by race. For those minority group members who do acquire housing, nonexclusionary discrimination may very well ensue, as actors with or without institutional power may engage in differential treatment to either re-establish the whiteness of the area or simply reinforce some status advantage within their own neighborhoods. These are by no means mutually exclusive aims.

Racially Transitioning/Integrated Space

When analyzing changes in the racial composition of neighborhoods, sociologists have for decades described the implications of areas approaching a minority "threshold"—a threshold wherein competitive processes and racial tensions will be triggered. Once the threshold is surpassed, the neighborhood will typically quickly transition into a segregated black space as whites flee to other neighborhoods. Realtors historically have both manipulated and taken financial advantage of whites' perceptions in these very regards by engaging in blockbusting.[1]

Hence, there is good reason to expect housing discrimination to vary significantly in areas approaching or at a threshold compared to predominantly white and black areas. As minorities increasingly gain access to certain areas, nonexclusionary discrimination—discrimination reflecting white efforts to maintain the status hierarchy—should be more obvious. Cases in these contexts will be characterized by racial coercion or intimidation from both neighbors and actors with institutional power (such as landlords) in an attempt to get minorities out or to at least remind them of where they are in terms of status.

Segregated Black Space

In segregated black areas, which also are apparent throughout the United States, there is little motivation on the part of residential whites to exclude or to harass minorities since minorities already make up the numerical majority of the area. One should thus expect significantly fewer cases of discrimination overall. Indeed, whites generally tend to avoid such areas given perceptions of crime and delinquency. There is also no logical reason why, for instance, landlords or neighbors (who may very well also be minorities) would discriminate with high minority composition contexts.

Particular forms of housing discrimination may nevertheless occur within segregated minority contexts. These forms will entail not exclusion but rather differential institutional treatment with the goal (by design or default) of financial exploitation of vulnerable populations. Here, we are referring to mortgage lending institutions, insurance companies, and realtors, each of whom have historically demonstrated a vested interest in unscrupulously targeting poor and minority neighborhoods for quick profit-making opportunities that are often class exploitive and racial discriminatory in nature (Ross and Yinger 2002; Yinger 1995).

Analyzing the Contexts of Housing Discrimination

We begin by examining the spatial patterning of serious cases of racial housing discrimination in figure 10.1 across the three spatial contexts discussed above for discrimination cases in which we currently have information pertaining to the neighborhood ($n = 602$). White contexts are defined as areas[2] in which 5 percent or less of the population is black, mixed contexts are those in which between 6 percent and 60 percent of the population is black, and black contexts are defined as areas in which 61 percent or more of the population is black.[3]

Notable is that the greatest percentage of serious cases of housing discrimination (53 percent) occur in mixed contexts that are undergoing racial transition and integration. On the other hand, 34 percent of the cases are located in predominantly white contexts, while only 13 percent are located in segregated black spaces. Hence, our theoretical expectations are confirmed in that, within our sample, discrimination cases are more likely in areas undergoing racial transition (as a result of increased racial threat and competition), followed by white contexts. Discrimination appears least likely to occur in predominantly black contexts.

Are similar differences found when we examine separately exclusionary ($n = 287$) and nonexclusionary ($n = 315$) discrimination? Figure 10.2 demonstrates that for both exclusionary and nonexclusionary discrimination, the most common contexts are those that are integrated or undergoing racial transition (52 percent of exclusionary cases and 55 percent of nonexclusionary

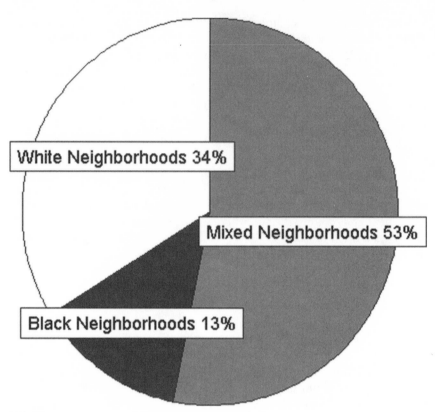

FIGURE 10.1
Percentage Breakdown of Distribution of Cases of Discrimination Across Contexts
(*n* = 602)

cases). Furthermore, white contexts contain the second greatest percentage of cases (37 percent of exclusionary and 31 percent of nonexclusionary cases), and black contexts hold the smallest (11 percent and 13 percent, respectively).

In both mixed and black contexts, nonexclusionary discrimination is more common than exclusionary discrimination (46 percent in mixed contexts and 43 percent in black contexts). This is not surprising. In areas undergoing racial transition, where blacks are obviously gaining access to the neighborhood, actors may be motivated to utilize nonexclusionary forms, such as harassment, differential treatment, and coercion in order to maintain the racial status hierarchy. On the other hand, in segregated black contexts, nonexclusionary discrimination may be more common because there is no motivation on the part of white actors to exclude blacks if the area is already predominantly black. Rather, we suspected and the data confirms[4] that the majority of these cases

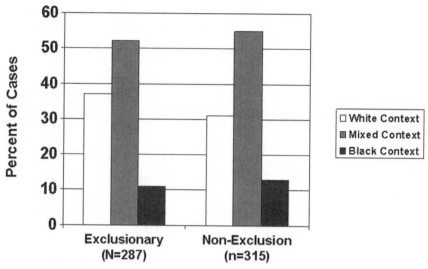

FIGURE 10.2
The Varying Contexts of Exclusionary and Nonexclusionary Discrimination

are characterized by discriminatory behaviors by institutionalized actors in the banking, lending, and insurance industries. Such actors, as confirmed by examination of case files, target disadvantaged populations—disadvantaged populations that very well may lack the resources or knowledge to prevent being taken advantage of.

In sum, the analysis above reveals that (1) both exclusionary and nonexclusionary discrimination appear to be most likely in areas undergoing racial transition and integration (mixed contexts) and least likely to occur in segregated black areas; and (2) discrimination in mixed and black segregated contexts is more likely to be characterized by nonexclusionary practices and behaviors, while discrimination in white contexts is more likely to be characterized by processes of exclusion. While these patterns are certainly informative, only a detailed examination of cases within each context reveals what these processes actually look like.

Protecting White Space

How does racial housing discrimination unfold in white areas characterized by the presence of few, if any black households? In the case of Kenneth, an African American male who attempted to rent an apartment in a privileged neighborhood in Cuyahoga Falls, Ohio (located in the Cleveland–Akron metropolitan statistical area), subtle tactics were utilized by the landlord. Kenneth repeatedly called the office of a newly constructed apartment complex to inquire about possibly renting a one-bedroom apartment. He left numerous messages, none of which were returned. Finally, Kenneth visited the property but was told that all apartments had been rented. However, as the apartment complex had only recently been open for rental, and after witnessing intensive repair work and painting of several of the apartments, Kenneth felt he was denied the opportunity to even apply for consideration solely because of his race.

After filing a complaint with a fair housing agency, two testers (one white and one black) with comparable human capital were sent to the property. The white tester was able to make an appointment to view the property only after the manager picked up the phone while the white tester was leaving a message. The black tester, in contrast, left numerous messages, never received a return call, and eventually visited the property only to be treated differentially. As noted in the case file, the experiences of the black and white tester were considerably distinct:

> The White tester was offered an application, but the Black tester had to ask for an application and he was denied an application as the Respondent allegedly had none available. The respondent also asked for a larger security deposit and monthly rent from the Black tester than the White tester.

Apartments were indeed available, yet the manager clearly had lied to Kenneth, the black tester. Furthermore, when prodded, the manager failed to provide any proof to the Ohio Civil Rights Commission (OCRC) in terms of the nonavailability of apartments, such as copies of the alleged leases. Hence, the OCRC concluded that Kenneth had, in fact, been discriminated against. This case demonstrates the subtle tactics some landlords will use to protect and preserve "white space." Exclusionary forms of discrimination that are subtle and more difficult to detect seem much more common in these areas.

In a more complicated case, presented in the last chapter, George, an African American male, filed a claim that he had been discriminated against by a manager at an apartment complex in a privileged neighborhood in the Cleveland–Akron metropolitan statistical area. He was approved to rent an apartment, but then was denied occupancy when the owner found out that he had a white, live-in girlfriend. In such a case, no claims of overt discriminatory acts such as the use of racial slurs are reported. Rather, the manager utilized more subtle tactics, such as claiming that George's roommate must also qualify to rent the apartment (though an investigation revealed this standard was not applied equally).

In more privileged contexts, institutionalized actors who wish to preserve white space may often be limited in fulfilling their desire to exclude as they may be very aware of the potential legal consequences if caught discriminating. On the other hand, when an opportunity presents itself, as in the case of George, actors may utilize forms of discrimination that appear legitimate rather than more overt forms such as the use of racial slurs and outright denial.

Discrimination in generally disadvantaged white areas, as the qualitative material suggests, tends to be much more explicit and is activated in unique ways, often by neighbors. As a case in point, in March of 2003, Venetia saw an advertisement in a local newspaper for a house for rent in her price range in a predominantly white, somewhat disadvantaged neighborhood in Canton, Ohio. She called her mom and asked her to drive out to the neighborhood with her to look at the house. As they inspected the exterior of the house, a white neighbor approached them stating that she "did not want people like you [Ventia] living in the neighborhood." Venetia later reported this to the owner of the home for rent, who did not live in the neighborhood. After examining Venetia's application, the owner offered to rent the house to Venetia. However, Venetia "was hesitant to rent a house in a neighborhood hostile towards individuals of color."

In this case, a neighbor blatantly warned a prospective tenant that she was not welcome there. While lacking institutional power to exclude, the neighbor, most likely unaware of fair housing laws, directly attempted to exclude blacks and to protect the whiteness of the neighborhood by warning Venetia that African Americans are not welcome. Despite the fact that the owner (who was not a neighborhood resident) offered the house, Venetia feared intimidation, threat, or even violence from the neighbor and others who did not want her there.

The above example is not to suggest that it is merely neighbors and residents that will actively attempt to exclude in working-class or poor white neighborhoods. Sometimes actors with institutional power will also blatantly exclude blacks from entering white areas (especially poor white neighborhoods), as in the case of Steve. He was told by the landlord of an apartment for rent, "the tenants that live here don't want niggers!"

Racial Transition, Integration, and Tension

As reported earlier, housing discrimination in more integrated contexts or contexts approaching a particular minority threshold tend to witness nonexclusionary tactics, such as harassment, coercion, intimidation, and violent threats. Discriminatory actors in such a context include those with and without institutional power. If they cannot stop African Americans from moving in, it seems, they at least try to preserve racial hierarchy in the neighborhood.

Dorothy and Devon Belter, residents of a neighborhood in Columbus, Ohio, undergoing racial transition, filed a complaint suggesting that they and other African American tenants in their apartment building were frequently intimidated, stalked, and threatened with eviction because of their race. Evidence collected by the OCRC investigator confirmed that the environment was indeed racist and hostile.

> The complainants . . . were constantly and viciously insulted by on-site management and . . . management has no respect for Black residents. . . . Complainants and other African Americans are being singled out by owners management, who uses the same ploy to force Black tenants to move.

The investigation also uncovered that several black residents were physically attacked by the white maintenance person on duty. Management, for their part, consistently ignored the problem.

As is apparent in the case above, racial threats and antagonism can and often do occur in transition areas. The magnitude of the stress and mental anxiety for blacks, caused by daily negotiations required to coexist with whites threatened by their presence, cannot be denied. With white institutional actors, such as the management in the case of Dorothy and Devon, failing to help and sometimes contributing to the averse situation, blacks often have no one to turn to for help in these contexts.

Such tension, as described above, is certainly clear in the case of Jordan and Jola, an African American couple that was served a three-day eviction notice from their apartment in an integrated and transitioning neighborhood in Cleveland. The rationale for their eviction surrounded the violation of the complex's pet policy. Yet,

> Witness substantiated that Rob Styler [white manager] stated that he wanted to "get the niggers out. And that where he came from, they knew to stay on the other side of the tracks." Evidence substantiates that Caucasian tenants who have received complaints about their dog, and who have violated the pet policy, have not been issued a three-day eviction notice.

Rob Styler's racist comments and actions clearly demonstrate his desire to maintain the status hierarchy of the neighborhood by harassing black residents and unfairly excluding them from the property. For him, blacks should know their place "on the other side of the tracks." Rather than being explicit in his attempt to evict them, however, he attempted to use a legitimate-appearing, arguably neutral policy to push Jola and Jordan out. This resonates, to a considerable degree, with particular findings presented earlier on race and sex discrimination at work. Specifically, bureaucratic procedure and policy, which is arguably neutral in tone, can be executed in targeted and discriminatory ways.

In some instances, white residents will take severe measures to ensure the status hierarchy of the transitioning neighborhood is maintained, as is readily apparent in the case of Ishon, a black male resident of a small apartment complex in a racially mixed neighborhood. In the charge affidavit filed with the OCRC, Ishon explains what occurred in his particular case.

> I had been a resident of the respondents for approximately 18 months. On February 4, 2002, White resident Stanley Brenant told me he was going to kill me. Mr. Brenant made this threat only to me and not the other residents, all of whom are White, who were standing around at the time. In response, I expressed related concerns about my personal safety to Housing Manager Sharon Hult [White]. She did nothing to address my concerns. As a result, I was forced to terminate my tenancy later that day.

The investigation of Ishon's claim of discrimination revealed he had repeatedly been subject to racial slurs and threats by Stanley Brenant and other white tenants, and that the housing manager of the complex failed to respond to his concerns or make any effort to prevent other tenants from illegally subjecting Ishon to a racially tainted environment. As a consequence of the discrimination, Ishon felt his only viable option to ensure his personal safety was to move. This case is particularly interesting in that the discrimination entailed an interaction of negligence on the part of the housing manager, an actor with institutional power, and harassment on the part of neighbors who held no real institutional power.

While the housing manager in the case above, Sharon Hult, was implicated for failing to be proactive in terminating the racially tainted environment created by other tenants under her supervision, sometimes actors embedded within institutions take a more active role in nonexclusionary discrimination. LaShandra and Jebin, an African American married couple were attempting to apply for a loan to purchase a home in a mixed neighborhood.

> They allege that they were subjected to more stringent screening standards than similarly situated white loan applicants. They contend that they were continually asked to verify income and sources of income over and over again, because, according to the loan agent, they had to make sure their money was not made illegally or from drugs.

Though LaShandra and Jebin ultimately secured the loan and were able to purchase the home, the investigation revealed that other, white applicants were not required to undergo the same level of scrutiny over sources of income. Hence,

Jebin and LaShandra were subjected to differential treatment in securing their loan as a result of embarrassing and stereotypical assumptions on the part of the lending agent regarding how African Americans secure income. In essence, LaShandra and Jebin were assumed guilty until proven innocent, in that they had to prove their income did not derive from the selling of illegal drugs.

While nonexclusionary forms of discrimination, such as the harassment experienced by Ishon or the differential treatment toward LaShandra and Jebin, are found in the majority of cases in mixed areas, in some instances whites take advantage, when the opportunity presents itself, to exclude blacks in both subtle and more overt ways. Toya, responding to an ad in a local paper in a racially mixed neighborhood in Cincinnati, Ohio, scheduled an appointment to view an apartment for her mother, Ruth. The investigator from the OCRC later reported:

> When they arrived to view the apartment, no one was there, although they saw an older man in front of the building who they thought was the owner of the property in question. Claimants allege that after noticing they were black, the man pulled off without keeping the appointment.

Toya and Ruth felt the owner ignored them after seeing they were black. After their claim was filed, a local fair housing agency conducted an audit on the property, in which a black and white tester were sent in. Results from the audit, in which the owner denied availability to the black tester yet professed availability to the white tester, provided significant evidence that the owner of the apartment building was actively, illegally excluding blacks.

The cases highlighted in this section reveal the complex and varying processes through which varying actors discriminate in areas with a heightened level of racial threat and competition, as a result of the racially mixed environment of the neighborhoods. The various manifestations of nonexclusionary and exclusionary discrimination revealed in these cases demonstrate the added burden African Americans clearly face in maintaining a peaceful presence within, or at times even gaining access to, contexts undergoing racial transition.

Discrimination in Segregated Black Space

Though only 13 percent of the serious cases of housing discrimination in the data occurred in segregated black contexts, historical evidence provides some insight into an economic motive for discrimination by institutional actors (who otherwise have little reason to exclude blacks from segregated black areas). Specifically, actors embedded in mortgage lending, insurance, and financial institutions have historically targeted relatively vulnerable minority populations, neighborhoods, and families. Typically, these nonexclusionary forms of discrimination include discrimination in the making of loans, refusal to provide homeownership insurance, purposeful misrepresentation of a home's value, and differential terms and conditions in refinancing.

Devonna, an African American female residing in a predominantly black census tract in a large metropolitan area filed a claim of discrimination after refinancing her home, noting that she was mislead in the terms of the loan.

> I live in a predominantly African American census tract and was targeted based on that data, and as a result, I was harmed. I was given a bad loan that did not benefit me. I paid very high closing costs, and received a bad appraisal that has resulted in me owing more than my home is worth. I also believe that I continue to be discriminated against with every payment I make on my refinance since it has put me in a vulnerable position financially.

Evidence collected by investigators substantiated that the corporation in charge of refinancing Devonna's home purposely falsely appraised it in order to maximize profits in the financing terms.

The loss of financial security and increased stress produced by the discriminatory acts toward Devonna were also likely experienced by Barbara, who filed a charge of discrimination while living in a similarly situated, predominantly black neighborhood.

> Complainant said she is going through a divorce and is refinancing her home mortgage with Colonial Bank. There was a "drive by" appraisal by Jim Swain for the Bank, where the home was appraised for $78,000. Complainant had an independent appraiser view the home, and it was appraised for $127,000. She believes her home was under appraised by the respondent because it is located in a predominantly African American community.

Evidently, African Americans are not able to escape discrimination, even in the context of segregated black neighborhoods. While institutional actors have little reason to exclude blacks from these areas, the financial gains from illegitimate and unfair financing, insurance, and mortgage-lending policies motivate these actors to consistently take advantage of vulnerable blacks through institutionalized processes of nonexclusionary discrimination.

Conclusion

The diverse sample of racial housing discrimination cases noted throughout this chapter illustrate the importance of considering the role of the spatial context in which housing discrimination occurs. Variations in the discriminatory foci, methods, and actors exist depending on neighborhood racial composition and socioeconomic status. White neighborhoods in general tend to exhibit greater levels of exclusionary discrimination. Such discrimination in more affluent white locales tends not to be overtly racist in form, but rather subtle—such as not returning phone calls or the differential enforcement of economic criteria. Disadvantaged white neighborhoods, in contrast, are characterized by more overt racial discrimination, such as the use of racial slurs, immediate eviction without just cause, and outright denial.

In contrast to disparately white areas, neighborhoods with sizeable or increasing black populations witness a greater overall tendency toward nonexclusionary forms of housing discrimination, often by neighbors and sometimes landlords. Here, the intent appears to be racial hierarchy maintenance in day-to-day interaction. Segregated black contexts, on the other hand, appear to be especially vulnerable to nonexclusionary discrimination toward home owners by banks and insurance companies. While the racial nature of such discrimination is not overt, its economically exploitive nature and implications for African Americans are obvious.

Our findings are, admittedly, only a starting point for those interested in understanding how inequality is related to space and to broad societal dynamics pertaining to competition and threat. Our reading of case materials suggests quite clearly that the character of discrimination itself may differ fundamentally at the local level. Certain areas witness efforts, subtle in the case of well-to-do white areas and more overtly racial in poorer white areas, to protect white space. In other areas, with some racial heterogeneity and change, the focus seems to be less so on the protection of the white spaces and more so on reifying racial hierarchy within a mixed environment. And, finally, minority neighborhoods, while lacking instances of what many would consider discrimination, remain especially vulnerable to economically exploitive and often organizationally based practices.

Future research, with sensitivity to neighborhood "types," might consider statistically modeling rates of discrimination within census tracts. The availability of the housing stock, the state of the urban economy, change in minority composition, average household income, the unemployment rate, the percentage of the population living in poverty, as well as the property and violent-crime rates could easily be included in such modeling—modeling that would not provide insight into the processes involved (our principal goal in this chapter) as much as empirical verification of the robustness of patterns highlighted across a variety of spatial and social contexts.

Greater insight into housing discrimination will ultimately require further analyses of who it affects and where and also how it unfolds, its forms, and its consequences for individuals and groups. Data and analyses, such as that which we have employed throughout this chapter, reflect an effort to address the former. As methods are refined further and data of established cases of discrimination become more widely available, we may eventually begin to move forward not only our knowledge of how individuals and organizations discriminate, but how the larger demographic and social contexts of neighborhoods contribute or mitigate the tendencies we find.

Notes

1. Blockbusting is characterized by a process whereby realtors convince residents in white neighborhoods that they should sell there homes before property values drop, as blacks are moving in. Typically, white residents panic and sell their homes for a low price. Realtors then re-sell the property to blacks at a much higher price, portraying the neighborhood as largely white and advantaged. Hence, as the neighborhood transitions from white to black, realtors who engage in blockbusting typically reap huge profits. For example, see Gotham 2002a; Massey and Denton 1993.

2. For this analysis, zip codes are used as a proxy for neighborhood contexts. Hence, racial composition was determined through 2000 U.S. Census calculations for the zip codes in which cases of serious housing discrimination were located.

3. To our knowledge, there is no apparent consensus on the appropriate boundaries for defining segregated white and black space, as well as space undergoing racial transition. However, the literature on racial preferences of whites and blacks in housing (see, for example, Krysan 2002; Krysan and Farley 2002) provides useful insight. Specifically, whites typically report feeling uncomfortable with more than a marginal (or token) representation of blacks in their neighborhoods. Hence, we define "token" representation as less than 5 percent, and believe that when the percentage of blacks in an area exceeds this amount, processes of racial threat and competition may be likely to ensue. However, once an area is populated by greater than 60 percent blacks, it is likely that these processes will subside as the area is now a segregated black space.

4. Actors implicated in over 50 percent of the cases of discrimination in segregated black areas are embedded within either a banking, lending, or insurance institution.

11

Housing and Sex Discrimination

with Griff Tester

Christina inquired about renting a house from Star Apartments. When Jason Michaels, the manager, learned that Christina was a single mother, he stated that "a male needed to live in the house to do chores such as mowing the lawn and shoveling snow." Jason rented the house to a man.

—civil rights investigative report

RACIAL DISCRIMINATION IN HOUSING, the principal foci of the two prior chapters, has received significant attention from social scientists and policy advocates alike. Other dominant forms of societal inequality such as sex discrimination, however, have garnered scant attention at most in the housing literature. This is quite unfortunate. As our earlier chapters on sex discrimination in employment established rather clearly, sex and often related statuses (maternity and pregnancy) continue to reflect key axes of stratification within society and within its institutional workings. Housing is no exception.

In her article "What Happened to Gender Relations on the Way from Chicago to Los Angeles?" Daphne Spain (2002) argues that women's experiences have been surprisingly ignored by researchers studying urban spaces. And, interestingly, scholarship on "gender and urban space has remained largely isolated in a parallel world of feminist scholarship" even though women's ability to control fertility and achieve economic independence through educational opportunities and increased labor force participation has had major impacts on urban spaces and continues to do so (Spain 2002; see also Spain 1992). These social changes impact public and private spaces, as well as gender relations.

Spain's (2002) gendered critique of the absence of women in the Chicago School's ecological theories of urban spaces to Los Angeles School's postmodern theories can be extended to research on housing discrimination and, potentially, patterns of residential segregation. Audit studies of housing discrimination and research on patterns of residential segregation, as reviewed in the prior two chapters, have tended to focus almost exclusively on the exclusion of racial and ethnic minorities. Seldom, however, have such studies tackled differential treatment of women and men in the housing arena. Indeed, while gender scholars have devoted significant attention to discrimination against women in the workplace, gender discrimination in housing has been largely ignored. Given that gender "acts as a fundamental principle for organizing social relations in virtually all spheres of social life" (Ridgeway and Correll 2004, 521), it seems plausible that gender inequality occurs in housing as well.

Why Gender Matters in Housing

Disparities and discrimination that women face in the workplace—ranging from firing to hiring, to promotion and demotion, to general and sexual forms of harassment—hold implications for women's housing choices given that income directly impacts an individual's neighborhood and housing choices. This is especially true for single women and women of color.

In addition to the economic realities women face when securing housing, they also likely face gendered stereotypes about their ability to be the "head of the household" as well as preconceptions about the "type of woman" that would want to be in this role. To be sure, a women's place was traditionally "in the home," but she was not seen as the "provider" of that home. And, even contemporarily, women tend to manage the home but do not economically control it. "In contrast, for men, home is a space in which they have ultimate authority, yet limited responsibility for the domestic and child-rearing duties that take place in it" (Mallett 2004, 75).

The unique economic realities that women face along with prevailing stereotypes may intertwine in unique ways with several implications for the inequalities they face in housing. What are woman's experiences in the housing arena, particularly when it comes to discrimination? In what ways might economic vulnerability or maternal status play a part in discriminatory experiences? Do women of color, given their economically vulnerable status and disproportionate headship of families face even greater obstacles than their white female counterparts?

In 1997, the United Nations Sub-Commission on Prevention of Discrimination and Protection of Minorities adopted a resolution that specifically addressed the issues of women and the right to adequate housing, recognizing that women face unique problems when trying to obtain housing, including poverty, domestic violence, social and economic access to property and credit, and the presence of children (Senders 1998). This is consistent with previous work on the residential mobility of single-parent women, which has found that "women fitting this description who attempt to move will often find housing choices limited, and mobility, the mechanism most frequently used to correct housing deficits, blocked" (Cook 1989, 572). Mobility for women, it appears, is most often blocked by barriers that include the woman's race, the presence of children, and low income.

Some studies of gender inequality, including analyses presented in chapters 3 and 4 of this book, suggest that women in general and women of color in particular are endangered and compromised by sexual assault, sexual harassment, and domestic violence (Texeira 2002; Kalof et al. 2001). "Race and gender are strongly linked to sexual harassment because they are key dimensions of social stratification. Because sexual harassment is about power, less powerful people (e.g., women, minorities, and younger individuals) [are] particularly vulnerable" (Kalof et al. 2001, 283). The limited research on sexual harassment in housing, conducted by legal scholars, suggests that housing agents, like employers, have power over tenants, especially poor tenants, and that these agents can exploit their power by demanding sexual favors or creating a hostile living environment (Stein 1999). Correspondingly, the meaning of home for women is extremely complex (Darke 1994), ranging from a "safe haven" or place of pride to a place of oppression, domestic violence, and/or resentment (Mallett 2004).

Gender is certainly one of the most fundamental divisions of our society (West and Zimmerman 1987). Cultural beliefs about gender affect the "distribution of resources at the macro level, patterns of behavior and organizational practices at the interactional level, and selves and identities at the individual level" (Ridgeway and Correll 2004, 510). The interactional level is particularly important because this is precisely where gender is maintained and reinforced (Ridgeway and Correll 2004; Ridgeway and Smith-Lovin 1999; West and Zimmerman 1987; Blau and Schwartz 1984). Our analyses in the remainder of this chapter delve into the very experiences women have with housing discrimination, the forms it takes, and what the residential and social psychological consequences are.

The Realities of Sex and Discrimination in Housing

We begin by examining all serious cases of discrimination in housing directed toward black and white women based on their sex or family status. Figure 11.1 reports that black women account for 62.2 percent of the serious cases of sex

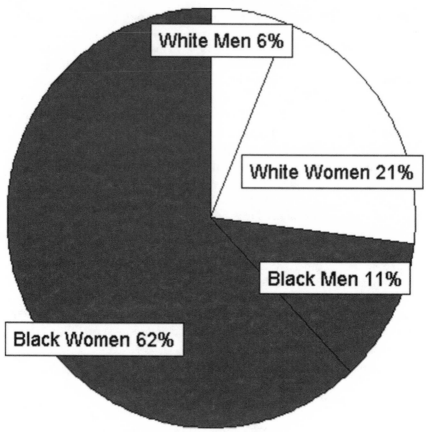

FIGURE 11.1
Distribution of Serious Sex and Familial Status Discrimination Cases by Sex and Race

and family status discrimination ($n = 601$). White women represent 20.5 percent. Black and white men, in contrast, only make up 11.3 percent and 6 percent of the sex and family status cases. Since black and white women, in fact, constitute 83 percent of all serious cases based on sex and family status, we focus attention on these in the qualitative examination that follows.[1]

Vulnerability to Housing Discrimination

Not surprisingly, women represent 83 percent of the sex discrimination cases filed ($n = 200$). Both exclusionary and nonexclusionary forms of discrimination against women make up these data. As was clearly the case with race, landlords and residential managers are the perpetrators in the overwhelming majority of the cases.

> Christina inquired about renting a house from Star Apartments. When Jason Michaels, the manager, learned that Christina was a single mother, he stated that "a male needed to live in the house to do chores such as mowing the lawn and shoveling snow." Jason rented the house to a man.

As Christina's experience demonstrates, there are gendered spaces surrounding the home and stereotypical beliefs about a woman's physical ability to take care of a residence. In addition to the persistence of such cultural views and stereotypes, women also face significant scrutiny about their ability to economically maintain a home, as in the case of Molly, below.

> Molly and her husband lived in a rented house for ten years during their marriage. After they divorced, Molly remained in the house for an additional two years, pre-paid as part of the divorce. When Molly's pre-paid rental period expired in March 2003 her landlord forced her to move. The investigation revealed that Molly was forced to move because of her sex, female.

Molly's rental history, before and after her divorce, was good and the landlord that evicted her was unable to provide any evidence to suggest that she would not continue to have a good rental history after the pre-paid rental period expired. Yet, the landlord evicted her, assuming that she, as a woman, would be unable to pay the rent.

While women face discrimination in the housing arena based solely on the fact that they are women, as the above examples suggest, the story of sex discrimination in housing is, in fact, often much more complex. Indeed, sex discrimination in housing usually intersects with issues pertaining to race and family status. Moreover, qualitative data garnered from the case files themselves suggest that social class is also playing a major role in these cases. This is quite consistent with the telephone audit study conducted by Massey and Lundy (2001).

It is important to note that housing charges can be filed on multiple bases (e.g., sex and race discrimination or sex and family status discrimination). Interestingly, white women who file sex discrimination charges almost always file solely on "sex." Men, regardless of race, rarely file a sex discrimination complaint that wasn't coupled with a charge of race discrimination.

The story is much more complex for African American women, who are just as likely to file a complaint based on their "sex" and "race" as they were to file a complaint based solely on their "sex." This suggests that African American women may be struggling to decide what the "primary" basis of discrimination

is. Black feminists, consistent with this point, have highlighted the complex nature of inequality and identity, especially for African American women, and
the fundamental difficulty individuals face of having to pick a "primary" status (Collins 1990; Crenshaw 1990).

African American women may slip through the legal cracks if their claims
are seen broadly as race and sex discrimination cases. For example, a black
woman's race discrimination claim could be dismissed if a housing provider
offers evidence that he is renting or has rented to black men. Alternatively, if
a black woman files a charge based on sex, such a claim could be discredited
with evidence that white women have been afforded housing at a given location. This may be especially true for housing cases since housing receives far
less public, academic, and political attention than employment-related discrimination. The cases analyzed here all had evidence to substantiate the complainant's charge of sex or sex and race discrimination. Notably, however, substantially more cases are dismissed every year for a lack of evidence.

Intersections of sex and race may go beyond being a black female too, as the
following example illustrates. Alicia, a white female, was told by a landlord
that he would not rent to a single woman, suggesting discrimination based
solely on sex. However, the landlord knew from a telephone conversation earlier that day that Alicia was a single woman, and only refused to rent to her
after meeting her and her biracial child.

Sexual Harassment in Housing

Sexual harassment is encompassed in federal and state laws—laws that prohibit sex discrimination in housings. Again, not surprisingly, women account
for the overwhelming majority of housing cases where the basis of charge is
sexual harassment. What is surprising is the fact that sexual harassment in the
housing arena has not received nearly as much attention by scholars, public-
policy makers, and the media, as workplace sexual harassment, especially
when one considers the added layers of threat and vulnerability involved in
housing-related sexual harassment.

Evidence demonstrates that the majority of cases of sexual harassment
occur after the woman has been housed, while fewer incidents of sexual harassment occur while the woman is attempting to secure housing. As with
general sex discrimination cases, the landlord or manager, was the perpetrator in most of these cases. But, as denoted in the following examples, other
housing staff are also involved. Women face many of the same situations of
sexual harassment where they live, or where they are attempting to live, as
they do in the workplace—cat calls, sexual comments, gestures, and so on in
an ongoing manner.

Laurie alleges, and evidence substantiates, that she has been repeatedly subjected to cat calls and whistles from Greg, the building maintenance person, while she has lived in the apartment complex. Laurie has complained to management but Greg has not stopped his behavior.

Similar to the workplace, unwanted sexual comments and gestures can create a hostile environment, in this case a hostile living environment. Yet, as Laurie's case demonstrates, there is a clear difference.

Laurie awoke to find Greg and another maintenance person in her apartment, without prior notification.

Greg had made sexually harassing comments to Laurie prior to this incident. Laurie's situation was not, unfortunately, a unique case in the data. Rhonda filed sexual harassment charges against her landlord stating that he verbally and physically intimidated her, stalked her, and entered her apartment without her permission or knowledge. Rhonda's and Laurie's claims were substantiated by investigators.

Numerous sexual harassment cases involve a landlord or another staff person entering women's apartments without permission. In all of these cases, the person entering the apartment without permission had a key, because of their institutional authority in the housing complex. Moreover, the perpetrator had previously sexually harassed the female target, as in Laurie's case, or began sexually harassing the female target upon entering her apartment.

Quid pro quo sexual harassment—when a benefit or consequence is tied to submitting to unwelcome sexual advances—is also evident in these data.

Since November 1998, Patricia's landlord repeatedly asked her out and even offered to buy her a ring and a car if she would marry him. When Patricia declined her landlord's advances, she was given an eviction notice.

Linda was a tenant in Mark's apartment complex for approximately three years. . . . Linda told Mark that she would be unable to pay the full amount of her rent. Mark responded by telling her that she could take care of the unpaid balance by having sex with him. When she told him "no," she was evicted.

Patricia was never late with her rent, and yet she was evicted. Linda had been late with her rent, but as the investigation revealed, she had been late and unable to pay the full amount of her rent in the past and had not been evicted or even threatened with eviction. Linda was evicted only after denying Mark's sexual advances. Once again, these were not isolated cases. Many cases involve quid pro quo sexual harassment. One woman, for instance, was denied repairs to her apartment because she refused her landlord's sexual advances, while another was offered a "discount" on her late fees if she performed oral sex on her landlord. She was evicted when she refused. Finally, another was informed that she could be late with her rent if she showed her breasts to her landlord. The fact that many of these cases involve quid pro quo sexual harassment revolving around late rent and "breaks" on security deposits and other housing fees suggests that economic vulnerability is a factor in many cases of sexual harassment in housing.

Another interesting and emergent finding, associated with the proximity of the harasser to the personal space of the women involved in housing cases and that may be somewhat unique to the housing arena, involves the victim's personal relationships. Some women's boyfriends were treated differently by landlords—landlords who would sexually harass the female target when the boyfriend was not present.

> On numerous occasions prior to August, Missy complained to her manager, Steven, that she felt that he made sexually inappropriate comments. . . . Missy states that Steven began treating her differently after observing a man at her apartment. Missy was given a warning when her male friend parked in a certain spot and another warning for being parked in the lot overnight.

The investigation substantiated that Missy had complained to Steven about sexual comments that he had made and that she was given lease violation warnings when her male friend parked in certain spots and left his car in the lot overnight. The investigation also found that Steven was aware of the fact that Missy often allowed her female friends to park in the same spots used by her male friend and allowed them to leave their cars in the lot overnight. Missy was never given a lease violation warning for the incidents involving her female friends.

Other women were evicted, or threatened with eviction, due to the appearance or presence of boyfriends/male friends, as noted by the example below, drawn from a letter written to the Ohio Civil Rights Commission (OCRC).

> [My landlord] has been sexually harassing me and I want something done about it. He is trying to evict me from [my apartment] unless I get rid of my boyfriend, who I have a five month old son with. He has said that I am very beautiful and that I could do better than my present boyfriend. When I was nine months pregnant [my landlord] wanted me to clean his house. I was practically due any day. I told my boyfriend what was happening, he confronted my landlord, and we were given an eviction notice. My landlord said I was not fair to him and treated him bad for telling my boyfriend about what he said. We have also made several police reports about him stalking us. One incident was at 1:30 a.m., when he was stalking the house by riding up and down the street several times and then sitting up on the corner and watching the house. Please help me with my situation.

Not only does this example demonstrate the consequences and degree of threat that many woman face in their neighborhoods and homes as a result of sexual harassment, but it also highlights the role of power and power differentials in the discrimination relationship. The complainant's landlord not only feels he can control who the female target is with by threats of eviction, but he feels that he can require her to clean his house when she is nine months pregnant, and not employed by him. Furthermore, he stalks the complainant even when her boyfriend is at her house, demonstrating his feeling of power over her and her boyfriend given his control of the residential complex.

Because of the unique nature of sexual harassment and the potentially severe consequences it may have for women, it is important to consider how race, family status, and class intersect in sexual harassment cases as well. African American women account for 66 percent of the sexual harassment cases. The following example, which is taken from the investigative report and the investigator's field notes, illustrates these intersections.

Natasha, a black female with children, lived in John Smith's apartment for nearly five years. Shortly after Natasha moved onto the property, John began sexually harassing her. Natasha stated dozens of examples of sexual harassment, both verbal and physical, but she did not report John's actions or move from his property.

During the investigation, when asked why she continued to live under these circumstances for approximately five years, she became visibly upset and explained that, "it was something I had to do for my children."

[Natasha] reports that [John] had "overlooked" her credit and rental history when applying for the apartment and he had often given her "a break" on her already reduced rent during months that she struggled financially. More importantly, Natasha stated that the apartment was in a good neighborhood with schools that were better than any schools her children had attended. On December 1, 1999, when [Natasha] entered her apartment she found [John] sitting on her couch masturbating. She left the apartment, and later filed charges against [John].

This particular case illustrates the vulnerability that many women face in the housing arena, especially when they are poor, African American, and supporting children. It also illustrates the conscious effort that some housing providers make when deciding who to house and how vulnerable they may be to sexual advances. Noteworthy in this regard is that during the investigation of Natasha's case, twelve other women, both current and past tenants, provided statements that mirrored Natasha's experience of sexual harassment while living at this particular housing complex. According to the investigator, all of the women were poor, African American women with children, even though the composition of the neighborhood would suggest a different racial and class makeup, and most of the women told similar stories about "doing what I had to do to provide for my children."

Welfare mothers most frequently cited "putting their children first" as a marker of a good mother, which is consistent with representation of all mothers, regardless of social class (Hayes 1996). This marker, however, can put some mothers in vulnerable and dangerous situations, as we see in the case of sexual harassment in housing. In her discussion of gendered spaces and gender stratification, Spain (1994, 110) points out "that women in traditionally male trades consider verbal harassment part of the price of learning a lucrative occupation." As Natasha's case demonstrates, in housing, "overlooking" sexual harassment may be the price some women feel they have to pay, not only to provide housing for themselves, but to be able to provide their children with a home in a good neighborhood and good schools.

There are certainly similarities between sexual harassment at work and in housing but there are also differences. In housing, as we have seen here, the perpetrator may have a key to the victim's home, which demonstrates the potential for additional layers of threat and vulnerability for women. In addition, the victim may not be able to remove themselves from the situation, given, among other things, the economic burden of moving, and the harasser may have more insight into the victim's personal life (Stein 1999). We are not suggesting that sexual harassment in housing is *more* threatening or dangerous than sexual harassment in the workplace, but we are suggesting that sexual harassment in housing has additional dimensions of threat and vulnerability for the women involved.

Family Status and Discrimination

As the discussion of sex and sexual harassment discrimination implied, the presence of children can create additional barriers for female heads of households and housing seekers. Unlike laws prohibiting sexual harassment in housing, which are subsumed under the sex basis, family status is a separate basis under federal and state fair housing laws. However, women, especially African American women, are disproportionately affected by family status discrimination—the presence of children under the age of eighteen. Women represented 86 percent of the serious cases of family status discrimination filed by individual women and men.[2] As figure 11.2 shows, 57 percent of these cases were filed by black women, compared to 11 percent filed by white

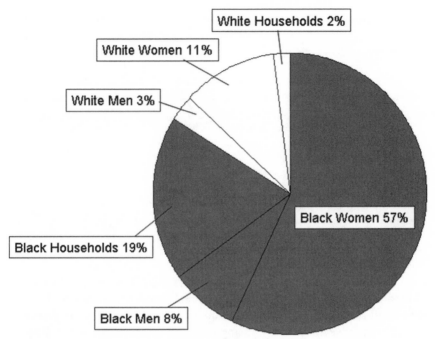

White Households 2%

White Women 11%

White Men 3%

Black Women 57%

Black Households 19%

Black Men 8%

FIGURE 11.2
Serious Cases of Discrimination Based on Familial Status

women. Black and white men accounted for 8 percent and 3 percent of the family status cases, respectively. Black couples or households represented 19 percent, while white couples or households only represented 2 percent.

As with sex discrimination, family status discrimination is multidimensional, involving both exclusionary and nonexclusionary forms of discrimination. Unlike sex and sexual harassment cases, however, most family status cases involve discrimination while attempting to secure housing. Further, the documents from the investigative case files demonstrate that landlords presented a variety of reasons for discriminating against families and individuals with children, ranging from assumptions about noise and property damage to stereotypes about single women raising children, especially boys. Housing providers also charge these families or individuals with children an additional fee per-month per-child, which is illegal.[3]

While federal and state laws permit senior or adult living facilities, which meet certain criteria, to prohibit children, it is illegal for general housing providers to do so. Yet, it is still not uncommon to see "for rent" signs and other advertisements that read "No Children" or "Adults Only." Many of the

family status cases are based on illegal advertisements or blatant denials, as the
following examples demonstrate.

> The Daily Newspaper permitted discriminatory advertising for rental of a single-
> family home to be carried in its classified section. The rental ad stipulates "no
> children."

> Bill, the owner, told fair housing testers that he advertised the unit as a one bed-
> room unit, when in fact it was a three bedroom unit, so that families with chil-
> dren would not call about the unit.

> In January 2000, Katrina Simons bought the building that Mindy, a single
> mother, had been living in for a number of years. Katrina Simons renewed the
> leases of all the tenants who were in the building before she bought it, except for
> some of the tenants with children. Katrina told Mindy's Section 8 Case Manager
> that "there are too many children on the property."

In each of the above cases the investigation revealed that family status discrimination occurred. The fact that individual housing providers and newspapers still run illegal, discriminatory advertisements suggest that there is a
lack of knowledge about fair housing laws and a general social acceptance,
or at least tolerance, of discrimination against families and individuals with
children.

Interestingly, some housing providers denied families with younger children while others denied older children. It appears that some housing
providers may associate noise with younger children and property damage
and delinquency with older children, especially boys. However, other housing
providers associated noise, property damage, and delinquency with all children, regardless of age or sex.

Although it is not clear why some housing providers associate problems
with children of certain ages while others are concerned with any and all children, it is quite obvious from the case data that the sex of the parent matters.
In the 1990s, which is the time period that encompasses the bulk of these
cases, single mothers were characterized as a serious social problem and threat
to domestic stability (Hancock 2004). As one landlord told a fair housing au-
ditor, "rental is not possible for a single woman with two children."

> The property is near where my sister lives. I saw a sign in front of the property
> regarding the availability for rental. There was a number and I called and left a
> message on [the landlord's] answering machine. The person I spoke to identified
> himself as Rich and during the conversation I let Rich know I had two children,
> a boy and a girl. Rich said he could not rent to me where a boy and girl would
> share the same bedroom.

Doris' case highlights the connection between gender, housing, and work. Later in her testimony, Doris discussed the importance of finding a place "near where my sister lives," because her sister watched her children while she worked.

The client-prejudice hypothesis suggests that housing providers may deny racial minorities housing out of fear of losing its white client base (Yinger 1998). In many of the cases the housing provider either directly or indirectly referenced noise and/or damage that children cause and their concern for other tenants living around families with children. However, like other forms of discrimination, these are assumptions based on stereotypes. Housing providers are permitted to evict disruptive families with children just as they are permitted to do so with individuals and families without children. More importantly, discrimination against families with children has a disparate impact on women, especially African American women. Indeed, as observed in figure 11.2, 84 percent of the family status charges were filed by African Americans. Therefore, fear of noise or delinquency, in many situations, may have more to do with the race of the children than simply the fact that they are children.

> Testers were told that the owner did not want children in the building. Black testers were told nothing was available, while white testers were told units were immediately available.

As the above example from an investigative file illustrates, there may,be an interaction affect of race and family status occurring. Other cases involved race and family status discrimination that occurred after the individual or families were housed. The following is the initial charge filed by Bernadette, a single mother who is African American.

> I believe that the manager of Two Pines Apartments, Fanny, treated my family, along with other African American families, differently because of our race. Each and every time there was an incident in the complex Fanny would blame the black children. Fanny would not respond to notices of damage done by white children. My children were blamed for things that happened while we were not in the complex. She reports these things to Section 8, which almost caused me to loose my Section 8 assistance. One of my white neighbors had a pool party without permission and her lease was renewed, while I was advised that my lease would not be renewed. Fanny complained to me about my children being too loud, yet the white children could horse around in the pool and make all kinds of noise and she would not say anything to them. She refused to give me a reference, which seriously impacted my ability to find assisted housing.

Distinct rules and policies regarding "play" and noise were applied differentially to children based on their race. However, the consequences went beyond rules children had to follow. Bernadette's lease was not renewed and management provided her a poor reference, which subsequently made her housing search more difficult. The following example illustrates a similar intersection of race and family status.

> Cathy Carter, White, viewed the house for rent, talked to the landlord, Gary Martin, about the lease and told him that she had children and a husband, who was at work. Gary Martin later called Cathy's husband, Desmond Carter, who is Black, and informed him that they got the house. After Desmond got off work, they met with Gary Martin to sign the lease. When Desmond approached Gary Martin in front of the house, Gary told Desmond that the house was rented already. Cathy approached Gary and stated "yes, you rented it to me and this is my husband, Desmond, who you spoke to over the phone." Gary Martin would not accept money from Desmond Carter but accepted it from Cathy. Also, Gary Martin would not allow Desmond to sign the rental agreement. The following day Gary Martin showed up at the Carter's home and returned the deposit he accepted from Cathy, stating he couldn't sleep all night because he was worried about their children walking down the long lane, which usually "gets snowed in pretty bad."

During the OCRC investigation, Gary Martin told the investigator that Cathy Carter misrepresented herself because she didn't tell him that she had a black husband and four black children. Gary was willing to rent to Cathy, who is white, until he saw her husband and her children. However, the initial reason Gary gave Cathy for denying her rental, which other landlords in other cases gave as well, was his concern for her children's "safety."

In general, the data suggest that poor African American women with children are more disadvantaged in the housing market than other groups, and that these disadvantages are rooted in stereotypes about these women. The persistence of such stereotypes should not come as a surprise, really. Research examining fifteen hundred race-related articles and images in twenty-eight metropolitan newspapers found that "Nearly 32% of all images in the series were of people of color in their 'social pathology' roles: welfare recipients, single mothers, public housing residents, and high school drop-outs" (Drew 2005, 21). Women of color were depicted through stereotypical norms, such as "welfare queen" and "baby machine." Evidence of these stereotypes and their potential impacts are certainly present in the housing cases referred to in this chapter.

Our research supports the findings of the individual audit studies, noted previously, while extending their insights to issues of sex and family status discrimination in housing. By doing so, we not only reveal the disadvantages that women face in the housing market, we also reveal the complex interplay between sex, race, social class, and family status.

Conclusion

Women face many disadvantages in the housing market. Not only do they represent the majority of sex discrimination cases, they also represent the overwhelming majority of family status discrimination cases. In addition, women are subjected to sexual harassment in and around their homes. Vulnerability to sexual harassment, as well as the other forms of discrimination discussed in this chapter, is especially high for African American and poor women. This is likely to do to disparities and discrimination that women in general, and poor women and women of color in particular, face in the labor market, as well as the cultural stereotypes that continue to be attached to these women.

Most of the discrimination that women face in the housing market comes from landlord and residential managers, who often perceive certain women as unable or unfit to physically or economically care for their homes. Other landlords or managers do not refuse to rent to women they perceive of as economically vulnerable. Yet, as many examples highlighted, they nevertheless use their control of housing to take advantage of these women in other ways.

This chapter began by looking at sex discrimination in housing. The story, however, goes beyond sex. Our analyses of sex discrimination cases, and particularly their complexities as revealed in case files, notes, and witness and victims' account, reveals that housing discrimination often involves a complex intersection of sex, race, family status, and social class. Race is certainly fundamental, as are its associations with social class, even in processes of sex and family status discrimination. Correspondingly, scholars and policy makers alike must be cognizant of these social statuses, the ways they intersect, and the implications for inequality generally and that pertaining to housing.

Notes

1. Of the sex and family cases, females account for 66 percent, males 12 percent, couples or households 7 percent, and fair housing groups 15 percent

2. As discussed earlier, fair housing groups can file cases and often conduct familial status audits. Of the serious familial status cases filed, 37 percent were filed by fair housing groups, second only to individual women (39.5 percent). Research is currently being conducted to determine who the cases were filed on behalf of, if a bona fide complainant was involved.

3. City and other local governments are permitted to have reasonable occupancy standards based on the square footage of a dwelling. In addition, housing providers are not permitted to deny children for "safety reasons." For example, one landlord denied a family with children rental because the apartment "had a second floor balcony," which he felt was dangerous for small children.

Conclusion

Throughout this whole ordeal, my education, experience, and knowledge
all seemed to have been of no consequence to the individuals in charge.

—Nancy Wilson, forty-five-year-old nurse

SOCIAL STRATIFICATION IS MORE than simply a remnant of historical exclusion
played out through slowly declining intergenerational disadvantages in, for
instance, education, skills, job experience, or wealth. It is also much more than
the culmination of individual proclivities toward work, residence, or education patterned by cultural lag and socialization processes. While individual
pathways, attributes, and preferences are unquestionably relevant, they are
only influential within the bounds and constraints of organizational and interactional social closure dynamics, including but not limited to contemporary discrimination.

Sociologists, at least in their theorizing, have largely concurred about the
importance of social closure generally, and the rigidity of social statuses in
particular. Yet, scholarship on persistent inequalities has analytically priori-
tized not processes of closure but instead the ways in which subordinate group
attributes (e.g., education, preferences, etc.) matter for contemporary status
and well-being. As noted by Tomaskovic-Devey, Thomas, and Johnson (2005)
in the preface to this book, this tendency is driven by the adoption of human
capital and status attainment assumptions pertaining to stratification—assumptions that, explicitly or by default, treat institutional and organizational
processes as relatively neutral. The social scientist is correspondingly left with
a theoretical orientation wherein individuals are conceived of as competing in

a largely meritocratic environment. Race or gender disadvantages, to the extent they exist, are merely residues. Racist and sexist structures, ideologies, differential organizational and institutional treatment, and discrimination by gatekeeping actors fall out of theoretical and empirical sight.

There are certainly important exceptions pertaining to the influence of queuing, job networks, segregation, and constraints on residential and workplace mobility.[1] Such work—work that indeed takes closure seriously in its theoretical orientation—nevertheless remains hard pressed to explicitly capture social closure processes, including, most fundamentally, discrimination. It is perhaps for this reason that that recent multi-methodological (see especially Pager 2003; Pager and Quillian 2005; Galster 1990b; Royster 2003) and qualitative, attitudinal work (notable in this regard are Bonilla-Silva 2003; Feagin 1991; Feagin and Eckberg 1980; Moss and Tilly 2001; Royster 2003; Pager 2003) has generated excitement in the field by providing a momentary window into the very discriminatory processes that scholars have only been able to speculate about.

As noted at the outset of this book, the sheer lack of data on, and limited capacity of researchers to gain entry into, everyday discriminatory encounters is a significant source of the problem. Lack of theoretical rigor is just as central. Indeed, with few exceptions (but see Feagin and Eckberg 1980; Reskin 2000, 2003), we seldom see scholars grapple conceptually with the questions of discrimination and social closure, as well as their forms and consequences. This may lead to theoretical and analytic blind spots. Indeed, taken-for-granted assumptions may develop. These are assumptions that lead us to believe that the forms of inequality that we can most easily measure in some objective fashion (e.g., wages) are most important, even for the subjective experiences of the groups and individuals we study.

From a "theoretical strength" standpoint, few studies have been able to convincingly demonstrate precisely how the process of discrimination, often inferred by an empirical association between a given x and a given y, is playing a part. To be sure, establishing causal associations, a primary goal in much stratification research, is essential for gauging support and the relative strength of a given theoretical argument. Equally important from a theory construction and validation standpoint, however, is the explication of process—the central goal of this book.

Outlined below are key themes that emerged from the chapters and their respective analyses. Findings, particularly with regard to racial and gendered processes of social closure, are discussed relative to existing research literatures. Confounding status intersections and potential variations by context are revisited as well. In this regard, the analyses reported throughout speak to complexities pertaining to status, discrimination, and social closure, as well as to historical and macrostructural dynamics that our analyses visit to some extent.

While our findings speak to specialty area literatures, they also inform sociological theorizing and conceptions of inequality more broadly. Broader lessons pertaining to human agency, discretion, and action in the stratification process are garnered from these analyses, as is insight pertaining to organizational constraint and culpability. We conclude by discussing these contributions, as well as the ways in which the processes of employment and residential discrimination represent an important snapshot of structural, interactional, and ideological processes within society at large.

Social Closure and the Study of Discrimination

In the introduction and chapter 1, we addressed the need to conceive of social closure broadly rather than constrained within the bounds of a specific outcome of interest (e.g., wages, mobility, etc.). Particularly important, with implications for both race and gender inequality in the contexts of both employment and housing, are issues of institutional access, treatment, and status hierarchy maintenance. Conceiving of social closure in this three-pronged manner broadens one's orientation toward the study of inequality and discrimination. Without doing so, we run the risk of falling victim to false divides in the literature—divides between those who suggest declines in ascriptive forms of inequality and those who see manifestations of race and gender inequality in most facets of everyday life.

Such divides exist, in our view, precisely because of limited discussion of the multidimensional nature of social closure. On the one hand, some focus on gender or race stratification within a given institutional context, captured through objectively measurable indicators of well-being (e.g., wages, mobility or position, residence). Others, however, remain more interested in inequalities played out in everyday interactions and encounters—encounters most often captured through retrospective narratives and qualitative interviewing. Finally, some analyses take as their principal foci institutional access, relying on either audit designs or life course narratives. What results are three distinct research foci that may reach quite varying conclusions—conclusions shaped by the form of closure that is being addressed. A classic example of such a divide is the question of whether race is declining in significance.[2]

By conceiving of social closure broadly from the outset, we leave open the possibility that inadequately theorized processes of discrimination and closure may be captured. The data we have employed throughout is especially notable in this regard, given its richness on the question of injury—not to mention the significant detail afforded on precisely what happened and its consequences. For both race and sex, discrimination impacts institutional access to both housing and employment. It also influences treatment within a given institutional environment once access has been obtained. And, finally, as revealed by the prevalence of harassment cases within both residential and workplace settings, status hierarchy maintenance is clearly an important part of the social closure story.

The General Character of Race and Sex Discrimination

In some ways, processes of social closure in employment and housing arenas seem quite parallel. Both minorities and women continue to face barriers in institutional access and treatment. Perhaps even more apparent in our analyses, both experience significant harassment within everyday workplace and residential encounters. This is particularly informative, given the virtual neglect of this form of inequality in standard empirical examinations of employment and housing inequality.

While harassment in both arenas makes up a significant portion of both race and gender discrimination cases, it is also woven throughout other discrimination claims—claims pertaining to differential mobility in employment, and especially expulsion from one's residence or job. This seems to suggest that, even in the contemporary era, some workplace and residential environments are highly charged in a race and gender sense and in ways that stratification research has not been able to empirically capture. In fact, it may be the case that by prioritizing individual background attributes in our modeling of objective and material workplace and residential outcomes, we are missing important, albeit sometimes informal, group dynamics that have very significant consequences for well-being—consequences that are perhaps even more significant to the victim, according to our qualitative accounts, than the objectively measurable inequalities that social scientists have tended to focus on.

Beyond experiencing harassment, African Americans and women also witness the application of differential criteria by gatekeepers—gatekeepers with significant discretion in both workplace and residential contexts. In employment, the invoking of soft skill criteria works to the disadvantage of women and minorities, who are often seen as less dependable albeit for distinct reasons (which we discuss momentarily). Indeed, two key insights emerged on the issue of managerial discretion. First, and quite consistent with what more quantitative scholars have inferred for some time, the use of soft skill criteria impacts women and minorities in job mobility. Wilson and McBrier (2005) refer to this as the particularistic mobility thesis. Others employing quantitative modeling, such as Huffman and Cohen (2004) and Prokos and Padavic (2005), concur that differential treatment by race and sex must be playing a role in high-status job attainment, as denoted below.

> Discrimination against workers—especially exclusion from better-paying jobs— is an important mechanism for the effect of black population size on the racial wage gap. (Huffman and Cohen 2004)

> We found the pay gap for scientists and engineers scarcely abated throughout the 1990s but that has less to do with an earnings glass ceiling barrier than with the likely presence of other, unmeasured, types of discrimination. (Prokos and Padavic 2005)

As many of our qualitative materials attest, gatekeeping actors exercise considerable agency when making promotion and hiring decisions, and invoke a relatively flexible set of filters for "who fits the job best" and "who might be best for the promotion." Given specific stereotypical assumptions about women and minorities, such subjectivity hardly tends to work in their favor.

Second, discretion is activated not only in the course of hiring or mobility decisions, but in the day-to-day monitoring of employees. This, according to our results, seems to have serious implications for women and minority employees who are policed more closely, and sanctioned more often and severely. In a very real sense, this is targeted workplace bullying, often carried out under the guise of following organizational procedures and rules.[3] The problem, of course, as many of our cases revealed, is when organizational procedures, policies, and penalties are followed only when convenient and when disparately applied to particular individuals and status groups. Disparate policing, characteristic especially of the race discrimination cases we examined, no doubt explains why discriminatory firing is so prevalent in these data.

Housing discrimination is also replete with moments of discretion that work to the significant disadvantage of minorities and women. The consequences, as revealed in both chapters 9 and 11, include both exclusion from housing and various forms of nonexclusionary discrimination. Landlords, complex managers, neighbors, and even banks and insurance companies, it appears, draw from biased assumptions pertaining to the economic security of prospective female and minority homeowners or tenants, differentiate in terms of terms and conditions, and also harass. It is notable that such things continue to occur despite nearly forty years of federal fair housing legislation and oversight.

Uncovering processes of housing exclusion, as we have done, informs prior work on segregation patterns and why they persist. Analyzing nonexclusionary forms of social closure in housing, not to mention sex-based discrimination, are two unique contributions of this project. These contributions broaden sociological understanding of the real complexities of housing discrimination, its forms, its implications for minority and female well-being.

The Gendered Character of Discrimination

Despite similarities in the realities of harassment, expulsion from work, or the denial of housing, the qualitative data clearly denote a racialized and gendered character to what we are describing. For women, several issues and patterns stand out. First, much of the discrimination women face is gendered. Stereotypical assumptions about women are employed by gatekeeping actors in employment and housing, women are often sexualized in both contexts, and issues of dependability linger in the minds of landlords and employers. In the aforementioned regards, we have seen that soft skill criteria and gatekeeper evaluation often work to the disadvantage of women over men in the mobility process, sometimes subtly and sometimes quite explicitly. Several of the employment and housing examples indeed denote how powerful actors periodically feel that women "just don't belong" in certain work environments, or are "just not dependable" as tenants without a male counterpart.

Maternity and pregnancy, in the case of employment, and family status, in the case of housing, likewise stand out as pivotal discriminatory issues, particularly in chapters 3, 5, and 6. Frankly, we were surprised at the extent to which this was the case. Clearly, maternity and pregnancy (or even potential future maternity or pregnancy) are considerations that some employers consider during hiring, when making promotion decisions, and in arbitrary firing. Such is the case within our data *despite the intent and goals of female targets to remain employed.* These are, in essence, stories of exclusion, forced demotion, and being pushed out of the labor market. Such realities, evidenced in countless case files, fly in the face of the neoclassic economic assumption that women merely choose, via socialization or life-course decisions, to opt out of productive work or mobility contests. In housing, discrimination on the basis of family status overwhelmingly impacts women, particularly women with small children. Such women, as denoted vividly in chapter 11, are vulnerable to exclusion, but also may become targets of sexual harassment by complex managers.

The fact that women are often sexualized in employment and residential contexts, either through general harassment or more obviously through explicit sexual harassment, is also clear. Indeed, approximately one-fourth of the randomly selected and context-coded cases pertaining to sex discrimination revealed some level of sexual harassment on the job. As chapter 4 denoted, the process of sexual harassment is complex, often stretching out over a significant period of time and usually evolving for the worse. Admittedly, there are workplaces (not represented in our data) wherein there is little tolerance for such conduct, and perpetrators may bear the brunt of organizational sanctions. Female efforts to resolve the harassment on their own, the significant psychological and job-related consequences of such harassment, and the virtual lack or organizational response in our data are nevertheless noteworthy, not to mention quite troubling. Somewhat surprisingly, and maybe even more disconcerting to some, is the fact that such harassment also occurs in women's residential lives. Residential complex managers are most often the perpetrators of sexual harassment in housing, and this proves especially troubling given their access to female targets' homes.

The Racial Character of Discrimination

Racial minorities, or in the case of our study in particular, African Americans, experience significant levels of discretionary sanctioning and policing while on their jobs. While some of this is tied to harassment on the job, there is no doubt that such policing is playing a large part in the levels of expulsion (or firing) of African American employees. Both African American men and women, as our examples have demonstrated, seem to be systematically targeted for oversight by supervisors—something one female victim referred to as "just watching." In some cases this targeted attention appears to be part of a plan to terminate the employee in question from the outset. In others, disparate oversight and then more harsh sanctions when policy is violated appear to be shaped by assumptions regarding black employees, including the view that they are more aggressive or inclined toward laziness while on the job.

In either scenario, the issue is disparate enforcement and policing relative to organizationally defined, "legitimate" policies and procedures. Indeed, it is not the policy itself that is in question, rather the extent to which it is followed and by whom. Here, again, discretion and arbitrary decision making by immediate supervisors is particularly key. The consequences, beyond the most obvious ones pertaining to demotion or job loss, are numerous and often devastating social psychologically. Victims become paranoid, perhaps with good reason, that they are being watched by several employees, absenteeism goes up as a result of stress, and in many cases workers relate ways in which their overall sense of dignity has been assaulted. They also recognize quite clearly the race-based nature of such treatment given observations that other employees routinely undertake the behavior in question, yet are never penalized.

Particularistic mobility processes and the invocation of soft skill criteria in job access and promotions are also revealed in our analyses of race, particularly in chapters 1, 5, 6, and 7. Here we see those in more powerful positions defining desirable job qualities informally or on the spot, and in a manner that undermines minority hiring and promotion. Whether such soft skills, such as communicative ability, confidence, and the ability to work with others, are important for a given job is a matter of debate. What is not in question, however, is the problematic nature of using such criteria arbitrarily to exclude some at the cost of others, particularly where there is either racist intent from outset or subjective interpretation invoked on the spot.

The use of particularistic criteria in evaluation is hardly isolated to the arena of employment. As chapters 9 and 10 note so clearly, landlords, complex owners, banks, and insurance companies also clearly employ differential criteria to distinguish between and discriminate against potential tenants or homeowners. Again, some of the examples we draw from suggested a preexisting racist intent on the part of gatekeepers. In other cases, the intent is unclear. There is nevertheless good reason to suspect that assumptions about black families, black females with small children, or single black males play a part in proclivities toward outright exclusion, steering, or more general differential treatment.

Quite notable throughout is the contemporary persistence of race-based discriminatory harassment—harassment that occurs both on the job and in minorities' everyday residential lives. Overt racist acts by coworkers, managers, neighbors, and landlords continue to occur, and obviously have profound consequences for the targets, including fear, insult, and a sense of indignity. Yet, such harassment does not have to be explicitly racist in tone. Rather, it may take the form of general taunting, systematic isolation on the job, or neglect of employee or tenant needs. This breeds frustration, no doubt, as well as overall stress. It is notable, throughout cases of harassment, that the harassment is often carried out over a significant time frame and that victims often attempt to rectify the situation themselves. It is often only after other options are exhausted, and a desperation point is reached, that an external discrimination charge is filed.

Processes of harassment are all but invisible in contemporary scholarship on employment and housing inequalities. The exception is recent work by Bonilla-Silva (2003) and Feagin and McKinney (2003). These scholars, relying on interviewing, describe the ways in which race is interwoven in everyday encounters and interactions. Our analyses, which draw from actual case histories of discrimination, support many of their insights, with a specific focus on workplace and residential contexts. Such harassment is clearly an affront to the victim's sense of dignity and is a formidable component to the social closure process itself.

One of the more interesting patterns revealed, in chapter 2 especially, is the disjuncture between what organizations say unfolded versus what actually occurred from the charging party's point of view, corroborated by eyewitness and investigator accounts. Whether we are talking about employers or residential complex owners, we see powerful agents consistently and overwhelmingly claim neutrality and objectivity, if not meritocracy, in their responses to charges of discrimination.[4] Referring to the treatment of the employee or tenant, the suggestion is typically made that "all are held to the same standard," that the victim simply did not meet the required criteria, or that misconduct on the part of the victim is really what drove the organizational decision. But, as we have seen, differential race-based treatment prevailed in the case determination, and the organization is either directly culpable or indirectly so via one of its agents. What is particularly notable here are the ways in which organizations themselves invoke claims of complete color blindness and meritocracy so prevalent in the larger society, even in the face of discrimination that clearly suggests otherwise.

We temper our conclusions pertaining to race-based patterns with the recognition that our case data are largely limited to African Americans given the state from which they are drawn. There is, however, little reason to believe that the patterns highlighted would not play out similarly in contexts that are largely Caucasian and Latino, for instance. In fact, we believe that many of the discriminatory processes revealed in our analyses—particularistic criteria, disparate policing of racial/ethnic minorities, and harassment on the job—likely prevail and shape minority employment and housing status in most U.S. contexts. The flavor of particularistic criteria may take on distinct forms, especially for language minorities. Yet, the role of discretionary decision making among gatekeepers will, in all likelihood, remain central. We hope that scholars will be able to access similar data in the future, but from state contexts with varying racial and ethnic compositions to see whether or not this is the case.

Contextual and Intersectional Complexities

Although there are racialized and gendered patterns to the processes we are describing, there are also contextual and intersectional dimensions that are no less sociologically relevant. Labor market variations in employment discrimination are afforded some attention in chapters 1, 3, and 5, while potential variations by compositional contexts are addressed explicitly in chapters 6 and

10. Although not our explicit theoretical focus in this book, such foci reflect our acknowledgment and effort to remain cognizant of structure in the face of more micro-oriented processes.

Interesting are variations in discrimination by economic sector generally, and between public and private sectors in particular. Discrimination toward women and racial minorities is quite pronounced overall in the low-wage service sector, as revealed earlier in figures 1.1 and 3.2. Yet, women and minorities are quite disproportionately represented in this sector to begin with. Once adjusted for sectoral representation overall, we see that discrimination charges are largely proportionate to overall female and minority representation. For minorities, the same pattern holds for the core sector, while for women, discrimination in the core sector—which contains traditionally male employment—remains disproportionately higher. All sectors, with the exception of the public (or state) sector, reveal disparate discriminatory firings relative to female and minority representation.

Chapter 5 teases out public–private distinctions in informative ways, showing how allocative discrimination in particular is more likely in the private sphere (figure 5.1). Discriminatory mobility processes, however, appear to be manifested more obviously in the public sector, while discriminatory expulsion is much more common in the private economic sector. It seems that employers in the private sector view workers as more expendable.

Such sectoral patterns should be interpreted with caution, to some degree, given potential biases in our data in terms of who files discrimination charges. Indeed, we have no doubt that such biases exist—biases that probably inflate public-sector claims (given higher education levels and more explicit promotion ladders) and that underestimate private-sector reports of discrimination.[5] Underestimation is particularly likely in the low-wage service sector, which hosts lower-status workers with less political knowledge of their legal rights. Results are nevertheless suggestive and informative relative to research that grapples with sectoral variations in minority and female job status and occupational rewards such as wages (for instance, Cohen 1988; Huffman and Cohen 2004).

Chapters 6 and 10 address the question of compositional effects and specifically whether or not race composition (in the case of housing and employment) or gender composition (in the case of employment) shape the degree and forms of discrimination that individuals and groups may encounter. As suggested in both chapters, the composition of a workplace or neighborhood will, by default, shape the odds of discriminatory encounters given the simple likelihood of contact. In isolated scenarios, where there is but one or a few minority or female employees, individuals are more easily identified and targeted for gendered treatment or heightened policing and oversight. Where integration prevails, so too may explicit competition and its manifestation in the form of mobility contests (and the associated discriminatory use of soft skills by gatekeepers in employment) or outright harassment (in employment and housing). Chapter 10 revealed an interesting third scenario that pertains to race and housing, namely segregated African American areas. Here, discrimination has less to do with systematic harassment or exclusion, and more to do with economic exploitation of a relatively vulnerable, poorer population. More analyses of what composition means to individuals and their interactions in the realms of work and housing are clearly warranted.

Analyses of intersectionalities, or the ways in which race, gender, and even social class and family status create unique configurations of discriminatory experiences, are explicitly dealt with in chapters 7, 8, and 11. These analyses reflect our sociological viewpoint that inequality is a complex phenomena, shaped simultaneously by multiple statuses and identities, and with implications for both how victims interpret discrimination and how perpetrators enact it. For women in employment, the focus of chapter 7, we find disparate patterns of discrimination based on both race and occupational status, as well as distinct interpretations of that discrimination. Black women are much more likely to experience and interpret discrimination in race rather than gender terms, perhaps owing to the fact that they are more likely to be in sex-segregated environments. Discriminatory firing and mobility processes prevail for these women, regardless of social-class status. For white women, in contrast, their sex is the primary foundation of the discriminatory experience, although notable variations exist in terms of how that discrimination is enacted. Pregnancy and maternity issues clearly stand out for middle- and upper-class females, and less so for lower-status white women.

Black men, as revealed in chapter 8, face a precarious historical legacy in employment, only complicated by contemporary experiences with discrimination. Particularly notable are social-class differences, captured by occupational status breakdowns. Lower-class black males face disparate levels of discriminatory expulsion related to disparate policing and sanctioning by managers and supervisors. Given their disproportionate representation at lower occupational levels, this perhaps explains why unstable career histories and unemployment remain such significant issues for black men. Middle-status black males, who work in skilled and semi-skilled occupational trades that are traditionally white and male, experience higher than average rates of harassment on the job, while those in the higher occupational echelons experience most commonly discrimination in mobility.

Finally, and no less notable, is the conflation of sex, race, social class, and family status in analyses of housing discrimination in chapter 11. Here we find disadvantages that are extraordinarily hard to dissect, that make these women particularly vulnerable to unscrupulous landlords, and that trigger a host of discriminatory behaviors including most obviously exclusion but also harassment. Seldom has sex and family status been considered in sociological research on housing inequality, and even rarer have been efforts to address such inequality with recognition of its complex, intersectional nature. Clearly, in the case of our analyses, discriminators draw from broad conceptions of what might be the ideal tenant. Poor black women with children are on the losing end of such culturally driven views, with consequences for housing denial and exclusion.

Theorizing Social Closure and Inequality

Beyond more concrete patterns and lessons, the analyses of discrimination presented in this book speak to several broader theoretical issues that warrant consideration, and that indeed should inform future research on topics of social closure and stratification, broadly. These theoretical issues center on (1) the role of human agency in our conceptions of inequality, (2) the role of organizational structure, constraint, and culpability in interaction and in the dynamics of stratification, and (3) the embeddedness of inequality in societal context. These discussions bring us full circle to the theoretical framing presented at the outset, and hopefully provide a framework from which future scholars can draw.

Human Agency and Inequality in Action

By virtue of the data that have been employed in the preceding pages and what they communicate, it is obvious that human action and agency are part and parcel of stratification maintenance, creation, and challenge. As the qualitative materials so poignantly suggest, human beings actively engage in reifying inequality within organizational and locational environments, and victims of inequality are much more than mere recipients of differential treatment. Victims, instead, often go through a series of steps to try to counter the inequality they are experiencing, including negotiation, avoidance, confrontation, and, in the case of filing a discrimination suit, politically and legally fighting what is unjust.

Although these points may seem all too obvious, it should be noted that the acknowledgment of such agency within sociological scholarship is relatively rare. Indeed, the distinctly human behavioral component is seldom woven into analyses of stratification aside from, perhaps, ethnographic analyses or research pertaining to collective behavior and social movements. This is unfortunate. Introducing some dimension of agency into our theoretical models provides leverage for talking about processes of inequality (rather then just relations and associations) and helps highlight ways in which individuals and groups play a part in producing (or reproducing) the structures within which they exist. Moreover, and perhaps more directly, introducing agency and interaction into overly structural accounts of inequality tempers relatively deterministic sociological claims.

The construct of social closure itself, when taken seriously, pushes us as researchers to highlight how interactions within and between social groups may be directed toward closure or resistance (usurpation). Such has been the principal aim of the preceding chapters. This is not to suggest, however, that scholars simply resort to interactional and ground-level analyses of inequality and human agency. This would be problematic as well. As noted within our theoretical framing in the introduction to this book, interactions pertaining to stratification which entail some agency by the actors involved are fundamentally constrained, at least to some degree, by the organizational, institutional, and even cultural structures that enfold them.

Organizational Structure, Constraint, and Culpability

As theoretically important as it is, the introduction of agency and action/interaction into our conceptions of stratification can render sociological theorizing relatively useless unless the framing, discussion, and analyses of relevant processes are placed within context. Indeed, without doing so, we resort simply to individual, unique stories with little in the way of generalizable lessons, theoretical growth, and predictive power. It is for this very reason that we embed our own analyses and conclusions regarding the interactional nature of discrimination and the agency of perpetrators and victims within broader research traditions emphasizing the potential influence of labor markets, compositional contexts, workplace structures, and residential environments.

As noted in some of our analyses, such structures may very well shape and condition the nature of discriminatory encounters. Although our intent from the outset has been to shed light on relevant interactions on the part of human actors, given that this is where the literature is sorely lacking, it is our position that such interactions and expressions of agency are fundamentally bounded and conditioned by the structures within which they exist. Workplace supervisors and landlords, for instance, activate discretion and potentially discriminatory criteria, but only to the extent that organizational structures, procedures, and rules give them the flexibility to do so. By default, this implicates organizations and institutions themselves in the inequalities that we have described. Conversely, there are certainly organizations and businesses, not represented in our data, wherein mandates and formalized procedures constrain actors—actors perhaps with a proclivity to discriminate—from doing so.

Obviously there is an interplay between expressions of human agency/discretion and the environments within which they are embedded. And, it is at the crux of this interplay where the most interesting sociological questions lie. How does the structure of workplaces or neighborhoods, for instance, alter the nature of individual and group interactions in a manner that reifies or mitigates prevailing stratification arrangements and social status hierarchies? Or, how might processes of social closure and related microlevel interactions reinforce or alter structural arrangements themselves? Whether one builds one's research question from micro to macro or from macro to micro, or defines the question itself in terms of agency to structure or structure to agency, does not really matter. What is more paramount is that theorists and researchers alike make explicit the ways in which human action, conditioned and constrained to some degree by structure, is responsible for the patterns they describe.

Inequality and Discrimination in Societal Context

The patterns, processes, and forms of inequality and discrimination that we have described are far reaching and beyond specific considerations pertaining to work and housing. There is no reason to believe that the differential treatment we have uncovered does not apply equally to other institutional domains including, for instance, education, politics, medical care, policing, and legal/judicial decisions. We know through prior research that race and gender inequalities exist within these arenas. Would it thus not make sense that gatekeeping discretion and differential evaluative processes might be contributing to these disparities? We believe so, and leave it to other scholars to distinguish precisely how.

Beyond formal institutional and organizational dynamics, many of the lessons garnered from our empirical analyses of employment and housing discrimination also hold implications for everyday encounters and interactions—encounters and interactions that may not be explicitly shaped or constrained by formalized rules, but that are no less influenced by broader societal and cultural views regarding women and racial ethnic minorities. Our findings suggest that actors within organizational, institutional, and even local environments oftentimes filter evaluations of others and their interactions with others through preset cultural views and stereotypes. Such beliefs are by no means the creation of a given workplace or neighborhood, but rather of societal culture and history. The implication of this is that all social interaction—formal and informal, context-specific or not—has the potential to recreate status hierarchies whether or not the parties involved are aware of it.[6] Remaining cognizant of any such preconceptions, particularly in the discretion we all utilize on a daily basis, may go a long way in ensuring that our own behaviors are not contributing to the sorts of inequalities that shape the everyday lives of women and minorities.

Notes

1. For examples of important discussions of closure processes, see especially Kmec (2003); Padavic and Reskin (2002); Tomaskovic-Devey (1993a, 1993b); Tomaskovic-Devey and Skaggs 2002; Martin (2004); Royster (2003); Petersen and Saporta (2004); Wilson (1997); Wilson and McBrier (2005).

2. Scholars embroiled in this particular debate often prioritize distinct empirical foci and methodologies, for instance. Some, using aggregate data on income, have suggested that indeed race is declining in significance. Others, focusing on everyday discriminatory encounters on the street, in neighborhoods, and in workplaces, in contrast, see race status as paramount to one's lived experience. These are, however, apples and oranges. The former is gauging a perhaps slow and steady decline in the direct effects of ascription in employment. The second is gauging whether status hierarchy maintenance on a day-to-day interactional level is still occurring. Both may, in fact, be correct.

3. For a broader discussion of workplace bullying and relevant organization and interactional processes, see Hodson, Roscigno and Lopez (2006).

4. Investigative materials often show that this is, in fact, not the case, otherwise a case would not receive a probable cause finding.

5. It is quite difficult to gauge where such biases may lie. To do so perfectly would necessitate information on all real world incidents of discrimination—something that will never be available. Indeed, there is every reason to believe that discrimination is much more prevalent than even our data can reveal, and that victims more often than not either never file charges or do not realize to begin with that they have been discriminated against.

6. This is precisely a point that Bonilla-Silva (2003) touches upon in his analyses of white attitudes toward racial inequality in particular. By adopting broader cultural notions of merit and a race-blind society, whites relieve themselves of culpability, and correspondingly detach from any questioning of their own views and potential treatment of racial/ethnic minorities.

Bibliography

Acker, Joan. 1990. "Hierarchies, Jobs, Bodies: A Theory of Gendered Organizations." *Gender and Society* 4: 139–58.

———. 1999. "Rewriting Class, Race and Gender: Problems in Feminist Rethinking." Pp. 44–69 in *Revisioning Gender*, edited by Myra Marx Ferree, Judith Lorber and Beth B. Hess. Thousand Oaks, CA: Sage.

Anderson, Elijah. 2001. "The Social Situation of the Black Executive: Black and White Identities in the Corporate World." Pp. 405–36 in *Problem of the Century: Racial Stratification in the Untied States*, edited by E. Anderson and D. S. Massey. New York: Russell Sage.

Anderson, Karen Tucker. 1982. "Last Hired, First Fired: Black Women Workers During World War II. *Journal of American History* 69:82–97.

Arrow, Kenneth. 1973. "The Theory of Discrimination." In *Discrimination in Labor Markets*, edited by Orley Ashenfelter and Albert Rees. Princeton, NJ: Princeton University Press.

Baldi, Stephane, and Debra Branch McBrier. 1997. "Do Determinants of Promotion Differ for Black and Whites?" *Work and Occupations* 24:478–97.

Balser, Deborah. 2002. "Agency in Organizational Inequality: Organizational Behavior and Individual Perception of Discrimination." *Work and Occupations* 29:137–65.

Becker, Gary S. 1971. *The Economics of Discrimination*. Chicago: University of Chicago Press.

Becker, Henry Jay. 1980. "Racial Segregation Among Places of Employment." *Social Forces* 58:761–76.

Beggs, John J. 1995. "The Institutional Environment: Implications for Race and Gender Inequality in the U.S. Labor Market." *American Sociological Review* 60:612–33.

Beggs, John J., Wayne J. Villemez, and Ruth Arnold. 1997. "Black Population Concentration and Black–White Inequality: Expanding the Consideration of Place and Space Effects." *Social Forces* 76:65–91

Beller, Andrea H. 1982. "Occupational Segregation by Sex: Determinants and Changes. *The Journal of Human Resources* 17:371–92.

Bendick Jr., Marc, and Charles W. Jackson. 1994. "Measuring Employment Discrimination Through Controlled Experiments." *Review of Black Political Economy* 23:25–49.

Bendick Jr., Marc, Charles W. Jackson, and Victor A. Reinoso. 1994. "Measuring Employment Discrimination Through Controlled Experiments." *Review of Black Political Economy* 23:25–48.

Benokraitis, Nijole V., and Joe R. Feagin. 1995. *Modern Sexism: Blatant, Subtle, and Covert Discrimination.* 2d ed. Upper Saddle River, NJ: Prentice Hall.

Berdahl, J. L., V. J. Magley, C. R. Waldo. 1996. "The Sexual Harassment of Men? Exploring the Concept with Theory and Data." *Psychology of Women Quarterly* 20:27–47.

Bertrand, Marianne, and Sendhil Mullainathan. 2004. "Are Emily and Greg More Employable Than Lakisha and Jamal?: A Field Experiment of Labor Market Discrimination." National Bureau of Economic Research: NBER Working Paper Series. Cambridge, MA.

Bianchi, Suzanne M., Melissa A. Milkie, Liana C. Sayer, and John P. Robinson. 2000. "Is Anyone Doing the Housework? Trends in the Gender Division of Household Labor." *Social Forces* 79:191–228.

Bibb, R., and W. Form. 1977. "The Effects of Industrial, Occupational, and Sex Stratification on Wages in Blue-Collar Markets." *Social Forces* 55:974–96.

Bielby, William T., and James N. Baron. 1986. "Men and Women at Work: Sex Segregation and Statistical Discrimination." *American Journal of Sociology* 91:759–99.

Blalock, Hubert M. 1967. *Toward a Theory of Minority Group Relations.* New York: Wiley.

Blankenship, Kim M. 1993. "Bringing Gender and Race In: U.S. Employment Discrimination Policy." *Gender and Society* 7:204–26.

Blau, Peter M. 1967. *Exchange and Power in Social Life.* New York: John Wiley & Sons.
———. 1977. *Inequality and Heterogeneity: A Primitive Theory of Social Structure.* New York: Free Press.

Blau, Francine D., and Andrea H. Beller. 1992. "Black–White Earnings Over the 1970s and 1980s: Gender Differences in Trends." *The Review of Economics and Statistics* 74:276–86.

Blau, F., and M. Ferber. 1987. "Occupations and Earnings of Women Workers." Pp. 37–68 in *Working Women: Past, Present, Future,* edited by K. S. Koziara, M. H. Moskow, and L. D. Tanner. Washington, DC: Bureau of National Affairs.

Blau, P., and J. E. Schwartz. 1984. *Cross-cutting Social Circles: Testing a Macrostructural Theory of Intergroup Relations,* Orlando, FL: Academic Press.

Bloch, F. 1994. *Antidiscrimination Law and Minority Employment.* Chicago: University of Chicago Press.

Blumer, Herbert. 1958. "Race Prejudice as a Sense of Group Position." *Pacific Sociological Review* 1:3–7.

Bonilla-Silva, Eduardo. 2003. *Racism Without Racists: Color-Blind Racism and the Persistence of Racial Inequality in the United States.* Lanham, MD: Rowman & Littlefield.

Borjas, George J. 1983. "The Measurement of Race and Gender Wage Differentials: Evidence from the Public Sector." *Industrial Labor Relations Review* 37:79–91.

Boswell, Terry. 1986. "A Split Labor Market Analysis of Discrimination Against Chinese Immigrants, 1850–1880." *American Sociological Review* 51:352–71.

Boswell, Terry, and Cliff Brown. 1999. "The Scope of General Theory: Methods for Linking Inductive and Deductive Comparative History." *Sociological Methods and Research* 28:154–85.

Bound, John, and Richard B. Freeman. 1992. "What Went Wrong? The Erosion of Relative Earnings and Employment Among Young Black Men in the 1980s." *The Quarterly Journal of Economics* 107:201–32.

Bourdieu, Pierre, and Jean-Claude Passeron. 1977. *Reproduction in Education, Society & Culture.* London: Sage.

Braddock, Jomills Henry, II, and James M. McPartland. 1987. "How Minorities Continue to Be Excluded from Equal Employment Opportunities: Research on Labor Market and Institutional Barriers." *Journal of Social Issues* 43:5–39.

Britton, Dana M. 2000. "The Epistemology of the Gendered Organization." *Gender and Society* 14:418–34.

Brown, Cliff. 2000. "The Role of Employers in Split Labor Markets: An Event Structure Analysis of Responses to AFL Organizing in Gary and Chicago, 1917–19." *Social Forces* 79:653–81.

Browne, Irene, and Joya Misra. 2005. "Labor Market Inequality: Intersections of Gender, Race and Class." *Blackwell Companion to Inequalities*, edited by Mary Romero and Eric Margolis.

Brownstein, Henry H. 2000. *The Social Reality of Violence and Violent Crime.* Needham Heights, MA: Allyn and Bacon.

Budig, Michelle J. 2002. "Male Advantage and the Gender Composition of Jobs: Who Rides the Glass Escalator?" *Social Problems* 49:258–77.

Budig, Michelle J., and Paula England. 2001. "The Wage Penalty for Motherhood." *American Sociological Review* 66:204–25.

Burbridge, Lynn C. 1997. "Black Women in the History of African American Economic Thought: A Critical Essay." In *A Different Vision: African American Economic Thought*, edited by Thomas D. Boston. London: Routledge.

Burstein, Paul. 1991. "Policy Domains: Organizations, Culture, and Policy Outcomes" *Annual Review of Sociology* 17:327–50.

Carrington, William J., and Kenneth R. Troske. 1995. "Gender Segregation in Small Firms." *The Journal of Human Resources* 30:503–33.

Chambliss, William J. 2001. *Power, Politics, and Crime.* Boulder, CO: Westview Press.

Charles, Camille Zubrinsky. 2003. "The Dynamics of Racial Residential Segregation." *Annual Review of Sociology* 29:167–207.

Chodorow, Nancy. 1987. "Feminism and Difference: Gender, Relation and Difference in Psychoanalytic Perspective." In *The Psychology of Women: Ongoing Debates*, edited by Mary Roth Walsh. New Haven: Yale University Press.

Clark, William. 1991. "Residential Preferences and Neighborhood Racial Segregation; A Test of the Schelling Segregation Model." *Demography* 28:1–19.

Cohen, Philip N. 1998. "Black Concentration Effects on Black–White and Gender Inequality: Multilevel Analysis for U.S. Metropolitan Areas." *Social Forces* 77:207–29.

Cohen, Philip N., and Matt L. Huffman. 2003. "Individuals, Jobs, and Labor Markets: The Devaluation of Women's Work." *American Sociological Review* 68:433–63.

Cohn, Samuel. 2000. *Race and Gender Discrimination at Work.* Boulder, CO: Westview Press.

Cohn, Samuel, and Mark Fossett. 1995. "Why Racial Employment Inequality is Greater in Northern Labor Markets: Regional Differences in White–Black Employment Differentials." *Social Forces* 74:511–42.

Coleman, Major G. 2003. "Job Skill and Black Male Wage Discrimination." *Social Science Quarterly* 84: 892–905.

Collins, Patricia Hill. 1990. *Black Feminist Thought: Knowledge, Consciousness, and the Politics of Empowerment.* Boston: Unwin Hyman.

Connell, Richard W. 1993. "The Big Picture: Masculinities in Recent World History." *Theory and Society* 22:597–623.

Cook, C. C. 1989. "The Role of Expectations in the 'Intention to Move' Among Single-Parent Families." *Environment and Behavior* 12:554–76.

Cotter, David A., Joan M. Hermsen, Seth Ovadia, and Reeve Vanneman. 2001. "The Glass Ceiling Effect." *Social Forces* 80:655–81.

Cotter, D. A., J. M. Hermsen, and R. Vanneman. 1999. "The Effects of Occupational Gender Segregation Across Race." *Sociological Quarterly* 44:17–36.

Crenshaw, K. 1990. "Demarginalizing the Intersection of Race and Sex: A Black Feminist Critique of Antidiscrimination Doctrine, Feminist Theory and Antiracist Politics." Pp. 195–217 in *The Politics of Law: A Progressive Critique*, edited by D. Kairys. New York: Pantheon.

———. 1998. "Demarginalizing the Intersection of Race and Sex: A Black Feminist Critique of Antidiscrimination Doctrine, Feminist Theory, and Antiracist Politics." In *Feminism and Politics*, edited by Anne Phillips. New York: Oxford University Press.

Crewson, Philip E. 1995. "A Comparative Analysis of Public and Private Sector Entrant Quality." *American Journal of Political Science* 39:628–39.

Cunningham, James S., and Nadja Zalokar. 1992. "The Economic Progress of Black Women, 1940–1980: Occupational Distribution and Relative Wages." *Industrial and Labor Relations Review* 45:540–55.

Cutler, D. M., and E. L. Glaeser. 1997. "Are Ghettos Good or Bad?" *Quarterly Journal of Economics* 112:827–72.

Darity, William A., Jr., and Patrick L. Mason. 1998. "Evidence on Discrimination in Employment: Codes of Color, Codes of Gender." *The Journal of Economic Perspectives* 12:63–90.

Darke, J. 1994. "Women and the Meaning of Home," in *Housing Women*, edited by R. Gilroy and R. Woods. London: Routledge.

Davis, Theodore J., Jr. 1995. "The Occupational Mobility of Black Males Revisited: Does Race Matter?" *The Social Science Journal* 32:121–35.

Daymont, Thomas N., and Paul J. Andrisani. 1984. "Job Preferences, College Major, and the Gender Gap in Earnings." *The Journal of Human Resources* 19:408–28.

De Coster, Stacey, Sarah Beth Estes, and Charles W. Mueller. 1999. "Routine Activities and Sexual Harassment in the Workplace." *Work and Occupations* 26:21–49.

Denton, Nancy A., and Douglas S. Massey. 1988. "Residential Segregation of Blacks, Hispanics, and Asians by Socioeconomic Status and Generation." *Social Science Quarterly* 69:797–817.

DiPrete, Thomas A., and Whitman T. Soule. 1988. "Gender and Promotion in Segmented Job Ladder Systems." *American Sociological Review* 53:26–40.

Dobbin, Frank, John Sutton, John Meyer, and W. Richard Scott. 1993. "Equal Opportunity Law and the Construction of Internal Labor Markets." *American Journal of Sociology* 99:396–427.

Drew, E. M. 2005. "Beyond Journalistic Jingoism: Journalism's 'Racial Projects' Reposition Race as a Central Organizing Principle in Daily Life." Paper presented at the annual meeting of the American Sociological Association, Philadelphia, PA.

DuBois, Cathy L. Z., Deborah E. Knapp, Robert H. Faley, and Gary A. Kustis. 1998. "An Empirical Examination of Same- and Other-Gender Sexual Harassment in the Workplace," *Sex Roles* 39:731–49.

Dyson, Michael Eric. 2004. "The Liberal Theory of Race." In *The Michael Eric Dyson Reader*, edited by Michael Eric Dyson. New York: Basic Civitas Press.

EEOC (U.S. Equal Opportunity Employment Commission). 2004a. "Employment Statistics." (1999 EEO-1 Aggregate Reports). Washington, D.C.: U.S. Equal Opportunity Employment Commission. http://www.eeoc.gov/stats/define.html (accessed November 2, 2004).

———. 2004b. "Enforcement Statistics." (Race-Based Charges FY 1992–FY 2003). Washington, D.C.: U.S. Equal Opportunity Employment Commission. http://www.eeoc.gov/stats/employment.html (accessed November 2, 2004).

———. 2005. Sexual Harassment Charges EEOC and FEPAs Combined: FY 1992–FY 2004. http://www.eeoc.gov/stats/harass.html (accessed May 2, 2005).

Elo, Irma T., and Samuel H. Preston. 2001. "The African American Population, 1930 to 1990." Pp. 168–223 in *Problem of the Century: Racial Stratification in the United States*, edited by E. Anderson and D. S. Massey. New York: Russell Sage.

Elvira, Marta M., and Christopher D. Zatzick. 2002. "Who's Displaced First? The Role of Race in Layoff Decisions." *Industrial Relations* 41:329–61.

Emerson, Michael O., Karen J. Chai, and George Yancey. 2001. "Does Race Matter in Residential Segregation? Exploring the Preferences of White Americans." *American Sociological Review* 66:922–35.

England, Paula. 1981. "Assessing Trends in Occupational Sex Segregation: 1900–1976." Pp. 273–99 in *Sociological Perspectives on Labor Markets*, edited by Ivar Berg. New York: Academic Press.

England, Paula. 1982. "The Failure of Human Capital Theory to Explain Occupational Sex Segregation." *The Journal of Human Resources* 17:358–70.

———. 1992. *Comparable Worth: Theories and Evidence*. Hawthorne, NY: Aldine de Gruyter.

England, Paula, Melissa A. Herbert, Barbara Stanek Kilbourne, Lori L. Reid, and Lori McCreary Megdal. 1994. "The Gendered Valuation of Occupations and Skills: Earnings in 1980 Census Occupations." *Social Forces* 73:65–99.

Farley, Reynolds. 1977. "Residential Segregation in Urbanized Areas of the United States in 1970: An Analysis of Social Class and Race Differences." *Demography* 14:497–518.

Farley, Reynolds, and William H. Frey. 1994. "Changes in the Segregation of Whites from Blacks During the 1980's: Small Steps Toward a More Integrated Society." *American Sociological Review* 59:23–45.

Farley, Reynolds, Charlotte Steeh, Maria Krysan, Tara Jackson, and Keith Reeves. 1994. "Stereotypes and Segregation: Neighborhoods in the Detroit Area." *American Journal of Sociology* 100:750–80.

Feagin, Joe R. 1991. "The Continuing Significance of Race: Antiblack Discrimination in Public Places." *American Sociological Review* 56:101–16.

Feagin, Joe R., and Douglas Lee Eckberg. 1980. "Discrimination: Motivation, Action, Effects, and Context." *Annual Review of Sociology* 6:1–20.

Feagin, Joe R., and Karyn McKinney. 2003. *The Many Costs of Racism*. Lanham, MD: Rowman & Littlefield.

Feagin, Joe R., and R. Parker 1990. *Building American Cities: The Urban Real Estate Game*. 2d ed. Englewood Cliffs, NJ: Prentice Hall.

Feagin, Joe R., and Hernan Vera. 1995. *White Racism: The Basics*. NY: Routledge.

Fernandez, J. 1975. *Racism and Sexism in White Corporations*. New York: John Wiley.

———. 1981. *Black Managers in White Corporations*. Lexington, MA: Lexington Books.

Fix, Michael, and Raymond Struyk, eds. 1993. *Clear and Convincing Evidence: Measurement of Discrimination in America*. Washington, DC: Urban Institute Press.

Floge, Liliane, and Deborah M. Merrill. 1986. "Tokenism Reconsidered: Male Nurses and Female Physicians in a Hospital Setting." *Social Forces* 64:925–47.

Forman, Tyrone A., David R. Williams, and James S. Jackson. 1997. "Race, Place, and Discrimination." *Perspectives on Social Problems* 9:231–61.

Foucault, Michel. 1980. *Power/Knowledge: Selected Interviews and Other Writings 1972–1977*. Edited by Colin Gordon. New York: Pantheon Books.

Friedman, Ray, Melinda Kane, and Daniel B. Cornfield. 1998. "Social Support and Career Optimism: Examining the Effectiveness of Network Groups Among Black Managers." *Human Relations* 51:1155–77.

Galster, George C. 1990a. "Racial Discrimination in Housing Markets during the 1980s: A Review of the Audit Evidence." *Journal of Planning Education and Research* 9:165–75.

———. 1990b. "Racial Steering by Real Estate Agents: Mechanisms and Motives." *Review of Black Political Economy* 19:39–63.

Gamson, William A. 1995. "Constructing Social Protest." Pp. 85–106 in *Social Movements and Culture*, edited by H. Johnston and B. Klandermans. Minneapolis, MN: University of Minnesota Press.

Giddens, Anthony. 1984. *The Constitution of Society*. Cambridge: Cambridge University Press.

Glassner, Barry. 1999. *The Culture of Fear: Why Americans Are Afraid of the Wrong Things*. New York: Basic Books.

Goffman, Erving. 1976. "Gender Display." *Studies in the Anthropology of Visual Communication* 3:69–77.

Goldin, Claudia, and Cecilia Rouse. 2000. "Orchestrating Impartiality: The Impact of 'Blind' Auditions on Female Musicians," *The American Economic Review* 90:715–41.

Gotham, Kevin Fox. 2000. "Racialization and the State: The Housing Act of 1934 and the Origins of the Federal Housing Administration (FHA)." *Sociological Perspectives* 43:291–316.

Gotham, Kevin Fox. 2002a. "Beyond Invasion and Succession: School Segregation, Real Estate Blockbusting, and the Political Economy of Neighborhood Racial Transition." *City and Community* 1:83–111.

———. 2002b. *Race, Real Estate, and Urban Redevelopment: The Kansas City Experience, 1900–2000.* New York: SUNY Press.

Gottdiener M., and J. R. Feagin. 1988. "The Paradigm Shift in Urban Sociology." *Urban Affairs Quarterly* 24:163–87.

Greenhaus, Jeffrey H., Saroj Parasuraman, and Wayne M. Wormley. 1990. "Effects of Race on Organizational Experience, Job Performance Evaluations, and Career Outcomes." *The Academy of Management Journal* 33:64–86.

Griffin, Larry J., Christopher Botsko, Ana-Maria Wahl, and Larry Isaac. 1991. "Theoretical Generality, Case Particularity: Qualitative Comparative Analysis of Trade Union Growth and Decline." *International Journal of Comparative Sociology* 32:110–36.

Griffin, Larry, and Charles C. Ragin. 1994. "Some Observations on Formal Methods of Qualitative Analysis." *Sociological Methods and Research* 23:4–21.

Grodsky, Eric, and Devah Pager. 2001. "The Structure of Disadvantage: Individual and Occupational Determinants of the Black–White Wage Gap." *American Sociological Review* 66:542–67.

Gruber, James E. 1998. "The Impact of Male Work Environments and Organizational Policies on Women's Experiences of Sexual Harassment." *Gender and Society* 12:301–20.

Gruber, James E., and Michael D. Smith 1995. "Womens' Responses to Sexual Harassment: A Multivariate Analysis." *Basic Applied Social Psychology* 17:543–62.

Gutek B. A., A. G. Cohen. 1987. "Sex Ratios, Sex Role Spillover and Sex at Work: A Comparison of Men's and Women's Experiences." *Human Relations* 40:97–115.

Haberfeld, Yitzhak. 1992. "Employment Discrimination: An Organizational Model." *The Academy of Management Journal* 35:161–80.

Hancock, A. M. 2004. *The Politics of Disgust: The Public Identity of the Welfare Queen.* New York: New York University Press.

Harknett, Kristen, and Sara S. McLanahan. 2004. "Racial and Ethnic Differences in Marriage after the Birth of a Child." *American Sociological Review* 69:790–811.

Harris, Kathleen Mullan. 1993. "Work and Welfare Among Single Mothers in Poverty." *American Journal of Sociology* 99:317–52.

Hayes, S. 1996. *The Cultural Contradictions of Motherhood.* New Haven: Yale University Press.

Heckman, James J. 1998. "Detecting Discrimination." *The Journal of Economic Perspectives* 12:101–16.

Hersch, Joni. 1991. "Male–Female Differences in Hourly Wages: The Role of Human Capital, Working Condtitions, and Housework." *Industrial and Labor Relations Review* 44:746–59.

Hodson, Randy. 1999. *Analyzing Documentary Accounts.* Thousand Oaks, CA: Sage.
———. 2001. *Dignity at Work.* Cambridge: Cambridge University Press.
Hodson, Randy, Vincent J. Roscigno, and Steven H. Lopez. 2006. "Chaos and the Abuse of Power: Workplace Bullying in Organizational and Interactional Context." *Work and Occupations* 33:382–416.
Hoffnar, Emily, and Michael Greene. 1996. "Gender Discrimination in the Public and Private Sectors: A Sample Selectivity Approach." *Journal of Socio-Economics* 25:105–14.
Huffman, Matthew L. 2004. "Gender Inequality Across Local Wage Hierarchies." *Work and Occupations* 31:323–44.
Huffman, Matt L., and Philip N. Cohen. 2004. "Racial Wage Inequality: Job Segregation and Devaluation Across U.S. Labor Markets." *The American Journal of Sociology* 109:902–36.
Hughes, Micheal, and Melvin Thomas. 1998. "The Continuing Significance of Race Revisited: A Study of Race, Class, and Quality of Life in America, 1972 to 1996." *American Sociological Review* 63:785–95.
Institute for Women's Policy Research. 2004. "The Gender Wage Ratio: Women's and Men's Earnings." http://www.iwpr.org/pdf/C350updated.pdf (accessed October 2004).
Jackson, Pamela Braboy, Peggy A. Thoits, and Howard F. Taylor. 1995. "Composition of the Workplace and Psychological Well-Being: The Effects of Tokenism on America's Black Elite." *Social Forces* 74:543–57.
Jacobs, David, and Robert M. O'Brien. 1998. "The Determinants of Deadly Force: A Structural Analysis of Police Violence." *American Journal of Sociology* 103:837–62.
James, Erika Hayes. 2000. "Race-Related Differences in Promotions and Support: Underlying Effects of Human and Social Capital." *Organization Science* 11:493–508.
Jencks, Christopher. 1992. *Rethinking Social Policy.* Cambridge, MA: Harvard University Press.
Jencks, C., and S. Mayer. 1990. "The Social Consequences of Growing Up in a Poor Neighborhood." In *Inner-City Poverty in the United States,* edited by L. Lynn Jr. and M. McGeary. Washington, DC: National Academy Press.
Johnson, William R. 1978. "Racial Wage Discrimination and Industrial Structure." *The Bell Journal of Economics* 9:70–81.
Kadushin, Charles. 1976. "Networks and Circles in the Production of Culture." *American Behavioral Scientist* 19:769–84.
Kain, John. 1992. "The Spatial Mismatch Hypothesis: Three Decades Later." *Housing Policy Debate* 3:327–460.
Kalof, L., K. K. Eby, J. L. Matheson, and R. Koska. 2001. "The Influence of Race and Gender on Student Self-Reports of Sexual Harassment." *Gender and Society* 15:282–302.
Kanter, Rosabeth Moss. 1993. *Men and Women of the Corporation.* New York: Basic Books.
Kaufman, Robert L. 1986. "The Impact of Industrial and Occupational Structure on Black–White Employment Allocation." *American Sociological Review* 51:310–23.
———. 2002. "Assessing Alternative Perspectives on Race and Sex Employment Segregation." *American Sociological Review* 67:547–72.

Kessler, Ronald C., Kristin D. Mickelson, and David R. Williams. 1999. "The Prevalence, Distribution, and Mental Health Correlates of Perceived Discrimination in the United States." *Journal of Health and Social Behavior* 40:208–30.

Kilbourne, Barbara, Paula England, and Kurt Beron. 1994. "Effects of Individual, Occupational, and Industrial Characteristics on Earnings: Intersections of Race and Gender." *Social Forces* 72:1149–76.

Kilbourne, Barbara, George Farkas,, Kurt Beron, Dorothea Weir, and Paula England. 1994. "Returns to Skill, Compensating Differentials, and Gender Bias: Effects of Occupational Characteristics on the Wages of White Women and Men." *American Journal of Sociology* 100:689–719.

Killingsworth, Mark R. 1987. "Heterogeneous Preferences, Compensating Wage Differentials, and Comparable Worth." *The Quarterly Journal of Economics* 102:727–42.

Kimmel, Michael S. 1994. "Masculinity as Homophobia: Fear, Shame, and Silence in the construction of Gender Identity." Pp. 119–41 in *Theorizing Masculinities*, edited by Harry Brod and Michael Kaufman. London: Sage.

Kimmel, Michael S., and Tyson Smith. 2005. "The 'Reasonable Woman' and Unreasonable Men: Gendered Discourses in Sexual Harassment Litigation." Pp. 143–66 in *In the Company of Men: Male Dominance and Sexual Harassment*, edited by James E. Gruber and Phoebe Morgan. Boston: Northeastern University Press.

King, Mary C. 1992. "Occupational Segregation by Race and Sex, 1940–88." *Monthly Labor Review* 115:30–38.

King, Mary C. 1995. "Black Women's Labor Market Status: Occupational Segregation in the United States and Great Britain." *Review of Black Political Economy* 24:23–44.

Kirschenman, Joleen, Philip Moss, and Chris Tilly. 1995. "Employer Screening Methods and Racial Exclusion: Evidence from New In-depth Interviews with Employers." Unpublished paper. New York: Russell Sage Foundation.

Kirschenman, Joleen, and Kathryn M. Neckerman. 1991. "'We'd Love to Hire Them, But . . .': The Meaning of Race for Employers." Pp. 203–32 in *The Urban Underclass*, edited by C. Jencks and P. E. Peterson. Washington, DC: Brookings Institution.

Kluegel, James R. 1978. "The Causes and Cost of Racial Exclusion from Job Authority." *American Sociological Review* 43:285–301.

Kmec, Julie A. 2003. "Minority Job Concentration and Wages." *Social Problems* 50:38–59.

Kochanek, K. D., J. D. Maurer, and H. M. Rosenberg. 1994. "Why Did Black Life Expectancy Decline from 1984 through 1989 in the United States?" *American Journal of Public Health* 84:938–44.

Kohlman, Marla R. 2001. *Locating Sexual Harassment within Intersections of Experience in the U.S. Labor Market.* Dissertation Abstracts International, A: The Humanities and Social Sciences 62:346.

Konrad, A. M., Linnenhan F. 1995. "Formalized HRM Structures: Coordinating Equal Employment Opportunity or Concealing Organizational Practices?" *Academy of Management Journal* 38:787–820.

Krieger, N., D. L. Rowley, A. A. Herman, B. Avery, and M. T. Phillips. 1993. "Racism, Sexism, and Social Class: Implications for Studies of Health, Disease, and Well-Being." *American Journal of Preventative Medicine* 9:82–122.

Krivo, Lauren, and Ruth D. Peterson. 1996. "Extremely Disadvantaged Neighborhoods and Urban Crime." *Sociological Forces* 75:619–48.

Krivo, Lauren, and Ruth D. Peterson. 2000. "The Structural Context of Homicide: Accounting for Racial Differences in Process." *American Sociological Review* 65:547–59.

Krysan, Maria. 2002. "Whites Who Say They'd Flee: Who Are They, and Why Would They Leave?" *Demography* 39:675–96.

Krysan, Maria, and Reynolds Farley. 2002. "The Residential Preferences of Blacks: Do They Explain Persistent Segregation?" *Social Forces* 80:937–79.

Laband, David N., and Bernard F. Lentz. 1998. "The Effects of Sexual Harassment on Job Satisfaction, Earnings, and Turnover among Female Lawyers." *Industrial and Labor Relations Review* 51:594–607.

Landry, Bart. 2000. *Black Working Wives: Pioneers of the American Family Revolution.* Berkeley: University of California Press.

LaPiere, Richard T. 1934. "Attitudes vs. Actions." *Social Forces* 13:230–37.

Lawler, Edward, Cecilia Ridgeway, and Barry Markovsky. 1993. "Structural Social Psychology and the Micro–Macro Problem." *Sociological Theory* 11:268–90.

Lee, Deborah. 2000. "Hegemonic Masculinity and Male Feminisation: The Sexual Harassment of Men at Work." *Journal of Gender Studies* 9:141–55.

Lee, Deborah. 2001. "'He Didn't Sexually Harass Me, as in Harassed for Sex. . . . He Was Just Horrible': Women's Definitions of Unwanted Male Sexual Conduct at Work." *Women's Studies International Forum* 24:25–38.

Lefebvre, H. 1991. *The Production of Space.* Oxford: Basil Blackwell.

Lens, Vicki. 2003. "Reading Between the Lines: Analyzing the Supreme Court's Views on Gender Discrimination in Employment, 1971–1982." *Social Service Review* 77(1):25–50.

Lieberson, Stanley, 1980. *A Piece of the Pie: Blacks and White Immigrants Since 1880.* Berkeley: University of California Press.

Logan, John R., Brian Stults, and Reynolds Farley. 2004. "Segregation of Minorities in the Metropolis: Two Decades of Change." *Demography* 41:1–22.

Long, James E. 1975. "Public–Private Sectoral Differences in Employment Discrimination." *Southern Economic Journal* 42:89–96.

Lynn, Richard, and Wei-Cheng Mau. 2002. "Why do Black American Males Earn Less than Black American Women? An Examination of Four Hypotheses." *The Journal of Social, Political, and Economic Studies* 27:307–13.

MacKinnon, Catherine. 1979. *Sexual Harassment of Working Women.* New Haven: Yale University Press.

Mallett, Shelley. 2004. "Understanding Home: A Critical Review of the Literature." *The Sociological Review* 52:62–89.

Marini, Margaret Mooney. 1989. "Sex Differences in Earnings in the United States." *Annual Review of Sociology* 15:343–80.

Marini, Margaret Mooney, and Pi-Ling Fan. 1997. "The Gender Gap in Earnings at Career Entry." *American Sociological Review* 62:588–604.

Martin, Patricia Y. 2004. "Gender as a Social Institution." *Social Forces* 82:1249–73.

Massey, Douglas S. 2005. "Racial Discrimination in Housing: A Moving Target." *Social Problems* 52:148–51.

Massey, Douglas, and Nancy Denton. 1993. *American Apartheid.* Cambridge: Harvard University Press.

Massey Douglas, and Garvey Lundy. 2001. "Use of Black English and Racial Discrimination in Urban Housing Markets: New Methods and Findings. *Urban Affairs Review* 36:452–69.

Massey, Douglas S., and Brendan P. Mullan. 1984. "Processes of Hispanic and Black Spatial Assimilation." *American Journal of Sociology* 89:836–73.

Maume Jr., David J. 1999a. "Glass Ceilings and Glass Escalators, Occupational Segregation and Race and Sex Differences in Managerial Promotions." *Work and Occupations* 26:483–509.

———. 1999b. "Occupational Segregation and the Career Mobility of White Men and Women." *Social Forces* 77:1433–59.

Maume, David J., Jr. 2004. "Wage Discrimination Over the Life Course: A Comparison of Explanations." *Social Problems* 51:505–27.

McBrier, Debra Branch, and George Wilson. 2004. "Going Down?: Race and Downward Occupational Mobility for White-Collar Workers in the 1990s." *Work and Occupations* 31:283–322.

McCall, Leslie. 2001. *Complex Inequality: Gender, Class, and Race in the New Economy.* New York: Routledge.

McGuire, Gail. 2002. "Gender, Race, and the Shadow Structure: A Study of Informal Networks and Inequality in a Work Organization." *Gender and Society* 16:303–22.

Meitzen, Mark E. 1986. "Differences in Male and Female Job-Quitting Behavior." *Journal of Labor Economics* 4:151–67.

Miller, Ann-Schwarz, and Wayne K. Talley. 2000. "Motor Bus Deregulation and the Gender Wage Gap: A Test of the Becker Hypothesis." *Eastern Economic Journal* 26:145–56.

Moss, Philip, and Christopher Tilly. 1995. "Skills and Race in Hiring: Quantitative Finds from Face-to-Face Interviews." *Eastern Economic Journal* 21:357–74.

———. 1996. "Soft Skills and Race: An Investigation of Black Men's Employment Problems." *Work and Occupations* 23:252–76.

———. 2001. *Stories Employers Tell: Race, Skill, and Hiring in America.* New York: Russell Sage Foundation.

Mueller, Charles, Toby Parcel, and Kazuko Tanaka. 1989. "Particularism in Authority Outcomes: The Case of Supervisors." *Social Science Research* 32:1–20.

Mueller, Charles, Stacy De Coster, Sarah Beth Estes. 2001. "Sexual Harassment in the Workplace: Unanticipated Consequences of Modern Social Control in Organizations." *Work and Occupations* 28:411–46.

Murphy, Raymond. 1988. *Social Closure: The Theory of Monopolization and Exclusion.* Cambridge: Oxford University Press.

Murrell, A. J. 1996. "Sexual Harassment and Women of Color: Issues, Challenges, and Future Directions." In *Sexual Harassment in the Workplace: Perspectives, Frontiers, and Response Strategies,* edited by M. S. Stockdale. Thousand Oaks, CA: Sage.

NCES (National Center for Education Statistics). 2005. *Gender Differences in Participation and Completion of Undergraduate Education and How They Have Changed*

Over Time. NCES 2005-169 by Katharine Peter and Laura Horn. Washington, DC: U.S. Government Printing Office.

Neumark, David, Roy J. Bank, and Kyle D. Van Nort. 1996. "Sex Discrimination in Restaurant Hiring: An Audit Study." *The Quarterly Journal of Economics* 111:915–41.

OECD. 2001. *The Well-Being of Nations: The Role of Human and Social Capital.* Paris.

Ohio Civil Rights Commission. 2004. "About OCRC." http://crc.ohio.gov/mission.htm (accessed November 2, 2004).

Olson, Craig A., and Brian E. Becker. 1983. "Sex Discrimination in the Promotion Process." *Industrial and Labor Relations Review* 36:624–41.

Olson, Walter K. 1997. *The Excuse Theory: How Employment Law Is Paralyzing the American Workplace.* New York: Free Press.

Olzak, Susan. 1990. "The Political Context of Competition: Lynching and Urban Racial Violence, 1882–1914." *Social Forces* 69:395–421.

Olzak, Susan, Suzanne Shanahan, and Candace West. 1994. "School Desegregation, Interracial Exposure, and Antibusing Activity in Contemporary Urban America." *American Journal of Sociology* 100:196–214.

Ondrich, Jan, Alex Stricker, and John Yinger. 1999. "Do Landlords Discriminate? The Incidence and Causes of Racial Discrimination in Rental Housing Markets." *Journal of Housing Economics* 8:185–204.

Ondrich, Jan, Alex Stricker, and John Yinger. 1998. "Do Real Estate Brokers Choose to Discriminate? Evidence from the 1989 Housing Discrimination Study." *Southern Economic Journal* 64:880–901.

Ondrich, Jan, Stephen L. Ross, and John Yinger. 2000. "How Common Is Housing Discrimination? Improving on Traditional Measures." *Journal of Urban Economics* 3:470–500.

Padavic, Irene, and David Orcutt. 1997. "Perceptions of Sexual Harassment in the Florida Legal System: A Comparison of Dominance and Spillover Explanations." *Gender and Society* 11:682–98.

Padavic, Irene, and Barbara Reskin. 2002. *Women and Men at Work.* Thousand Oaks, CA: Pine Forge Press.

Page, Marianne. 1995. "Racial and Ethnic Discrimination in Urban Housing Markets: Evidence from a Recent Audit Study." *Journal of Urban Economics* 38:183–206.

Pager, Devah. 2003. "The Mark of a Criminal Record." *American Journal of Sociology* 108:937–75.

Pager, Devah, and Lincoln Quillian. 2005. "Walking the Talk? What Employers Say Versus What They Do." *American Sociological Review* 70:355–80.

Paglin, Morton, and Anthony M. Rufolo. 1990. "Heterogeneous Human Capital, Occupational Choice, and Male-Female Earnings Differences." *Journal of Labor Economics* 8:123–44.

Park, Hyunjoon, and Gary D. Sandefur. 2003. "Racial/Ethnic Differences in Voluntary and Involuntary Job Mobility among Young Men." *Social Science Research* 32: 347–75.

Parkin, Frank. 1974. "Strategies of Social Closure in Class Formation." In *The Social Analysis of Class Structure,* edited by F. Parkin. London: Tavistock Publications Limited.

———. 1979. *Marxism and Class Theory: A Bourgeois Critique.* Cambridge: Tavistock.

———. 1982. "Social Closure and Class Formation." Pp. 175–86 in *Classes, Power, and Conflict: Classical and Contemporary Debates*, edited by Anthony Giddens and David Held. Berkeley: University of California Press.

Peoples, James, Jr., and Wayne K. Talley. 2001. "Black–White Earnings Differentials: Privatization versus Deregulation." *The American Economic Review* 91:164–68.

———. 2002. "Privatization, City Residency, and Black–White Earnings Differentials Evidence from the Public Sector." *Review of Industrial Organization* 21:251–70.

Petersen, Trond, and Ishak Saporta. 2004. "The Opportunity Structure of Discrimination." *American Journal of Sociology* 109:852–901.

Pfeffer, Jeffrey, and Yinon Cohen. 1984. "Determinants of Internal Labor Market Arrangements in Organizations." *American Sociological Review* 29:550–72.

Phelps, Edwin, 1972. "The Statistical Theory of Racism and Sexism." *American Economic Review* 162:659–66.

Pierce, Jennifer L. 2003. "Racing for Innocence: Whiteness, Corporate Culture, and the Backlash Against Affirmative Action." *Qualitative Sociology* 26:53–70.

Pinderhughes, Howard L. 1993. "The Anatomy of Racially Motivated Violence in New York City: A Case Study of Youth in Southern Brooklyn." *Social Problems* 40:478–91.

Prokos, Anastasia, and Irene Padavic. 2005. "An Examination of Competing Explanations for the Pay Gap Between Scientists and Engineers." *Gender and Society* 19: 523–43.

Quinn, Beth. 2002. "Sexual Harassment and Masculinity: The Power and Meaning of Girl Watching." *Gender and Society* 16:386–402.

Ragin, Charles. 1987. *The Comparative Method*. Berkeley: University of California Press.

Ragin, Charles C., Susan E. Mayer, and Kriss Drass. 1984. "Assessing Discrimination: A Boolean Approach." *American Sociological Review* 49:221–34.

Reid, Lori. 2002. "Occupational Segregation, Human Capital, and Motherhood: Black Women's Higher Exit Rates from Full Employment." *Gender and Society* 16:728–47.

Reid, Lori L., and Irene Padavic. 2005. "Employment Exits and the Race Gap in Young Women's Employment." *Social Science Quarterly* 86:1242–60.

Reskin, Barbara F. 1988. "Bringing the Men Back In: Sex Differentiation and the Devaluation of Women's Work." *Gender and Society* 2:58–81.

———. 1993. "Sex Segregation in the Workplace." *Annual Review of Sociology* 19:241–70.

———. 2000. "The Proximate Causes of Employment Discrimination." *Contemporary Sociology* 29:319–28.

———. 2003. "Including Mechanisms in Our Models of Ascriptive Inequality." *American Sociological Review* 68:1–21.

Reskin, Barbara F., Debra B. McBrier, and Julie A. Kmec. 1999. "The Determinants and Consequences of Workplace Sex and Race Composition." *Annual Review of Sociology* 25:335–61.

Reskin, Barbara F., and Irene Padavic. 1988. "Supervisors as Gatekeepers: Male Supervisors' Response to Women's Integration in Plant Jobs." *Social Problems* 35:536–50.

Reskin, Barbara F., and Patricia A. Roos. 1987. "Status Hierarchies and Sex Segregation." Pp. 3–21 in *Ingredients for Women's Employment Policy*, edited by Christine Bose and Glenna Spitze. Albany, NY: State University of New York Press.

———. 1990. *Job Queues, Gender Queues: Explaining Women's Inroads into Male Occu-pations*. Philadelphia, PA: Temple University Press.

Riccucci, Norma M. 1990. *Women, Minorities and Unions in the Public Sector*. New York: Greenwood Press.

Richman, Judith A., Kathleen M. Rospenda, Joseph A. Flaherty, Sally Freels, and Ken Zlatoper. 2004. "Perceived Organizational Tolerance for Workplace Harassment and Distress and Drinking Over Time [Harassment and Mental Health]." *Women and Health* 40:1–19.

Ridgeway, C. L., and S. J. Correll. 2004. "Unpacking the Gender System: A Theoreti-cal Perspective on Cultural Beliefs and Social Relations." *Gender and Society* 18:510–31.

Ridgeway, C. L., and L. Smith-Lovin. 1999. "The Gender System and Interaction." *An-nual Review of Sociology* 25:191–216.

Risman, Barbara J. 2004. "Gender as a Social Structure: Theory Wrestling with Ac-tivism." *Gender and Society* 18:429–50.

Robinson, Corre L., Tiffany Taylor, Donald Tomaskovic-Devey, Catherine Zimmer, and Matthew W. Irvin. 2005. "Studying Race or Ethnic and Sex Segregation at the Establishment Level: Methodological Issues and Substantive Opportunities Using EEO-1 Reports." *Work and Occupations* 32:5–38.

Roediger, David R. 1991. *The Wages of Whiteness: Race and the Making of the American Working Class*. London: Verso.

Rogers, J. K., and D. Henson. 1997. "Hey, Why Don't You Wear a Shorter Skirt? Struc-tural Vulnerability and the Organization of Sexual Harassment in Temporary Cler-ical Employment." *Gender and Society* 11:215–37.

Roscigno, Vincent J., and James Ainsworth-Darnell. 1999. "Race, Cultural Capital, and Educational Resources: Persistent Inequalities and Achievement Returns." *Sociology of Education* 72:158–78.

Roscigno, Vincent J., and Cynthia D. Anderson. 1995. "Subordination and Struggle: Social Movement Dynamics and Processes of Inequality." *Perspectives on Social Problems* 7:249–74.

Roscigno, Vincent J., and William F. Danaher. 2001. "Media and Mobilization: The Case of Radio and Southern Textile Worker Insurgency, 1929–1934." *American So-ciological Review* 66:24–48.

Roscigno, Vincent J., and Randy Hodson. 2004. "The Organizational and Social Foun-dations of Worker Resistance." *American Sociological Review* 69:14–39.

Roscigno, Vincent J., and Donald Tomaskovic-Devey. 1994. "Racial Politics in the Con-temporary South: Toward a More Critical Understanding." *Social Problems* 41:585–607.

Rosenberg, Janet, Harry Perlstadt, and William R. F. Phillips. 1993. "Now That We Are Here: Discrimination, Disparagement, and Harassment at Work and the Experience of Women Lawyers. *Gender and Society* 7:415–33.

Rospenda, Kathleen M., Judith A. Richman, and Stephanie J. Nawyn, 1998. "Doing Power: The Confluence of Gender, Race, and Class in Contrapower Sexual Harass-ment." *Gender and Society* 12:40–60.

Ross, Catherine, and John Mirowsky. 1996. "Economic and Interpersonal Work Rewards: Subjective Utilities of Men's and Women's Compensation." *Social Forces* 75:223–46.

Ross, Stephen L., and Margery A. Turner. 2005. "Housing Discrimination in Metropolitan America: Explaining Changes Between 1989 and 2000." *Social Problems* 52: 152–80.

Ross, Stephen L., and John Yinger. 2002. *The Color of Credit: Mortgage Discrimination, Research Methodology, and Fair Lending Enforcement.* Cambridge, MA: MIT Press.

Royster, Deirdre A. 2003. *Race and the Invisible Hand: How White Networks Exclude Black Men from Blue-Collar Jobs.* Berkeley: University of California Press.

Rundblad, Georganne. 2001. "Gender, Power, and Sexual Harassment." In *Gender Mosaics*, edited by Dana Vannoy. Los Angeles: Roxbury Publishing Company.

Sackett, Paul R., Cathy L. Z. DuBois, and Ann Wiggins Noe. 1991. "Tokenism in Performance Evaluation: The Effects of Work Group Representation on Male–Female and White–Black Differences in Performance Ratings." *Journal of Applied Psychology* 76:263–67.

Sampson, Robert J. 1995. "Unemployment and Imbalanced Sex Ratios: Race-Specific Consequences for Family Structure and Crime." Pp. 229–54 in *The Decline in Marriage Among African Americans*, edited by M. B. Tucker and C. Mitchell-Kernan. New York: Russell Sage.

Sanchez, Juan I., and Petra Brock. 1996. "Outcomes of Perceived Discrimination among Hispanic Employees: Is Diversity Management a Luxury or a Necessity?" *The Academy of Management Journal* 39:704–19.

Schuman, Howard, Charlotte Steeh, and Lawrence Bobo. 1985. *Racial Attitudes in America: Trends and Interpretations.* Cambridge, MA: Harvard University Press.

Schuman, Howard, Charlotte Steeh, Lawrence Bobo, and Maria Krysan. 1997. *Racial Attitudes in America: Trends and Interpretations.* Cambridge, MA: Harvard University Press.

Semyonov, Moshe, Rabeca Raijman, and Anat Yom-Tov. 2002. "Labor Market Competition, Perceived Threat, and Endorsement of Economic Discrimination Against Foreign Workers in Israel." *Social Problems* 49:416–31.

Senders, M. 1998. "Women and the Right to Adequate Housing." *Netherlands Quarterly of Human Rights* 16:175–200.

Shih, Johanna. 2002. " '. . . Yeah, I Could Hire This One, But I Know It's Gonna Be a Problem': How Race, Nativity and Gender Affect Employers' Perceptions of the Manageability of Job Seekers." *Ethnic and Racial Studies* 25:99–119.

Simpson, George E., and J. Milton Yinger. 1985. *Racial and Cultural Minorities: An Analysis of Prejudice and Discrimination.* New York: HarperCollins.

Smith, Ryan A. 1997. "Race, Income, and Authority at Work: A Cross-Temporal Analysis of Black and White Men (1972–1994)." *Social Problems* 4419–37.

———. 2001. "Particularism in Control over Monetary Resources at Work: An Analysis of Racioethnic Differences in the Authority Outcomes of Black, White, and Latino Men." *Work and Occupations* 28:447–68.

———. 2002. "Race, Gender, and Authority in the Workplace: Theory and Research." *Annual Review of Sociology* 28:509–42.

Smith, Shanna L., and Cathy Cloud. 1996. "The Role of Private, Nonprofit Fair Housing Enforcement Organizations in Lending Testing." Pp. 589–610 in *Mortgage Lending, Racial Discrimination, and Federal Policy*, edited by J. Goering and R. Wienk. Washington, DC: Urban Institute Press.

Snow, David A., and Robert D. Benford. 1992. "Master Frames and Cycles of Protest." Pp. 133–55 in *Frontiers in Social Movement Theory*, edited by A. D. Morris and C. M. Mueller. New Haven: Yale University Press.

Soule, Sarah A. 1992. "Populism and Black Lynching in Georgia, 1890–1900." *Social Forces* 71:431–49.

Spaights, Ernest, and Ann Whitaker. 1995. "Black Women in the Workforce: A New Look at an Old Problem." *Journal of Black Studies* 25:283–96.

Spain, Daphne. 1992. *Gendered Spaces*. Chapel Hill: University of North Carolina Press.

———. 1994. "Safe Havens for Cleveland's Virtuous Women." *Journal of Planning History* 3:267-91.

———. 2002. "What Happened to Gender Relations on the Way from Chicago to Los Angeles?" *City and Community* 1:155–67.

Squires, Gregory D. 2003. "Racial Profiling, Insurance Style: Insurance Redlining and Uneven Development of Metropolitan America." *Journal of Urban Affairs* 25:391–410.

Squires, Gregory D., and William Velez. 1987. "Insurance Redlining and the Transformation of an Urban Metropolis." *Urban Affairs Quarterly* 23:63–83.

———. 1988. "Insurance Redlining and the Process of Discrimination." *Review of Black Political Economy* 16:63–75.

Stein, Laura W. 1999. *A Documentary History: Sexual Harassment in America*. Westport, CT: Greenwood Press.

Steinberg, Ronnie J., L. Haignere, and Cynthia H. Chertos. 1990. "Managerial Promotions in the Public Sector: The Impact of Eligibility Requirements on Women and Minorities." *Work and Occupations* 17:284–301.

Stockdale, Margaret S. 2005. "The Sexual Harassment of Men: Articulating the Approach-Rejection Theory of Sexual Harassment." Pp 117–42 in *In the Company of Men: Male Dominance and Sexual Harassment*, edited by James E. Gruber and Phoebe Morgan. Boston: Northeastern University Press.

Stainback, Kevin, Corre L. Robinson, and Donald Tomaskovic-Devey. 2005. "Race and Workplace Integration: A Politically-Mediated Process?" *American Behavioral Scientist* 48:1200–1228.

Taeuber, Karl E. 1965. "The Effect of Income Redistribution on Racial Residential Segregation." *Urban Affairs Quarterly* 4:5–14.

Tam, Tony. 1997. "Sex Segregation and Occupational Gender Inequality in the United States: Devaluation or Specialized Training?" *American Journal of Sociology* 102:1652–92.

Testa, Mark, and Marilyn Krogh. 1995. "The Effect of Employment on Marriage among Black Males in Inner-City Chicago." Pp. 59–95 in *The Decline in Marriage Among African Americans*, edited by M. B. Tucker and C. Mitchell-Kernan. New York: Russell Sage.

Texeira, M. T. 2002. "Who Protects and Serves Me? A Case Study of Sexual Harassment of African American Women in One U.S. Law Enforcement Agency." *Gender and Society* 16:524–45.

Thomas, David A. 1990. "The Impact of Race on Managers' Experiences of Developmental Relationships (Mentoring and Sponsorship): An Intra-Organizational Study." *Journal of Organizational Behavior* 11:479–92.

Thomas, Melvin, Cedric Herring, and Hayward Derrick Horton. 1994. "Discrimination over the Life Course: A Synthetic Cohort Analysis of Earning Differences between Black and White Males." *Social Problems* 41:608–28.

Tienda, Marta, and D. Lii. 1987. "Minority Concentration and Earnings Inequality: Blacks, Hispanics, and Asians Compared." *American Journal of Sociology* 93:141–65.

Tolnay, Stewart E., and E. M. Beck. 1995. *A Festival of Violence: An Analysis of Southern Lynchings, 1882–1930.* Champaign, IL: University of Illinois Press.

Tomaskovic-Devey, Donald. 1993a. *Gender and Racial Inequality at Work.* Ithaca: ILR Press.

———. 1993b. "The Gender and Race Composition of Jobs and the Male/Female, Black/White Pay Gaps." *Social Forces* 92:45–76.

Tomaskovic-Devey, Donald, Melvin Thomas, and Kecia Johnson. 2005. "Race and the Accumulation of Human Capital Across the Career: A Theoretical Model and Fixed Effects Application." *American Journal of Sociology* 111:58–89.

Tomaskovic-Devey, Donald, and Vincent J. Roscigno. 1996. "Racial Economic Subordination and White Gain in the U.S. South." *American Sociological Review* 61: 565–89.

Tomaskovic-Devey, Donald, and Sheryl Skaggs. 2002. "Sex Segregation, Labor Process Organization, and Gender Earnings Inequality." *American Journal of Sociology* 108:102–28.

Turner, M., M. Fix, and R. Struyk. 1991. *Opportunities Diminished, Opportunities Denied.* Washington, DC: The Urban Institute.

Turner, Margery Austin, Raymond J. Struyk, and John Yinger. 1991. *Housing Discrimination Study: Synthesis.* Washington, DC: U.S. Department of Housing and Urban Development.

Uggen, Christopher, and Amy Blackstone. 2004. "Sexual Harassment as a Gendered Expression of Power." *American Sociological Review* 69:64–92.

U.S. Census Bureau. 2000a. "Population and Household Economic Topics: Ohio Quick Facts." Washington, DC: US Bureau of the Census. http://www.census.gov/population/www/index.html (accessed December 20, 2004).

———. 2000b. QT-P29: Industry by Sex for Ohio. Generated from Summary File 3. Data accessible on-line at http://www.census.gov.

———. 2003. "Occupations: 2000, Census 2000 Brief," by Peter Fronczek and Patricia Johnson. http://www.census.gov/prod/2003pubs/c2kbr-25.pdf (accessed 2003).

Vallas, Steven P. 2003. "Rediscovering the Color Line Within Organizations: The 'Knitting of Racial Groups' Revisited." *Work and Occupations* 30:379–400.

Wakefield, Sara, and Christopher Uggen. 2004. "The Declining Significance of Race in Federal Civil Rights Law: The Social Structure of Employment Discrimination Claims." *Sociological Inquiry* 74:128–57.

Waldo, C. R., J. L. Berdahl, and L. F. Fitzgerald. 1998. "Are Men Sexually Harassed? If So, by Whom?" *Law and Human Behavior* 22:59–79.

Wallace, Phyllis. 1973. "Employment Discrimination: Some Policy Considerations." Pp. 155–75 in *Discrimination in Labor Markets*, edited by Orley Ashenfelter and Albert Rees. Princeton, NJ: Princeton University Press.

Wasti, S. Arzu, and Lilia M. Cortina. 2002. "Coping in Context: Sociocultural Determinants of Responses to Sexual Harassment." *Journal of Personality and Social Psychology* 88:394–405.

Weber, Max. 1978. *Economy and Society: An Outline of Interpretive Sociology*. Berkeley: University of California Press.

Welsh, Sandy. 1999. "Gender and Sexual Harassment." *Annual Review of Sociology* 25: 169–90.

Welsh, Sandy. 2000. "The Multidimensional Nature of Sexual Harassment: An Empirical Analysis of Women's Sexual Harassment Complaints." *Violence Against Women* 6:118–41.

Welsh, Sandy, M. Dawson, and A. Nierobisz. 2002. "Legal Factors, Extra-Legal Factors, or Changes in the Law? Using Criminal Justice Research to Understand the Resolution of Sexual Harassment Complaints." *Social Problems* 49:605–23.

West, Candace, and Don Zimmerman. 1987. "Doing Gender." *Gender and Society* 1:121–51.

West, Cornel. 1999. "Race and Modernity." In *The Cornel West Reader*, edited by Cornel West. New York: Basic Civitas Books.

Western, Bruce. 2002. "The Impact of Incarceration on Wage Mobility and Inequality." *American Sociological Review* 67:526–46.

Wiener, Richard L., Linda Hurt, Brenda Russell, Kelley Mannen, and Charles Gasper. 1997. "Perceptions of Sexual Harassment: The Effects of Gender, Legal Standard, and Ambivalent Sexism." *Law and Human Behavior* 21:71–93

Williams, Christine. 1992. "The Glass Escalator—Hidden Advantages for Men in Female Professions." *Social Problems* 39:253–67.

Williams, Christine, Patti A. Giuffre, and Kirsten Dellinger. 1999. "Sexuality in the Workplace: Organizational Control, Sexual Harassment, and the Pursuit of Pleasure." *Annual Review of Sociology* 25:73–93.

Williams, David R. 1995. "Poverty, Racism and Migration: The Health of the African American Population." In *Origins and Destinies: Immigration, Race and Ethnicity in America*, edited by S. Pedraza and R. Rumbaut. Belmont, CA: Wadsworth.

———. 1999. "Race, SES, and Health: The Added Effects of Racism and Discrimination." In *Socioeconomic Status and Health in Industrial Nations: Social, Psychological and Biological Pathways*, edited by N. E. Adler, M. Marmot, B. S. McEwen, and J. Stewart. New York: New York Academy of Sciences.

Williams, David R., and Chiquita Collins. 1995. "U.S. Socioeconomic and Racial Differences in Health: Patterns and Explanations." *Annual Review of Sociology* 21:349–86.

Wilson, Franklin D., Marta Tienda, and Lawrence Wu. 1995. "Race and Unemployment: Labor Market Experiences of Black and White Men, 1968–1988." *Work and Occupations* 22:245–70.

Wilson, George. 1997. "Pathways to Power: Racial Differences in the Determinants of Job Authority." *Social Problems* 44:38–54.

Wilson, George, and Debra Branch McBrier. 2005. "Race and Loss of Privilege: African American/White Differences in the Determinants of Job Layoffs From Upper-Tier Occupations." *Sociological Forum* 20:301–21.

Wilson, George, Ian Sakura-Lemessy, and Jonathan P. West. 1999. "Reaching the Top: Racial Differences in Mobility Paths to Upper-Tier Occupations." *Work and Occupations* 26:165–86.

Wilson, William J. 1978. *The Declining Significance of Race.* Chicago: University of Chicago Press.

———. 1987. *The Truly Disadvantaged: The Inner City, the Underclass, and Public Policy.* Chicago: University of Chicago Press.

———. 1996. *When Work Disappears: The World of the New Urban Poor.* New York: Knopf .

Wise, Sue, and Liz Stanley. 1987. *Georgie Porgie: Sexual Harassment in Everyday Life.* Canada: HarperCollins.

Wood, Robert G., Mary E. Corcoran, and Paul E. Courant. 1993. "Pay Differences among the Highly Paid: The Male–Female Earnings Gap in Lawyers' Salaries." *Journal of Labor Economics,* 11:417–41.

Xu, Zu, and Ann Leffler. 1992. "Gender and Race Effects on Occupational Prestige, Segregation, and Earnings." *Gender and Society* 6:376–92

Yinger, John. 1986. "Measuring Discrimination with Fair Housing Audits: Caught in the Act." *American Economic Review* 76:881–93.

———. 1991. "Acts of Discrimination: Evidence for the 1989 Housing Discrimination Study." *Journal of Housing Economics* 1:318–46.

———. 1995. *Closed Doors, Opportunities Lost: The Continuing Costs of Housing Discrimination.* New York: Russell Sage Foundation.

———. 1998. "Evidence on Discrimination in Consumer Markets." *Journal of Economic Perspectives* 12:23–40.

Yoder, J. D. 1991. "Rethinking Tokenism: Looking Beyond Numbers." *Gender and Society* 5:178–92.

———. 1994. "Looking Beyond the Numbers: The Effects of Gender Status, Job Prestige, and Occupational Gender-Typing on Tokenism Processes." *Social Psychology Quarterly* 57:150–59.

Young, Iris M. 1990. Justice and the Politics of Difference. Princeton: Princeton University Press.

Zax, Jeffery S. 1989. "Quits and Race." *The Journal of Human Resources* 24:469–93.

Zemans, Frances Kahn. 1983. "Legal Mobilization: The Neglected Role of the Law in the Political System." *American Political Science Review* 77:690–703.

Zwerling, Craig, and Hilary Silver. 1992. "Race and Job Dismissals in a Federal Bureaucracy." *American Sociological Review* 57:651–60.

Index